Visions and Prophecies

Visions and Prophecies

By the Editors of Time-Life Books

TIME-LIFE BOOKS, ALEXANDRIA, VIRGINIA

CONTENTS

CHAPTER 1

Seeing into the Future

istory is full of astonishing predictions about the shape of things to come. But few have been more precise or disturbing than the prophecy reportedly delivered by Jacques Cazotte at a dinner party in Paris, early in 1788.

Some time afterward, one of those present, Jean-François de La Harpe, wrote a detailed account of what he claims was said. It was evidently a lively evening. The host was a distinguished nobleman noted for his polished wit, and he had invited an equally luminous company: writers, courtiers, lawyers, members of the French Academy, and ladies of title, all of whom were known for their conversational gifts and high spirits. Cazotte himself was a well-known writer, author of the occult romance *Le Diable Amoureux,* "The Devil in Love." The dinner was sumptuous, the wine flowed freely, and everyone competed to be more outspoken and irreverent than his or her neighbor. No topic was considered sacred. The ladies listened to delightfully wicked stories without blushing, religion was mocked, the iconoclastic philosopher Voltaire was extolled. All agreed that revolution must soon come to France and that it should be welcomed as a new broom that would sweep away superstition and fanaticism.

It was then that Cazotte is said to have stilled the laughter by declaring: "Ladies and gentlemen, be content. You will yet see, every one of you, that great revolution for which you are so eager. You know, I am something of a prophet, and I assure you, you shall all see it." He went on to describe, in chilling detail, exactly how the impending revolution would affect each of those around the table.

"You, Monsieur de Condorcet, will die prone on the stone floor of a prison cell. You will perish of a poison you will have taken to cheat the executioner. And you, Monsieur de Champfort, will cut your veins twenty-two times with a razor, and still you will not die—until some months later. As for you, Monsieur de Nicolai, you will die on the scaffold. And you, Monsieur Bailly, also on the scaffold." As he continued, people began to whisper, "It is easy to see the man's mad." And "Don't you see he is joking? His jokes, you know, always have something eerie, fantastic, about them." La Harpe, a noted freethinker, objected that Cazotte had not predicted his fate.

"Ah, for you," replied Cazotte, "I foresee something even more extraordinary: You will become a Christian." At this, the entire table burst out laughing. Declared Champfort: "What a relief. If we are not to perish until La Harpe becomes a Christian, then we are practically immortal!"

"And what of the ladies?" demanded the Duchesse de Grammont. "Surely, we shall not be harmed in this revolution of yours?" Replied Cazotte: "Your sex, ladies, will offer you no protection in this bloodbath. You, Madame la Duchesse, and many other ladies will be taken to the scaffold in the executioner's cart, with your hands tied behind your backs, like common criminals." And as the company seethed with disbelief, he delivered his last and most horrible prophecy. "I must tell you this: No one will be spared. Not even the king and queen of France!"

If this story is true—and it was supported, but only after the revolution had played itself out, by several witnesses—it surely ranks among the most accurate prophecies ever recorded. For within five years, Jacques Cazotte's vision had been fulfilled in almost every detail. The French revolution, which began in 1789 with the highest ideals, was transformed into an orgy of violence and bloodletting. Cazotte's dinner companions met the fates he supposedly had predicted. But he had not foretold his own grim destiny: death under the guillotine in 1792.

When Cazotte described himself as "something of a prophet," he laid claim to one of the oldest titles in history. Every age has had its visionaries, seers who seem to possess a kind of second sight that enables them to peer through chinks in the wall of time.

Some have said their knowledge comes from God. Others believe they have uncanny powers of foresight denied to the average person.

But for most people, the godlike ability to foresee tomorrow has always seemed to hang, tantalizingly, just out of reach. Lacking prophetic vision, many have turned to divination—the art of discovering hidden knowledge through the interpretation of omens and symbols. Humanity's attempts to know the unknowable by such means are reflected in some of its earliest artifacts: Babylonian models of a sheep's liver, marked with instructions for diviners; Chinese animal bones, inscribed with predictions. Some methods have become so esoteric that they require years of study: the Tarot cards, for instance, or the sixfold symbols of the *I Ching*. Others have focused on the here and now; those who seek clues to human personality in physical characteristics, for example, have kept systems such as palmistry thriving for centuries.

It is not the present but the future that holds the greatest allure for would-be soothsayers. And they are not interested in just any future, but in the fascinating matter of human fate—be it the destiny of an individual or of a nation. Even the farmer, hoping to gauge the morrow's weather by the behavior of birds, is really asking what is going to happen to him. Will his crops and hopes wither beneath an unremitting sun, or will his fields turn lush from nurturing rain and bring a rich harvest?

Indeed, many future events are quite predictable. We know that the sun will rise in the east tomorrow; we also know that we will die. Occurrences such as these follow easily observable natural patterns. We can also fore-

tell events statistically. Within a few thousand, for example, we can number the people who will die in highway accidents in the coming year. And we know that the iron law of averages dictates that in that same year, a major earthquake will strike somewhere in the world, as will a devastating drought. But unique features of such events are impossible to foresee by any explainable means. On what day, at what hour, will I die? Where on the globe will the earthquake hit? No science yet exists that can answer these crucial questions.

Outside the scientific realm, however, in the misty land of the paranormal, many people have claimed to possess the vision denied to mere scientists and scholars. One such was John William Dunne.

In January 1901 the no-nonsense British soldier was convalescing on the Italian Riviera, recovering from wounds suffered during the Boer War in South Africa. One night he dreamed he was back in Africa, in a dusty Sudanese town, when three ragged explorers arrived. The next morning Dunne saw a headline in an English newspaper that announced the arrival of the paper's overland expedition in Khartoum. The description of their physical condition and hardships en route corresponded almost exactly to what Dunne had dreamed. It was as though he had already read the account. Other dreams followed: A volcanic blast destroyed an island town; a rubber factory burned. Again, the visions were echoed in the next day's headlines.

Dunne thought that many people probably had prophetic dreams—but forgot them on waking or failed to understand their significance. In the course of a pioneering career in aeronautics, during which he designed Britain's first military airplane, he experimented with influencing and recording his dreams. In 1927 Dunne wrote *An Experiment with Time*, in which he maintained that dreams are a mingling of images of past and future, useful as a predictive tool to anyone having the patience to record and analyze them. Time is multidimensional, he wrote: Events exist before they occur in the conventional sense, and we move up to them—just as we can move up to or around a physical object. In dreams, he believed, we break out of our human habit of viewing past, present, and future as a stream flowing in only one direction and are able to dip into a wider pool of knowledge.

Some readers found Dunne's book enthralling. The British writer J. B. Priestley, for example, hailed it as "one of the most fascinating, the most curious, and perhaps the most important books of this age." Others, though, found it a confusing jumble of science and philosophy. But the questions he raised about the true nature of time echoed those asked by physicists.

Nothing in either Newton's or Einstein's universe requires time to flow in only one direction. Problems in classical physics work just as well if time is reversed, and Einstein, of course, showed that time is relative to the observer: Two people—one stationary, one moving at very high speed—could see the same events proceeding in a different order. The great physicist personalized this finding in a letter to a deceased friend's sister. "Michele has left this strange world just before me," wrote Einstein. "This is of no importance. For us convinced physicists the distinction between past, present and future is an illusion, although a persistent one."

In positing his novel notion about the nature of time, Dunne raised the age-old issue of fate versus free will. If people really could see the future, was the future then predetermined? Or was it a mass of alternate possibilities from which to choose? To take just one graphic example, was the *Titanic* destined to sink, or might the captain, forewarned by prophecy, have set a different course and have thereby avoided the iceberg?

Such questions have loomed especially large in cases of what might be called "pure" prophecy, when a visionary claims to know the future through direct revelation. In the long history of second sight, perhaps the most common explanation for such unsettling knowledge is a religious one. Many ancient prophets claimed that theirs was the voice of God—or gods—merely funneled through a human mouthpiece. And if lowly humans were to take steps to avoid a

fate that had been thus predicted, they would seem to be contravening the divine will.

In Babylon, supposedly god-inspired kings may have been the first prophets. In the Gilgamesh epic, believed to have been first recorded as long ago as 2000 BC, the semi-divine ruler dreams about an upcoming fight; his mother, a goddess, tells him that he and his enemy will then become fast friends. And it came to pass, just as Gilgamesh had been told in his dream.

The legendary Sumerian king Enmenduranna, who was supposed to have lived before the Flood, was said to have codified the rules of prophecy. Certainly the seer's art was well developed by the time of the First Dynasty of Ur, around 2500 BC. Prophecies were delivered in the name of the ruler and said to be inspired by the gods, but they were made by professional seers, who developed a number of divinatory systems involving inspection of sheep's livers and other natural objects.

The Illusion of Time

Soothsaying calls into question the nature of time itself. For if the future can be seen, then it must already exist, as part of some coherent structure of time.

Albert Einstein *(right)*, the father of modern physics, posited that there is no absolute time. Rather, he said, time changes with the motion of a particular observer. We treat time as though it were linear, one thing leading to another. But Einstein showed that past, present, and future need have no fixed status. In theory, at least, it is possible to perceive them in varying order—future before present, for instance.

Einstein's theory draws no conclusion about seeing the future. In fact, he was not much interested in such

things. Still, the theory profoundly affected the most influential modern thinker to concern himself with metaphysics: psychologist Carl Jung.

Einstein and Jung knew each other in Zurich in the days when the great physicist was refining his special theory of relativity. And, said Jung, "It was he who first started me off thinking about a possible relativity of time as well as space, and their psychic conditionality." Einstein had unveiled a theoretical world where cause need not precede effect. Years later, Jung adapted the idea in his theory of synchronicity, suggesting that meaningful coincidences occur through some mechanism outside the realm of cause and effect.

In Egypt, a priestly caste arose to interpret dreams, which were said to bear messages from the gods. These priests practiced primarily in two remote temples of the sun-god, Amun-Re: one in Natopa, the other far out in the Libyan desert, twelve days' journey from the capital at Memphis. People feared dreams almost as much as they did spirits, and believed that a correct interpretation could help to defuse the dream's potential threat. The priests who performed this task were especially cautious when called upon to decipher the pharaoh's dreams. So, according to the biblical account, it was only Joseph, a captive Israelite, who would explain the Egyptian ruler's dream of the seven fat and seven lean cows, and the seven good and seven thin ears of corn. The astute prediction—seven years of plenty, followed by a similar time of famine—was accompanied by the wise advice to lay up stores of corn.

The Bible, particularly the Old Testament, contains numerous reports of prophets whose privileged relationship with God allowed them to face the future with confidence. Israel's seers were known as *nabhi,* "called persons" on whom the spirit of God apparently had breathed, and their chief functions were to teach, to encourage, and to warn the people what would happen if the deity was defied. Around 800 BC, Amos, a simple shepherd's son, reportedly prophesied that "Jeroboam shall die by the sword and Israel shall surely be led away captive out of their own land. Therefore shall I cause you to go into captivity beyond Damascus, saith the Lord. . . ." Jeroboam was another name for the northern kingdom of Israel, and some years after the prophecy, in 721 BC, its ten tribes were indeed conquered and transported to Assyria. The Bible also relates how other prophets, including Jeremiah, Habakkuk, and Ezekiel, were divinely inspired to foretell the downfall of Assyria, the Babylonian invasion, the devastation of Judah, and the Babylonian captivity. Like so many accounts of prophecy, however, these statements were written down long after the predicted events had occurred, leaving their veracity in question for those without implicit faith.

The ancient Greeks had no sacred books like the Bible to guide their destinies. Priests administered sacred rites and sacrifices, but offered no guidance on personal crises or issues of state. When such advice was needed, the questioner would instead visit an oracle, a shrine where such questions were put to a god through a human medium. These temples existed throughout Greece. Most were consecrated to Apollo, the son of Zeus and the Greek god most associated with prophecy. And none enjoyed greater fame than the Delphic Oracle.

The ruined Temple of Apollo at Delphi can still be seen, in a setting of great natural beauty on the slopes of Mount Parnassus, just north of Athens. Today, the few local inhabitants depend on the tourist trade, but for a thousand years, from the sixth century BC until the coming of Christianity in the fourth century AD, this famed oracle drew the rich and famous from all over the Greek world. Delphi grew fat from their patronage.

The temple's origins are lost in myth. Greeks believed that the earth-goddess Ge and her daughter Themis had given answers (also called oracles) at this spot, which was then called Pytho, before Apollo took possession by slaying a great she-dragon. And archaeologists have found the remains of a sanctuary dedicated to Apollo that dates back to the eighth century BC.

So great was Delphi's fame that legends have obscured its true character. The Greek historian Herodotus claimed that the medium, usually titled the Pythia, spoke in a trance induced by natural gases seeping through the rocks. Her mutterings were interpreted by priests who rendered them in deliberately vague verse. However, recent scholars have found that most responses were in fact straightforward commands on religious matters and, less frequently, on public or private affairs. Few were in verse, and these dated from the later years. Declares one researcher: "A close study of all reliable evidence . . . reveals no chasm or vapors, no frenzy of the Pythia, no incoherent cries interpreted by priests. The Pythia spoke clearly, coherently, and directly to the consultant in response to his question."

Sometimes, in fact, she may have spoken more directly than she intended. According to one tale, Alexander the Great was told that he had come to Delphi on a day that the Pythia did not prophesy. When the impatient soldier grabbed the priestess and dragged her toward the tripod on which she delivered her pronouncements, the woman gasped, "My lad, you are invincible"—which was answer enough for him.

Although Delphi was the most celebrated of Greek oracles, it was also the most costly. At the height of its fame, the minimum rate for oracles was the equivalent of two days' pay for the average Athenian—to which the visitor would have to add offerings and travel expenses. States were charged ten times that amount; moreover, they could consult the Pythia only on the seventh of the month, the date of Apollo's birthday.

A more democratic alternative to Delphi was located in the Temple of Zeus at Dodona, far to the west. Petitioners there wrote questions on thin lead strips that were rolled up, numbered, and placed in a jar, from which they were drawn one at a time by the priestess. Queries had to be phrased to allow a yes or no answer. Hundreds of these strips have survived. One man wanted to know if he should marry, another if he should take up sheep farming; a town in the province of Thessaly asked whether it should invest funds collected in the name of its goddess.

Following the conquests of Alexander the Great in the fourth century BC, population and wealth flowed from Greece into its colonies in Asia Minor, and new oracles superseded those of Delphi and Dodona. Claros, on the west coast of what is now Turkey, was popular with the newer Greek settlers. Cities that consulted the oracle of Claros would often organize an annual civic outing, which included a choir that sang a hymn to Apollo. The inquirers were led, by night and in single file, through a subterranean maze of corridors to a vaulted hall. There they waited in the flickering light of torches, while the medium retired to an underground fountain whose bubbling waters were reputed to inspire the prophecy. So theatrical a setting may have

Secrets of the Maya's Calendar

Europeans and Americans pack time in parcels. We treat time as linear expanses with beginnings and ends—days, weeks, months, years, centuries—each a package to be filled with events and stowed away, each to be replaced on time's conveyor belt by a new and empty segment, more or less identical to the one that went before and the one to follow.

The ancient Maya of Central America saw things quite differently. For them each day was unlike any other, a unique entity pregnant with meaning and demanding divination. The Maya, whose obsession with time created the most accurate calendar in history, did not see time as a procession of linear starts and stops. Rather, it was a system of interlocking wheels where gods, humans, and nature meshed in perpetual concert.

Using exact calculations of the earth's rotation and of the lunar and solar cycles, the Maya actually created not one calendar but two: a solar one of 365 days and a sacred one of 260 days. The two interlocked to create fifty-two-year cycles.

The precision of these two calendars was essential, since time and religion were inextricable and coexistent for the Maya. Each day, year, decade, century, and millennium had its own god, and these divine bearers engaged in a circular and perpetual relay race, passing time intervals from god to god. Diligent calculations made by the Mayan astronomer-priests supplied information as to which gods bore each day—knowledge that was crucial to undertaking right actions, offering proper propitiation, and attuning oneself to the cycles of nature. A day was not an empty package to be filled but, rather, a precise potential to be realized.

Only four major writings from the Maya's Classic Period (AD 250 to 900) survived the Spanish conquest of Central America. Shown here is a portion of one of them. Known as the Madrid Codex, it is a sort of farmer's almanac painted by an ancient scribe on a twenty-two-foot length of fig-bark paper and is stored at Madrid's Museo de América.

Mayan priests used the codex in divination rites to discover which days were auspicious or ill-favored for such workaday pursuits as rainmaking, planting, hunting, weaving, and beekeeping. The document is made up of rows of glyphs, which accompany pictures of gods or beasts. Each of the twenty days in a Mayan month had its own name, and the codex glyphs name the days over and over through the 260-day cycle of the religious calendar.

In divination, priests probably counted out kernels from a random pile of corn while reading the codex from right to left. One kernel was removed from the pile for each day. The day reached when the pile was exhausted yielded the augury. The panel shown at right, for example, depicts the god of death, who is adorned at the head, wrists, and ankles with bells that the Maya called "death eyes." Over his head is a glyph that foretells sickness or death. Running out of corn on this glyph was very bad luck.

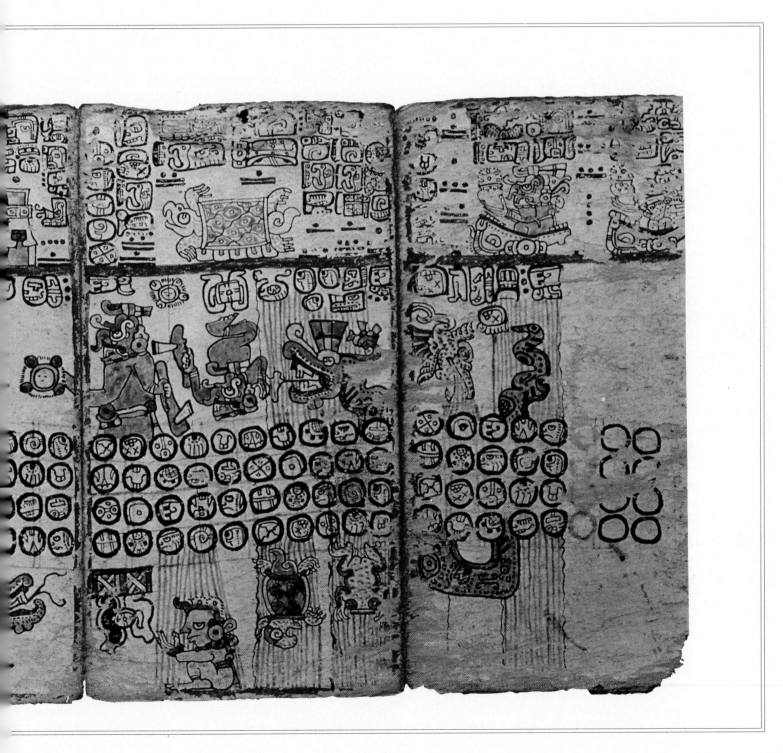

encouraged deception. One Cynic philosopher, who received a promise of rewards after toil, discovered that the identical message had been given to many others—and that all had suffered toil without reward.

The Roman Empire had its share of soothsayers and diviners, but few prophets of the fame and influence of Delphi. Not until the fall of Rome and the rise of Christianity in Europe did prophecy become as pervasive as it had been in the classical world.

Perhaps because of the Church's emphasis on sin and damnation, Christians of the so-called Dark Ages were easily swayed by prophecy based on portents of doom. The biblical Book of Revelation predicts the advent of a thousand-year period—or millennium—of righteousness during which Christ will rule on earth. Many of the faithful became convinced that this Second Coming would logically arrive in, or just before, the year 1000. Apparently most of these people did not believe they were holy enough to be included in the new kingdom and therefore viewed the Millennium as the end of the world. In the waning years of the tenth century, a succession of supposedly portentous events—including an eclipse of the sun, a particularly harsh winter, plague, an eruption of Vesuvius, and invading armies—strengthened the mood of fatalism.

As the dread year approached, people throughout Europe were seized by panic. Sure that the end was nigh, Christians abandoned their farms and villages to gather beneath crucifixes, praying for mercy. Some of the devout sold their property and joined pilgrimages to Jerusalem to await the coming of the Lord. Intoning hymns, they watched the skies, expecting them to open and reveal the Son of God.

When the new century dawned without incident, daily life resumed and apprehensions over the Millennium were largely put aside. The Church, however, continued to be the focus of prophecies of other kinds. Claiming to speak to angels, the fifteenth-century French peasant Joan of Arc, for example, predicted the defeat of the English invaders and the restoration of the king of France. Through her inspired leadership in battle, she fulfilled her own prophecy, was

martyred at the stake, and eventually was canonized as Saint Joan. An Italian hermit named Bartolomeo Brandano was imprisoned in Rome in 1517 for his denunciation of alleged papal sins and his prediction that a "trans-Alpine nation" would devastate that city. There had been no invasion of Rome for five centuries, but in just ten years the forces of the Holy Roman Empire—a federation primarily of Germanic principalities—swooped down from the north and overran the city. Brandano, vindicated, was released from prison by imperial troops.

Far more secular in her outlook was England's legendary sixteenth-century seer Mother Shipton. Intriguing stories of her remarkable prophecies have circulated since the seventeenth century, but no one knows for certain whether such a woman ever existed. By some accounts, she was born in Yorkshire in 1488, the daughter of a witch. Perhaps taking after her mother, the seer was reputedly "larger than common, her body crooked, her face frightful, but her understanding extraordinary."

She supposedly foretold the final downfall of Thomas Wolsey, the statesman and cardinal who was among the richest and most powerful men in England until he ran afoul of his monarch, Henry VIII. In 1529, stripped of all offices except the archbishopric of York, Wolsey was on his way to that city when Mother Shipton is said to have announced that he would never enter York. Hearing this, the story continues, Wolsey vowed that she would be burned as a witch when he did arrive, and he sent three members of his entourage to investigate. She calmly bade them welcome, offered them cake and ale, and demonstrated her power by casting a linen kerchief on the fire and retrieving it unsinged. Wolsey came to within eight miles of his cathedral city but was summoned back to London by the king to face a charge of treason; he died on his way to the capital.

Other prophecies attributed to Mother Shipton were published starting a century or so after her death. At times she seems to have had extraordinary insights: "Carriages without horses shall go, / And accidents fill the world with

woe. / Around the earth, thoughts shall fly / In the twinkling of an eye. . . . / The world to an end shall come, / In eighteen hundred and eighty one."

These verses have often been quoted as extraordinary examples of foresight, detailing the existence of railways and the telegraph centuries before their invention. However, as the editors of the London journal *Notes & Queries* disclosed as long ago as 1873, these and other Mother Shipton prophecies were in fact fabricated by a British bookseller, Charles Hindley, who in 1862 published them as a reprint of a pamphlet that he claimed had first appeared in 1684.

Even so, it is said that many provincial Britons feared that the world would indeed end, just as the discredited Mother Shipton prophecy had it, in 1881. And even today, Hindley's acknowledged fakeries are sometimes cited as evidence that a sixteenth-century British seer foretold the coming of such things as automobiles, radio, and aircraft.

The stories about the dubious Mother Shipton fade next to the fame of her contemporary, the French physician Michel de Nostredame. Unlike the Englishwoman, Nostredame was widely known in his own time, and his life is fairly well documented. Under the name of Nostradamus, he became a prophet for his era and for every generation since, more acclaimed—and more denounced—than any other seer.

Michel de Nostredame was born in 1503 at Saint-Rémy-de-Provence to a Jewish family that had converted to Christianity. A precocious boy, Michel learned classical languages, mathematics, and astrology from his grandfather; studied liberal arts at the University of Avignon; and then switched to medicine and enrolled at the University of Montpellier. Although he eventually abandoned his medical career in favor of prophecy, he was for a time a gifted physician who devised a number of unusual pharmaceutical preparations; one he used was rose pills, made from roses plucked before dawn. The fact that Nostradamus refused to bleed his patients at the slightest hint of illness, a common practice, may also have contributed to his success.

The young Nostradamus had no sooner obtained his license than he made his mark as a healer, successfully treating victims of the plague that ravaged Montpellier and

An illustration from a fourteenth-century Italian manuscript of Dante's Inferno reflects the poet's hearty contempt for fortune-tellers. He consigns them to hell with their heads twisted to face forever backward, a punishment for the arrogance they exhibit in aspiring to God's prescience.

other cities of the region. In about 1532 he married a young woman "of high estate, very beautiful and very amiable," according to a contemporary account. They had children, and Nostradamus seems to have enjoyed three years of happiness. Then the plague returned with renewed virulence. Nostradamus, who had saved so many, was unable to cure his own wife and children, and they died painfully.

Deeply depressed, Nostradamus spent the next six years wandering around France and Italy, consulting with other doctors and learned men. Once, he is said to have given a striking demonstration of the prophetic gifts that would win him lasting fame. According to accounts of that time, Nostradamus encountered a humble Franciscan monk while traveling through Italy and bowed down before him, addressing the startled young cleric as "Your Holiness." In 1585, years after the seer's death, the former swineherd Felice Peretti—by then a cardinal—was elected Pope Sixtus V.

Many such stories arose as testimony to Nostradamus's alleged second sight. In one account, the visionary was challenged by a skeptic, the Seigneur de Florinville, while staying at his chateau in the province of Lorraine. "Here are two pigs, one black, one white," declared de Florinville. "Foretell their future."

"You will eat the black one, a wolf will consume the other," replied the seer. Determined to prove him wrong, the lord told his cook to slaughter and serve the white pig

for dinner that night. After the roast had been served, de Florinville claimed victory, but Nostradamus insisted that his prediction had been correct. Finally the nobleman summoned his cook to settle the matter. The chef admitted that a wolf cub had entered the kitchen and eaten the white pig, and the black one had been prepared in its stead.

Returning to Provence in about 1544, Nostradamus resumed his successful career as a healer, traveling wherever there was a call for his services. But in 1547, the wanderer finally settled in the small town of Salon, in the heart of Provence. There he remarried and began to compose prophecies, drawing on his accumulated knowledge and books on astrology and magic. His first of several best-selling almanacs—pamphlets purporting to prophesy events for the coming year—appeared in 1550. But he soon went far beyond this narrow scope and turned to producing his famous collection of prophecies known as *Centuries*, which seems to look all the way to the year 3797.

Centuries, so called because the prophecies were assembled in groups of 100—except for one set that contains only 42—would eventually consist of 942 four-line verses, or quatrains, that appear to forecast events from around 1560 to the end of the world. The first were written in 1555; others were added later. The verses are deliberately obscure. Couched in a French that was already archaic in the sixteenth century, they are interlarded with words from other languages, as well as with anagrams, obscure images, and terms the seer apparently invented. Nostradamus claimed that he could have put a date on each verse but chose not to, in order to protect himself from charges of being a sorcerer.

Probably the most famous of the quatrains is one that is said to have caught the eye of the French queen Catherine de Médicis: "The young lion shall overcome the old / On the field of war in single combat; / He will pierce his eyes in a cage of gold. / This is the first of two loppings, then he dies a cruel death."

The poem sounded like an uncanny echo of an earlier prediction by the astrologer Gauric, who reportedly had warned Catherine's husband, King Henry II, that he must avoid "single combat in an enclosed place, especially near his forty-first year," for he risked injury or death from a blow to the head. Nostradamus was summoned to the court in Paris, where it is said he further predicted that three of Henry's sons would become kings. During that visit, he reportedly embellished his own legend with some off-the-cuff clairvoyance. Late one night a royal page who had lost a valuable hound came to the seer's door. Hearing only the knocking and without opening the door, Nostradamus snapped, "What is it you want, O page of the king? You make a deal of noise for a lost dog!" He told him, correctly, that the beast could be found on the road toward Orléans.

In the summer of 1559, his prophecies concerning the royal family began to fall into place. At a tournament held in Paris to celebrate a pair of royal weddings—Henry's daughter Elizabeth was married (by proxy) to Philip II of Spain, his daughter Marguerite to Henry of Navarre—the king ignored the warnings and rode against Montgomery, the captain of his Scottish Guard. At the third encounter, the captain's lance penetrated Henry's visor and pierced his eye. The king died in agony ten days later. And it came to pass, as well, that Henry's sons reigned in turn—and perished—as Francis II, Charles IX, and Henry III, whose murder in 1589 would be interpreted by some as the second of the "two loppings" referred to in the Nostradamus quatrain.

Skeptics have pointed out that there is no documentation of the face-to-face prophecy regarding Henry's children; in any case, untimely death was hardly an unexpected occurrence at the time, even—or perhaps especially—among royalty. On the other hand, believers can cite quatrains that they say refer to the fates of Henry's offspring. To that, skeptics can retort that each of the quatrains, because of the obscure language employed by their author, can be interpreted and translated in any number of ways.

Critics have also questioned specific details of Nostradamus's best-known prophetic quatrain. At forty, Henry was only six years older than his opponent; his visor, they say, was not gilded; a tournament ground can hardly be called "a field of battle"; and elsewhere in *Centuries,* the word *classes*—translated variously in this case as loppings, fractures, or wounds—is used to signify a fleet of ships. Furthermore, in a verse written later, Nostradamus seems to predict a bright future for Henry II. For most students of the seer, however, the verse remains one of his most impressive pieces of prediction.

There is no limit to the ingenuity of interpretations of Nostradamus. He has been credited with foreseeing the Great Fire of London, the French Revolution and the flight of Louis XVI, aerial warfare, communism, nuclear warfare, and the rise and fall of Hitler. Watergate, the Egyptian-Israeli peace accords, and the AIDS epidemic are a few of the more modern linkages. Enthusiasts have found in the quatrains references to rockets ("machines of flying fire"), submarines ("iron fish," usually bent on war), and various aspects of air travel, from the practical necessities—Nostradamus seemingly recognized that pilots needed oxygen and a radio for communications—to the more philosophical reflection that "the world becomes smaller."

Some of these interpretations seem to involve a willful

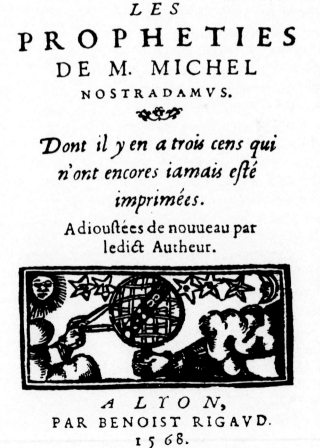

The first edition of Nostradamus's complete prophecies (right) was published posthumously in France in 1568, and the enigmatic and controversial quatrains have been in print ever since. Above, an eighteenth-century portrait by an unknown artist depicts the seer with what scholars believe is a telescope, symbolizing his astral preoccupations. The device is an anachronism; astronomers of Nostradamus's day had no telescopes.

ignorance of historical fact. For instance, verses referring to "Hister" have been translated by some commentators as referring to Hitler; however, Hister was simply the Latin name that Nostradamus used for the river Danube. Indeed, in one quatrain, the seer refers to the completion of a bridge across the Hister.

Still other quatrains that have been considered to be farsighted may actually refer to contemporary events with which Nostradamus should have been familiar. Skeptics cite the quatrain that purportedly depicts the Great Fire of London, down to the date, "twenty-three the sixes," or 1666. (To arrive at the year, believers multiply twenty by three, add a pair of sixes, and note that it was common in Nostradamus's time to omit the first digit of a date.) The verse's forecast of the fall of a lady from a high place has traditionally been interpreted as a reference to St. Paul's Church, which was so ravaged by the flames that it was torn down. But skeptics suggest that Nostradamus more likely referred to Queen Mary of England, known as Bloody Mary, who was at the time executing numbers of heretics, often in groups of six. Although Mary did not die until 1558, after the verse was printed, it would not have been particularly insightful in that turbulent era to predict a ruler's downfall or death.

Nostradamus enthusiasts have also applied many of the same prophecies to different historical events. For example, the quatrain about the birth "near Italy" of an emperor, "less a prince than a butcher," has been understood as an allusion to both Hitler and Napoleon—although, as

Prophecy at War

Nostradamus's persistent influence rests partly with his ambiguity: For years, people of various persuasions have managed to read something meaningful into his cryptic verses.

During World War II both Germany and Great Britain enlisted the seer for their own ends. "Nostradamus Predicts the Course of the War" is the English title of a pamphlet (above) produced by British intelligence in March of 1943; the document was meant to cause consternation in the enemy's homeland by predicting Hitler's doom. The Third Reich already had come up with Nostradamus adaptations of its own and planned to airlift into France copies of selected quatrains that supposedly forecast German victory.

It appears the leaflets were never used, however, perhaps because of France's quick surrender. And the small number of British pamphlets smuggled into Germany had no appreciable effect.

skeptics are quick to note, the geographic definition is broad enough to cover half a dozen countries, and the description could also be taken as a reference to Ferdinand II, a Holy Roman emperor of the early seventeenth century. Similarly, the following quatrain has invited more than one plausible interpretation: "The sermons from the Lake of Geneva annoying, / From days they will grow into weeks, / Then months, then years, then all will fail, / The Magistrates will damn their useless laws."

Did Nostradamus intend this as a blast against his contemporary, John Calvin, whose sermons from Geneva were provoking intense controversy? Or was the quatrain, as later commentators have claimed, a farsighted glimpse of the Geneva-based League of Nations—which, in the late 1930s, degenerated into an impotent debate society? Or could it, perhaps, be both? Such ambiguities, and the vast and obscure opus that the seer left behind, will no doubt continue to fascinate future generations of Nostradamus's readers.

Nostradamus, Jacques Cazotte, and other European prophets reflected in their dramatic predictions the death of monarchs, the rise and fall of empires. In the United States, prophecy took on a characteristically utilitarian bent. In the nineteenth century, for example, America would witness the career of a remarkable New World visionary: Andrew Jackson Davis, who came to be known as the Poughkeepsie Seer.

Davis was born in 1826, at Blooming Grove in New York's Orange County. His childhood was difficult and pe-

*Exotic German-born seer Terfren Laila, whose name in
Hindu supposedly means "then the sun rises over the mountain," claimed she
predicted Hitler's fall shortly after he came to power in the 1930s.*

nurious. His mother had no education; his father was a drunkard who scraped together a living first as a weaver and then as a shoemaker. But it seems that young Davis found a way to transcend his surroundings. After a day spent alone in the fields, he claimed to have heard voices and seen visions—one of which advised the family to move to Poughkeepsie. Thinking that prospects might indeed be better there, his shiftless parents made the move in 1838.

In the early 1840s, Davis began to dabble in the newly popular art of mesmerism, or hypnotism. A Poughkeepsie tailor put him into what he described as "magnetic sleep," in which state Davis claimed that the human body became transparent to him, enabling him to diagnose diseases and prescribe cures. At eighteen, the dreamy boy wandered from his home in a trance, during which he experienced a profound state of mental illumination. He claimed that during this trance he had met Galen, the Greek-born physician of the second century AD, and the Swedish mystic Emanuel Swedenborg, who died in 1772.

His rise to prominence began in 1845, when the fledgling seer took up with a Bridgeport, Connecticut, musician and amateur hypnotist who put him into a series of magnetic sleeps. While in this trancelike state, Davis began dictating to a scribe, the Reverend William Fishbough. For fifteen months this dictation continued, sometimes, according to a knowledgeable witness, in near-fluent Hebrew. The transcript was published in the year 1847 as *The Principles of Nature, Her Divine Revelations, and a Voice to Mankind*. This inspirational work had an extraordinary affinity to Swedenborg's writings, which Davis steadfastly maintained he had never come across.

The book was an interesting mixture of foresight and mysticism. For instance, Davis announced the existence of nine planets before even the eighth had been verified. At the same time, however, he predicted that advanced forms of humanity would be found on Mars, Jupiter, and Saturn.

Davis's work was hardly done, however. In *The Penetralia; Being Harmonial Answers to Important Questions*, published in 1856, he turned to earthly prophecy. He asserted

that technological progress would bring spiritual development and forecast horseless carriages—"moved by an admixture of aqueous and atmospheric gases"—traveling at high speeds on good roads. He also foresaw "spacious saloons, almost portable dwellings, moving with such speed, that perhaps there will be advertisements—'Through to California in four days!'"

To be sure, this was written at a time when railway lines from the East had already reached the banks of the Mississippi, but the quickest route from New York to California was still by ship around the tip of South America. Davis's vision of the future also included prefabricated apartment buildings, a phonetic spelling system, and a kind of typewriter that would print a person's ideas as readily as a piano expressed harmonies. "A glorious period is before mankind," he announced with the faith characteristic of his age. "It will be a kind of material heaven—a preparation for the Spiritual Harmonium."

Davis's books sold well, and the seer worked tirelessly for decades, lecturing, writing, and prescribing cures. It is said that Edgar Allan Poe was one of the many people influenced by his grand vision. Davis died in 1910, the owner of a small Boston bookshop and author of more than thirty books on spiritual matters.

From somewhat the same mold as Davis was the humble dreamer Edgar Cayce, who was born in Kentucky in 1877, a half century after Davis. Cayce came to be known as the "sleeping prophet" because he dictated his predictions—and his medical treatments—while in a trance. When he awoke he had no recollection—or even understanding—of what he had said. More than 14,000 such "readings," as he called them, were transcribed up to his death in 1945 and are now stored at the Virginia Beach, Virginia, headquarters of the Association for Research and Enlightenment, founded by Cayce in 1934.

Best known during his lifetime as a healer, Edgar Cayce also made predictions about the future. Among other things, he claimed to have foreseen the Wall Street crash of

1929. In April of that year, a broker consulted him about a dream, and Cayce declared that there would be a panic on Wall Street and other financial centers. Prices would fluctuate over a period of six months and then collapse. On October 29, Black Friday, came the crash. Many of Cayce's other visions were apocalyptic scenes of natural upheaval around the year 2000. Earthquakes, he predicted, would shatter the western part of the United States, cause massive flooding in Japan, and change the geography of Europe. The lost continent of Atlantis would rise from the floor of the ocean. In 1936 Cayce saw himself reborn in the year 2100, flying across North America at fantastic speed and exploring a devastated New York City.

Skeptics maintain that Cayce's record as a healer and prophet has been exaggerated by his faithful followers, and they dismiss some of his accurate predictions of wars and earthquakes as lucky guesses. To have prophesied a second world war in June 1931 was no great feat, they argue; the entire decade was full of such prognostications of global conflict. It was bound to happen sooner or later, and Cayce did not specify a date. As for his many other prophecies of late-twentieth-century disaster, time will tell.

Critical as some people have been of Edgar Cayce's track record, no one ever accused him of cashing in on his apparent abilities. As the century has progressed, however, a number of self-proclaimed seers have found some measure of fame and fortune, usually through the medium of the tabloid newspaper. Perhaps the best known of these popular prophets is Jeane Dixon, who has achieved both wealth and celebrity from her syndicated columns and television appearances.

Dixon claims to see the future in several ways: through visions in the air, through pictures in a crystal ball, and sometimes through a form of clairvoyance when she touches a subject's fingertips. Her fame rests largely on her assertion that she predicted the assassination of President John F. Kennedy. A number of legends have grown up around this insight. According to a rather breathless biographer, Dixon repeatedly predicted that the president would be shot, and as the time approached, she pinpointed it to the day and the place and even sought to warn the ill-fated chief executive.

The truth, however, seems far less dramatic and far less emblematic of Dixon's prophetic powers. Her only recorded prediction of the president's death is one printed in *Parade* magazine in 1956. In that article, written by Washington correspondent Jack Anderson, Dixon announced that the 1960 election would be dominated by labor and won by a Democrat who would be assassinated or die in office, not necessarily in his first term. Dixon also seems to have hedged her bets. In 1960 she predicted alternately—and incorrectly—that Richard Nixon would win the presidency that year.

Jeane Dixon is a staunch anti-Communist, and many of her prophecies seem to have been colored by her personal beliefs. Repeatedly she extolled Richard Nixon ("our last hope") while failing to predict the Watergate scandal and his resignation from the presidency. During the 1950s she forecast Soviet invasions of Iran and Palestine; in the late 1960s she saw the "ever-increasing presence of Russian submarines near the Bolivian coastline" as part of a "grand design" for world domination. (She was uncertain why they were menacing Bolivia, overlooking the fact that the country is landlocked.) Dixon has also said that by 1990 the Soviets will be in the final phase of "absorbing the Western Hemisphere by all means necessary including an atomic war if needed."

It is easy enough to make fun of such speculations and to list the predictions that fell wide of the mark. It seems unlikely that a comet will hit the world, or that the United States will experience germ warfare by China or have a woman president—all in the 1980s—as she once said would happen. And it is doubtful that even her most fervent supporters are much worried by her claim that the dread Antichrist was born in the Middle East on February 5, 1962.

Taken as a whole, Jeane Dixon's record is so inconsistent as to cast considerable doubt on her apparent successes. She claims, for example, to have forecast the disaster at

Edgar Cayce, who would eventually become the most influential modern American seer, was working as a photographer when this picture—believed to be a self-portrait—was taken in 1917.

Cape Kennedy in January 1967, when a fire in the *Apollo* command module took the lives of three astronauts. There was no written record of this prediction until after the event, however, and she failed to foresee the even more tragic disaster of 1986 in which the space shuttle *Challenger* exploded soon after launch, killing all seven aboard. Dixon accurately predicted Senator Robert F. Kennedy's assassination in 1968, but so did many others, Kennedy among them. Just two weeks before he died, he told French writer Romain Gary, "I know there will be an assassination attempt sooner or later."

In a way, Jeane Dixon and her fellow tabloid seers have chance on their side. A prophet who claims that in the upcoming year there will be, somewhere in the world, a major earthquake, a political assassination, or an airline disaster, is likely to prove successful. And for all that, the penalties of failure are slight. In ancient times, seers could be put to death for their mistakes; today's prophets risk nothing worse than ridicule. Moreover, as a number of skeptical observers have pointed out, the public tends to remember the one accurate prediction and to forget the thousands of inaccurate ones. Any self-professed prophet who foretells enough future events, particularly if the details are sufficiently vague, will hit the bull's-eye occasionally.

Alan Vaughan is a contemporary psychic who is candid enough to admit that some of his major predictions have missed the mark. One of his confessed failures occurred in San Francisco, the one large American city to have been devastated by an earthquake in this century. Fears of another major tremor constantly recur. In early 1969, for some reason, disaster scenarios proliferated: Prophets of doom seemed to emerge from every quarter, each with a different date for an impending catastrophe. To avoid possible panic—and promote his city in the bargain—Mayor John Alioto declared that San Francisco would survive and announced an earthquake party to be held at the Civic Center on April 18. It was to begin at 5:13 a.m.—sixty-three years to the minute after the last big quake. The

Probably America's best-known purported prophet, Jeane Dixon is also a prolific writer. Among the six volumes she has published are an astrological cookbook and a book for casting dogs' horoscopes.

party was a huge success, and the many predictions of disaster went unfulfilled.

Two years later, however, a big earthquake did strike —in the San Fernando Valley, far to the south. This event stirred a fresh wave of prophecy in San Francisco, and Alan Vaughan entered the sweepstakes with a confident prediction that a small quake would occur on May 22, at 5:18 p.m. It did not. Admitted Vaughan, "Either my method doesn't work, or I got the wrong year."

Geologists, using the best scientific tools at hand,

Your Fortune in a Cookie

Since gastronomy conveys it into the world of believer and skeptic alike, the fortune cookie is among the most common of all fortune-telling devices. Few take it seriously, perhaps, but hardly anyone leaves a Chinese meal without first reading the slip of fate tucked inside the ubiquitous dessert.

The humble cookie claims aristocratic origins among the upper classes of ancient China. There, a much-loved game involved writing essay topics on slips of paper and tucking them into tea cakes. Players would pluck out the topics and compete among themselves to write the best essay.

Chinese tea cakes may have presaged them, but in their familiar modern form the cookies owe more to California than to Canton. Los Angeles and San Francisco have vied for recognition as their original home (a mock court ruled in San Francisco's favor in 1983), and several Chinese-Americans—and at least one Japanese-American—have claimed to be their creator. In any case, the cookies first appeared in California just after the turn of the century, and their popularity was immediate. While most are purchased commercially, they can also be made at home (below). Fortune-cookie messages range from the trite ("Wealth will be yours") to the aphoristic ("A good name is better than gold") to the slightly ribald ("The redhead at the next table is dynamite"). They may also be political or social. The late Lyndon B. Johnson used the cookies to promote at least one of his political campaigns. And, during the 1960s, it was the fleeting fashion at some debutante parties to have specially made fortune cookies dictate dancing partners for the various guests.

The composers of cookie fortunes are many and various. Canton-born George Cheng, a major manufacturer of the cookies for many years, received cookie wisdom from a wide cross-section of acquaintances in Los Angeles, where his business was based. Contributors included one homemaker who turned out fortunes steadily for more than fifteen years. She was, Cheng opined, probably the best-read author in the state of California.

DO-IT-YOURSELF FORTUNE COOKIES

Ingredients: 2 eggs, 1/2 cup sugar, 1 teaspoon vanilla extract or 1/2 teaspoon almond extract, 1/4 cup vegetable oil, 1/2 cup cornstarch, 1/4 cup water

Beat the eggs in an electric mixer. Add the sugar and beat again at high speed until mixture is thick and foamy. Stir in the extract and fold in the oil. In a separate bowl, combine the water and a small amount of the egg mixture with the cornstarch. Stir together until smooth, then add to the rest of the egg mixture.

Heat a griddle over medium heat, then drop on tablespoonfuls of batter, spreading them with the back of the spoon into four-inch circles. Cook about 2½ minutes on each side, turning with a spatula, or until the cookies are golden with lightly browned edges. Working with one cookie at a time, remove them from griddle, place the fortunes in the cookies' centers, then pinch the cookie edges together and pull the corners toward each other for the proper shape.

seem to have a better track record than any psychic at predicting earthquakes. And it is not unlikely that human intelligence, ingenuity, and imagination are stronger forces than supposed supernatural insight when it comes to predicting the future. Leonardo da Vinci, who lived from 1452 to 1519 and was the most versatile genius of the Italian Renaissance, turned his own imaginings into sketches—of such things as helicopters and machine guns—centuries before technology began to catch up with his visions. The English philosopher and statesman Sir Francis Bacon, born in the reign of Queen Elizabeth I, ranged almost as widely. He scoffed at prophecies, though, considering them fit only for "winter talk by the fireside." But in his book *The New Atlantis,* published posthumously in 1626, he foresaw the possibility of the telephone and the refrigerator, of hybrid agriculture and the desalination of seawater.

It is often the specialists, blinkered by practical knowledge, who fail to foresee the dramatic advances to come. In 1928, for example, the American radio pioneer Lee De Forest declared, "While theoretically and technically television may be feasible, commercially and financially I consider it an impossibility, a development of which we need waste little time dreaming." Early in 1945, Admiral William Leahy, who served as chief of staff to President Franklin Roosevelt during World War II, assayed the prospects for the atomic bombs that would soon devastate Hi-

roshima and Nagasaki and declared: "The A-bomb is the biggest fool thing. The bomb will never go off and I speak as an expert on explosives." Sir Richard van der Riet Woolley, Britain's astronomer royal, dismissed the notion of space travel as "utter bilge" just months before the Russians launched their earth-orbiting *Sputnik* satellite in 1957.

Jules Verne, the French writer who is deservedly known as the father of science fiction, had better luck as a prognosticator. Indeed, he gave a fairly accurate account of the first manned space flights more than a hundred years in advance, coming intriguingly close to some of the key details of the Apollo moon exploration program in his novels *From the Earth to the Moon* (1865) and *Round the Moon* (1870). Verne's spacecraft, the *Columbiad,* took off from Florida and splashed down in the Pacific, where its three-man crew was rescued by an American ship. Verne calculated that the trip from earth to moon would take 97 hours and 13 minutes. *Apollo 11's* total flight time was just over 195 hours, an average of 97 hours 39 minutes each way. Both the real and the fictional craft were equipped with rockets to escape the lunar orbit and slow down reentry; both the *Columbiad* and *Apollo 13* suffered a life-threatening loss of oxygen in flight. However, Verne could not entirely escape the assumptions of his time: His astronauts wore smoking jackets and reclined on tufted velvet couches. And they were propelled from the earth not by rocket motors but, like an artillery shell, from a huge gun barrel buried in the earth.

Verne firmly believed that, as he put it, "What one man can imagine, another man can do." And his account of space travel did in fact fire the imagination of the Russian rocket-pioneer Konstantin Tsiolkovsky, who also wrote science fiction on the exploration of space. Another visionary writer, H. G. Wells, had a similar impact. In 1913, he described a future nuclear war in *The World Set Free.* Almost twenty years later, the noted Hungarian physicist Leo Szilard read the novel and later claimed that it provoked him to think about the power that could be generated by a nuclear chain reaction. Szilard went on to collaborate with Enrico Fermi, developing the nuclear reactor that made possible the world's first atomic bomb.

Leonardo da Vinci did not construct the airscrew he sketched in 1488, but he envisioned its role in human flight.

Men and women of the modern world are no less curious about the future than the ancient Egyptians and Greeks who pondered dreams or consulted oracles. In these latter days, however, prediction has increasingly become a team effort, conducted by groups of researchers with number-crunching computers. But governments and industries that commission studies from the Rand Corporation, SRI International, and other such think tanks are acting from some of the same impulses that led Roman emperors and medieval kings to seek the services of astrologers and soothsayers. We need to know, as much as they did, the probability of an uprising, the size of the harvest, the chances of an enemy attack and how best to avert it.

For all the computers and masses of data at their command, professional futurists—as the modern oracles are often called—struggle with a host of problems. Called upon to predict everything from next year's weather to the political situation in the twenty-first century, they may be contending with too many variables for even the most powerful computer to handle.

Often they lack crucial information, and even when dealing with much the same data, they tend to come up with wildly different conclusions. In 1972, for example, the largely European experts who formed a futurists' forum known as the Club of Rome predicted a catastrophic drop in population and industrial capacity within the next hundred years if present trends continue. But the equally distinguished prognosticator Herman Kahn was far more upbeat during a 1982 address in Arizona. He attacked the Club of Rome's continuing gloomy forecasts, insisting that we are in fact living through the most exciting period of change in history. "One hundred years from now," Kahn declared, "mankind will be everywhere numerous, everywhere rich, everywhere largely in control of the forces of nature."

Only time, of course, will tell which of these long-range global visions will come to pass. Meanwhile, many paranormalists will continue to believe that the prophetic powers reportedly shown by Nostradamus and others represent untapped abilities of the human mind. Perhaps, they argue, we should have less faith in nonpsychic experts and more trust in our own powers of intuition. They suggest that people with prophetic talents be encouraged and trained in different fields of expertise and that a consensus of their forecasts be sought. The wheel would be brought full circle, from dreaming kings awaiting God's guidance to scientists trusting their intuition to bridge the gaps in their data. Some people, these paranormalist are convinced, can breach time's barriers and discern what will come in what is now.

Jules Verne's fiction described a voyage to the moon a century before the fact. This engraving from an 1865 French edition of From the Earth to the Moon shows the spaceship he imagined hurtling moonward. Visionaries such as Leonardo da Vinci and Verne did not claim to be prophets.

CHAPTER 2

Omens and Auguries

The legend began one night in the early 1600s on the remote Scottish isle of Lewis. According to the traditional account, a hearty Highland woman named Mrs. Mackenzie was grazing her herd of cattle alongside an old graveyard, when all at once the entire crop of tombstones wavered, creaked, and toppled to the ground. As Mrs. Mackenzie watched in frozen fascination, ghosts floated out of the ground and flew swiftly away.

More intrigued than afraid, the Scottish woman waited to see what would happen. An hour later all the ghosts but one had returned from their wanderings in the mortal realm. Mrs. Mackenzie then placed her staff over the last open grave. Finally, the wraith of a young woman appeared and shrieked, "Lift your distaff from my grave and let me enter my dwelling of the dead!" "I shall do so," said the staunch Mrs. Mackenzie, "when you explain to me what detained you so long after your neighbors."

"My journey was much farther than theirs," replied the shade. "I had to go all the way to Norway. I am a daughter of its king and was drowned while bathing. My body was carried out to sea and eventually swept onto the shore not far from here, where it was found and interred in that grave. Now please remove your distaff so that I may once more take my rest."

Mrs. Mackenzie did so, and before the dead princess sank back into the earth, she said, "In remembrance of me, and as a small reward of your courage, I shall tell you where you will find something of rare value. If you will search in that loch over there, you will come across a small round blue stone. Give it to your son, who by it shall see into the future."

Mrs. Mackenzie found the mysterious treasure and presented it to her son. When he peered through a hole in the center of the stone, he found that the phantom had spoken the truth. Using this curious stone, a simple object drawn from nature, he could slice through the veils of time and divine what was to come, thus fulfilling one of humanity's most ancient dreams.

This tale typifies the legends that sprang up around the obscure Rennaissance seer Kenneth Mackenzie—or Coinneach Odhar, as he preferred to be called in Gaelic. Very little is known of the man himself, but records of the sixteenth-century Scottish parliament contain an order, sent to authorities in the county of Ross, to prosecute the wizard Coinneach Odhar. Presumably, this led to his execution. And it would not be surprising if his crime had been the widespread practice of scrying—divination by gazing into shining surfaces. Nor would it be unusual for a man of that era to claim second sight, an ability that many Scots still believe to be their birthright. The wizard of parliamentary record differs from the story's prophet in one key aspect, however: He lived almost a century before the events related in the Coinneach Odhar legend, a fact that only adds to the mystery surrounding him.

The seer was said to have announced his prophecies in a manner that daunted even his detractors, and his predictions were nothing if not dour. One day, while walking across a large field in Drummossie, he supposedly fell down and wailed, "This black moor shall be stained with the best blood in the Highlands. Heads will be lopped off by the score, and no mercy will be shown or quarter given on either side." He was kneeling on Culloden Moor, the future site of the terrible massacre of the Scots during the rebellion of 1745-46.

Word of his uncanny success is said to have elevated Odhar from a local curiosity to a man of great renown and status. He began to predict the future, charging high fees to rich families on the Scottish mainland. For all his apparent powers, however, Odhar's vanity may have prevented him from predicting his own demise. One day at the height of his fame, he was summoned to Brahan Castle, near Dingwall, by Isabella, the wife of the third earl of Seaforth. The earl was long overdue from a journey to Paris, and the countess was beside herself with worry. She begged Odhar to use his powers to alleviate her fears.

According to the story, the seer gazed through his stone and then broke into a lewd grin. "Madam," he said, "there is no need to worry concerning your husband's welfare. He is well and merry." Isabella pressed

for more details, which he refused to give. Finally, when she resorted to threats, he snapped back that in his vision he had seen the earl in a sumptuous Parisian salon with his arms around another woman.

After a moment of silence, the countess spoke. "You have sullied the good name of my lord in the halls of his ancestors, and you shall suffer the most signal vengeance I can inflict"—death on the pyre. The earl returned from Paris as Odhar was being taken to be burned alive. Upon hearing the news, and knowing Odhar's words to be true, he rode off to stay the execution.

Meanwhile, Odhar, who had been sure that the countess would, upon reflection, reduce the initial sentence, at last realized that she was determined to carry out her threat. In fear and rage he is said to have cried out the final prophecy that earned him the title of the Brahan Seer: "I see in the far future the doom of the race of my oppressor. I see a chief, the last of his house, both deaf and dumb. He will be the father of four sons, all of whom he will follow to the tomb. The remnant of his possessions shall be inherited by a white-coifed lassie from the East, and she is to kill her sister." Isabella was so incensed by this that she ordered her men to carry out the execution by thrusting Odhar headfirst into a barrel lined with sharp stakes and filled with burning tar. The earl was too late to halt this grisly deed. A few years afterward, Isabella threw herself out of the castle tower to her death.

One by one, each element of Odhar's reputed dying prophecy came to pass. An earl of Seaforth born in 1754 lost his hearing to scarlet fever when he was about twelve. Each of his four sons died young, and after those tragedies, he also lost his power of speech. He died on January 11, 1815, and one of his daughters returned to Scotland not long afterward from her home in India, where her husband had recently died; she was dressed in traditional white mourning clothes. The woman eventually remarried, and since there were no male heirs, the Seaforth lands passed to her and her second husband. One day, the carriage she was driving overturned and killed her sister, thus concluding the last act of the predicted tragedy.

Many of Odhar's alleged prophecies came true years after his death. He supposedly predicted that the eight-ton Stone of Petty, situated well inland, would end up in the sea—as it did, after a hurricane in 1799 struck the area and apparently dislodged the stone. And there are those who maintain that one legendary prediction may yet come to pass. Coinneach Odhar is said to have foretold that "a dun hornless cow will appear in Minch and will make a bellow which will knock the six chimneys off Gairloch House. The whole country will become utterly desolated, after which deer and other wild animals shall be exterminated by horrid black rain." Some doomsayers see the dun hornless cow as a nuclear submarine and the bellow as a nuclear explosion with its consequent devastation and fallout. Intriguingly enough, Gairloch House had no chimneys at the time of this prophecy; today it has six.

One thing missing from the Brahan Seer tales is a detailed discussion of Odhar's mystical blue stone. But if it fit the pattern of other time-honored tools of divination, the scrying stone was not so much a magic talisman as it was a device that allowed a powerful intellect to focus its concentration. Nature supplied humankind's first symbols of hidden knowledge—stones, water, flowers, birds, clouds—and in seeking to divine messages from them, our ancestors may have taken their earliest steps down the road to the sciences of biology, geology, and even meteorology.

In the modern world, reading tea leaves and gazing into crystal balls are two of the more familiar methods of natural divination, but there are many other traditional techniques, each with its own title ending in "mancy," a suffix based on the Greek word *mantis*, meaning "diviner" or "prophet." Capnomancy is the practice of reading portents in the way rising smoke drifts in the wind; apantomancy explores the significance of meeting animals—giving rise, for example, to the notion that if a black cat crosses your path, bad luck is on its way. Anthropomancy, perhaps the darkest art of all, is divination through human sacrifice. Happily, most forms of natural divination seem more bizarre than sinister *(page 35)*.

Divination from nature may be rooted in ancient shamanic rituals. For at least 25,000 years, shamans have played their part as priests, magicians, and healers. Portraits of entranced shamans decorate the walls of Stone Age caves; even today, in parts of Asia, the Arctic, and the Americas, these supposed magicians practice their arts.

This bronze model of a sheep's liver served as a guide for ancient Etruscans learning the complex art of hepatoscopy, or "liver gazing." Each of the model's forty segments, as well as the raised areas, is associated with a different god or element of nature.

Central to shamanic belief is the idea that a sacred living spirit inhabits all of the natural world, even the stones. Shamans undergo intense physical trials to gain an understanding of this force, an understanding that is said to enable them to discern the future. As one modern Siberian Chukchee shaman has said: "On the steep bank of a river, there exists life. A voice is there and speaks aloud. I saw the master of the voice and spoke with him. He subjugated himself to me and sacrificed to me. He came yesterday and answered my questions. The small gray bird with the blue breast comes to me and sings shaman songs in the hollow of the bough, calls her spirits, and practices shamanism."

As Western cultures developed and codified such techniques, divination became more formal. The early Greeks and Romans, for instance, assumed that almost every natural event was a sign from the gods. Hence any unusual happening, from a hailstorm to the birth of a deformed calf, was deemed an urgent message from on high.

To be sure, there was frequent evidence of the fallibility of divination. In one notable example, the Athenian general Nicias was seeking in 413 BC to capture Syracuse in a sea battle, only to be thwarted by the city's brave defenders. On the night the Greek ships were poised to retreat, the full moon that would have guided them home was extinguished by an eclipse. The sailors panicked. Nicias summoned a diviner, but since his usual seer had recently died, he had to rely on an unseasoned substitute who explained the eclipse as a directive from the gods to delay the retreat for twenty-seven days, or one cycle of the moon. Accepting his judgment, the Athenians remained, only to be crushed by the vengeful Syracusans. Twenty-seven thousand soldiers died, and the remaining 13,000 ended their lives in slavery. Nicias was killed and his body displayed on the city wall.

In ancient Rome, divination split into several distinct functions. Chief among these was augury. Regarded at the time as a profound science, augury was the study of eclipses as well as of thunder, the behavior of birds and animals, and other natural signs, called auspices. Augurs sought divine approval for the decisions and actions of society's leaders. Since elections, consecrations, and declarations of war could be held in abeyance until they were augured auspicious, these seers exerted enormous control over the lives of citizens and the fates of the communities.

Augurs in early Rome adopted many of their practices from the older Etruscan culture, passing their intricate system orally from generation to generation. As time went by, augury became institutionalized in the Roman Republic, and augurs were gathered into a formal college, along with the pontiffs, who administered public ceremonies, and the keepers of the Sibylline books (a collection of ancient oracular prophecies). The augurs' readings were recorded and stored, with the subsequent outcomes, in secret archives.

To take important auspices, the blindfolded augur would go with a magistrate to some outdoor setting. The official would then survey the land and sky and tell the augur what he saw, while the augur explained its meaning. To Roman augurs, lightning was considered a direct communication from Jupiter, the father of all gods, and lightning bolts were interpreted according to the sector of the sky from which they struck. Bolts from the east were good, those from the west were bad, and those from the north

A comet is said to have warned Montezuma of impending
danger shortly before the coming of Hernán Cortés in 1519, as depicted in this
sixteenth-century illustration. Called smoking stars by the Aztecs, such
celestial fireworks were considered the gravest of portents, often seen as omens of doom.

were the most portentous. Hence, northwestern lightning, meaning especially bad news, was greatly feared. Occasionally, though, the message was more direct. A bolt is said to have struck a statue of Caesar Augustus, actually melting the first letter of the word *Caesar*. Since the letter *C* was the Roman numeral for 100, his augurs predicted that he would live only 100 more days—as he supposedly did.

In another form of Roman augury, alectryomancers kept their eyes on common roosters. These augurs drew a circle in the dirt and divided it into pie segments with a letter of the alphabet in each one. After they scattered feed on this emblem, the rooster ate his way around the circle; the order of the lettered segments from which it took the grain spelled out the answers to augurs' questions.

Perhaps the most elaborate form of classical divination was the inspection of the entrails of sacrificed animals for signs of the gods' wishes. Called haruspicy, this practice came to the Greeks and Romans from either the Etruscans or the earlier cultures of Babylonia and Assyria. Its underlying theory was that when an animal—usually a sheep or an ox—was sacrificed, it was absorbed by the god to which it had been offered, creating a direct channel to the deity. By

44 Ways of Looking Ahead

Over the centuries an astonishing variety of natural objects and occurrences have been used as means of divining the future. The sampling below provides an overview of some of the most common—and more curious—modes of prophecy.

Aeromancy—by the observation of atmospheric phenomena.

Alphitomancy—by the swallowing of a specially baked barley loaf.

Axinomancy—by a stone balanced on a red-hot ax.

Austromancy—by the study of winds.

Botanomancy—by the burning of briar or vervain branches.

Cephalomancy—by boiling a donkey's head.

Ceromancy—by the observation of the shapes formed by dripping melted wax into water.

Chalcomancy—by interpreting the tones made by striking copper or brass bowls.

Chresmomancy—by the utterances of a person in a frenzy.

Cromniomancy—by observing the growth of specially prepared onions.

Daphnomancy—by the sound of burning laurel leaves.

Felidomancy—by the behavior and actions of cats.

Floromancy—by the study of flowers or plants.

Gelomancy—by the interpretation of hysterical laughter.

Gyromancy—by the mutterings of those exhausted by wild dancing.

Halomancy—by casting salt into fire.

Hippomancy—by observing the gait of horses during ceremonial processions.

Ichthyomancy—by the examination of fish, living or dead.

Lithomancy—by the reflection of candlelight in precious stones.

Lychnomancy—by watching flames of three candles forming a triangle.

Macharomancy—by swords, daggers, and knives.

Margaritomancy—by the action of a charmed pearl in a covered pot.

Metopomancy or Metoposcopy—by the lines on a person's forehead.

Myomancy—by the sounds, actions, or sudden appearance of rats or mice.

Nephelomancy—by the movement and shape of clouds.

Oenomancy—by the color, appearance, and taste of wines.

Omphalomancy—by contemplation of one's own navel.

Oneiromancy—by the interpretation of dreams and night visions.

Onychomancy—by the reflection of sunlight on fingernails.

Ophiomancy—by the study of serpents.

Ovomancy—by observing the shapes formed by dropping egg whites into water.

Phyllorhodomancy—by the sounds of rose leaves clapped against the hands.

Podomancy—by study of the soles of the feet.

Scapulomancy—by the markings on the shoulder bone of an animal.

Sciomancy—by the size, shape, and changing appearance of shadows of the dead.

Selenomancy—by the phases and appearances of the moon.

Sideromancy—by the shapes formed by dropping dry straw onto a hot iron.

Splanchomancy—by examining the entrails of sacrificial victims.

Sycomancy—by the drying of fig leaves.

Transataumancy—by events seen or heard accidentally.

Tyromancy—by the coagulation of cheese.

Uromancy—by inspection of urine.

Xylomancy—by interpreting the appearance of fallen tree branches or observing the positions of burning logs.

Zoomancy—by reports of imaginary animals, such as sea monsters.

---

opening the carcass, the haruspex presumed to peek inside the god's mind and watch the future being created.

Their assumptions may have been dubious, but if nothing else, ancient haruspices learned anatomy. In Babylonian and Etruscan ruins, archaeologists have discovered remarkably accurate models of livers, covered with inscriptions pertaining to gods and the heavens. Apparently, haruspices were particularly interested in the *processus pyramidalis,* the liver's pyramid-shaped projection. A large one was taken as a sign of good tidings, but a cleft one meant disruptions ahead. Indeed, several days before March 15, 44 BC, Spurinna Vestricius, Julius Caesar's haruspex, discovered that the liver of a sacrificed bull had no processus pyramidalis at all and warned his patron to watch out for his life. Caesar ignored this timely advice and died as predicted on the infamous Ides of March, of twenty-three dagger wounds inflicted by a group of his closest associates.

In time, haruspices succeeded augurs as the leading official government diviners, but eventually both practices degenerated into superstition, commercialism, and outright fraud. In one instance, a Greek haruspex named Soudinos, to encourage an army that was going into battle, inked the phrase "victory of the king" in reverse on his palm. When he lifted the liver out of its carcass, this war cry was "miraculously" on the organ, spurring the soldiers to battle. Whether they were indeed victorious is not recorded.

Outside the centers of Mediterranean culture, less-civilized peoples practiced their own forms of divination. In stark contrast to the Greeks and Romans, who generally conducted their elaborate rituals in glistening marble temples, the Druids of northern Europe celebrated their mysteries deep in the primeval forests. In the darkling shade of spreading oaks, novices were initiated into Druidical orders by tutelage that lasted as long as twenty years.

The Druids were the spiritual leaders of the Celts, a people who, before the Roman conquests, could be found in Spain, France, Germany, Britain, and as far east as Poland and Turkey. Celts often claimed an inherited characteristic

Divining among the Dogon

Sixty miles south of the river Niger, in one of the most parched and inhospitable regions of the earth, a West African tribe called the Dogon has endured for more than four centuries, largely untouched by the passage of time. As many as 300 small Dogon villages range across a ninety-mile stretch of rocky terrain, which is flanked to the west by towering sandstone cliffs and to the east by a vast, sandy plain.

The Dogon have not only survived but prospered in this challenging region, developing a culture uniquely suited to the burning landscape that surrounds them. But they take no personal credit for their accomplishments, however great or small. For when hundreds of lives depend on methods of planting and harvest or the health of one small child is in question, the Dogon rely on ancient methods of divination to render the critical decisions affecting their tribe.

Their belief in prophetic powers is evident at the festive open-air markets held every fifth day—the final day of the Dogon week. There, village fortune-tellers sit alongside purveyors of meats and spices, ready to dispense wisdom. For a few coins, they will shake a handful of cowrie shells into a straw basket and read the customer's future in the patterns.

Matters of graver import are left to the magical powers of the sand fox. The small, sandy-colored animals that freely roam the surrounding desert are thought to be the earthly emissaries of Ama, the supreme Dogon god. To open a channel to Ama, diviners etch symbols and patterns into the sands outside their villages, then scatter peanuts to lure the foxes. By careful reading of the creatures' trails over the sand drawings, the Dogon find the answers and insights that have sustained them for generations.

A Dogon fortune-teller sits placidly amid the spirited hubbub of market day, ready to foretell the future with a toss of his cowrie shells (inset). The smallest detail is critical to a careful reading, including whether a shell lands face up or face down.

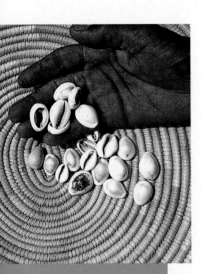

To prepare for the nocturnal arrival of a sand fox, a Dogon elder traces rectangular grids in the sand; each is then filled in with symbols representing the question to be addressed. The next morning, the diviner will study the animal's tracks (inset) to gain wisdom on such matters as fertility, agriculture, and medicine.

they called *an-da-sheal-ladh*, ''the two sights,'' but its mature exercise was a privilege reserved for Druids.

What little we know of this select class comes largely from classical authors. Druids formed a Celtic priesthood, responsible for passing along traditional lore, administering justice, overseeing religious ceremonies, and performing divinations. But the Romans looked upon the priests as primitive and abhorrent, particularly when they discovered that Druidical methods of divination included human sacrifice. In peacetime, the Druids sacrificed pairs of white bulls, but when at war, they dispatched captured enemies or criminals. The hapless ''offerings'' were confined within gigantic wicker sculptures, which were then burned. As the flames mounted, the priests would calmly practice their pyromancy and anthropomancy, reading the future in the smoke and flames and in the screams of their victims.

As the Romans conquered more of the Celtic domain, they tried to wipe out such practices. Later, Christian missionaries continued the effort, even ordering the wholesale slaughter of wrens, birds prized by the Celts because their twitterings were thought to contain prophecies.

ut the old ways may not have been completely crushed by the military might of the Romans and the weight of Christianity. Some believe the most famous of all magicians, Merlin of the King Arthur legend, may have been a Druid who practiced as late as AD 500. Even today, members of an English cult claiming Druid ancestry perform ancient rituals during the summer solstice at Stonehenge, erroneously thought by some to have been built by Druids as a ceremonial center.

Druids and augurs may no longer play an important role in society, but their divinatory advice lives on, especially in folk beliefs about the significance of weather, plant, and animal omens. Four-leaf clovers continue to represent good luck, and a stork flying over a house is still supposed by some to proclaim an imminent pregnancy.

Ancient legends recount how those who ignored the wisdom of animals did so at their peril. On the eve of a sea

On a Mexico City street corner, Lucerito the Trained
Canary selects at random a card that will reveal the fortune of a passerby
who has paid a few pesos to the bird's owner.

The art of reading coffee grounds, demonstrated by these Frenchwomen in 1909, is similar to that of reading tea leaves. The sediment is the key; ancient Romans read the dregs of wine.

battle with the Carthaginians, Claudius Pulcher, a headstrong Roman naval commander, chose to ignore a rather pointed animal omen: The sacred chickens on his ship stopped eating. "Throw the damn chickens into the sea!" he shouted. "If they won't eat, let them drink!" The Roman sailors followed their leader's bidding and were badly beaten by the Carthaginians.

Long after formalized augury died out, the behavior of birds interested omen watchers. In England, for instance, ravens still have special significance. A family of them has occupied the Tower of London for centuries, and it is generally supposed that if they ever fly off, the royal family will die out. By the same token, it is said that Britain's dominion over the fortress of Gibraltar will end if the native population of Barbary apes deserts the rocky peninsula.

Many people still believe animals to be prescient and their actions full of divinatory significance. Such beliefs may be fostered by the fact that many animals have far greater powers of sight, hearing, and smell than humans do. Dogs, for example, are supposed to be able to predict the death of their masters, but perhaps they are merely detecting subtle chemical changes in the body; it may be that the supposed psychic power of these loyal pets is nothing more than a keen sense of smell.

Even insects are said to have powers of foresight. The clicking of the so-called deathwatch beetle was once believed to foretell death in the home it infested. This alleged harbinger was taken quite seriously in the eighteenth century. As the Englishman Duncan Campbell wrote scornfully in 1732, "How many people have I seen in the most terrible palpitations, for months together, expecting every hour the approach of some calamity, only by a little worm which breeds in an old wainscot, and, endeavoring to eat its way out, makes a noise like the movement of a watch."

Ideas about the supposed wisdom of plants have also persisted into modern times. Many people, for example, still believe that laurel thrown on a fire portends good if it crackles and evil if it burns silently—a notion that may be rooted in the days of the Roman Empire, when there was a laurel grove in the capital composed of trees planted by each emperor as he ascended to the throne. But in AD 68, the last year of Emperor Nero's life, the entire grove withered and died, heralding the demise of the line of Caesars.

The use of plants in divination was formalized in the mid-eighteenth century when the Frenchman Rinoir Montaire, a professor at the University of Lyons, devised a briefly popular system known as the Floral Oracle. His clients chose flowers from a large bouquet, their selections supposedly showing underlying characters and future careers. The thistle, not surprisingly, denoted a surly temperament, while a scarlet geranium, for more obscure reasons, revealed stupidity. The subject who picked an apple blossom would become a lawyer; a lily pointed toward politics.

Among the most sought-after forms of divination are those that predict the weather. Even in the technologically advanced twentieth century, accurate weather prediction is important; in previous eras, more affected by the whims of nature, it was a vital skill. Forecasters of old scrutinized everything from the behavior of heavenly bodies to the appetites of fleas for clues to the next day's rain or shine.

On occasion, such predictions threw whole societies into turmoil. In one such case, an almanac published in 1499 by one Johannes Stöffler predicted that a planetary convergence on February 2, 1524, would cause a European reenactment of Noah's flood. As the date approached, as many as 137 pamphlets on the coming disaster were in circulation. The people of Toulouse, France, built and stocked enormous arks. The margrave of Brandenburg, Germany, collected a number of fellow citizens and retreated to the hilltop of Kreuzberg, near Berlin—only to climb down again after it became clear that no flood would occur.

For all of the technology and human energy devoted to it, modern meteorology is still a young and uncertain science. The first barometer, built by Galileo's student Evangelista Torricelli in the seventeenth century, could indicate weather trends for just a day or two in advance, and even today's meteorologists, equipped with many more-sophisticated instruments, will admit that the soundness of their forecasts diminishes to zero for predictions made more than five to ten days in advance.

Given the gap between the desire for perfect weather forecasts and the means to achieve them, it is no surprise that weather folklore has survived through the ages. One time-honored method relies on a calendar of predictions based on saints' days. According to this system, if there is a frost on Saint Sulpicius's day (January 17), it will be a fine spring, whereas if Saint Vincent's day (January 22) is sunny, the following season will be good for wine crops. Also surviving are hundreds of folk sayings based on the behavior of virtually every common animal. "When cockroaches fly, rain will come," claims one adage. "Sharks swim out to sea when a wave of cold weather approaches," says another.

And many Americans still believe that when the woolly caterpillar's brown band is wide, a mild winter lies ahead.

In the words of one weather researcher, most such beliefs "crumple by the weight of their own demerit" when tested. But not all of them are inaccurate. Unlike other forms of divination, which presuppose a certain degree of blind faith, the objective validity of some of these natural indicators has been examined by scientists. Biologists claim that birds do in fact fly closer to the ground before a storm, just as folklore has it. It seems they find the low-pressure air preceding a storm uncomfortable and seek lower altitudes where the pressure is more to their liking.

Indeed, the raw materials of meteorology—temperature, humidity, air pressure, and wind speed—can all be discerned by keen observers of nature without complicated instruments. Mare's tails (wispy cloud trails) usually precede a warm front, while cold fronts are often signaled by a mackerel sky (bunches of puffy, altocumulus clouds).

And Jesus' declaration to the Pharisees, "When it is evening, ye say, it will be fair weather: for the sky is red," is still valid. Actually, the red referred to in many sayings is closer to pink, for pink sunsets signal dry weather ahead, the color being caused by sunlight passing through dust. The light of a blood-red sunset shines through water vapor, a sign of wet weather to come.

Recognizing that such sayings are often accurate, scientists have augmented their earthquake research with serious studies of folklore, including the observation of abnormal animal behavior and other changes in nature as a means of early quake detection. In China, for example, where earthquakes are frequent and often devastating, the government has enlisted as many as 100,000 amateur earthquake watchers, who monitor warning signs such as shifting water levels.

That such traditional signs can be valid indicators of impending seismic upheavals was amply shown in early 1975, when seismologists measuring vibrations within the earth found evidence that a major quake would strike near the port city of Yingkow. At about the same time, local citizens began to witness nature's own indicators: Wells bubbled, rats and mice staggered around in the open as if drugged, and snakes emerged from their winter holes to freeze to death on the surface. On February 4—as anomalous animal behavior increased along with seismic activity—the citizens of Yingkow were evacuated. That evening, a monstrous earthquake demolished the city.

As tempting as it may be to ascribe psychic powers to animals, more mundane explanations may serve. Under certain atmospheric conditions, for example, human beings can hear particularly loud sounds from 600 miles away. An animal with much better hearing than humans may well sense the sound waves of breaking earthquakes while they are still rumbling deep below the earth's crust.

Most people living in earthquake zones would surely feel more confident relying for their warnings on the work of scientists rather than on the antic behavior of snakes, rats, and mice; reliance on natural omens to predict the weather has also waned. At the same time, however, divination through observing natural occurrences has evolved into more symbolic forms, involving the supposedly psychic powers of the human mind.

One technique is known as tasseography, or more humbly, tea-leaf reading. The practice is thought to have evolved from the more venerable geomancy—divination through the patterns of shifting sand or pebbles cast on the ground. Along with tea drinking itself, the art may have been born in ancient China, but the modern world came to know it through the tea-loving British. Today, Ireland is said to boast the best contemporary tea-readers, and even some Irish Catholic priests have their tea leaves read on occasion—though all in a spirit of fun.

In the United States, tasseography is often practiced in the ubiquitous Gypsy tearooms of larger cities, where a hostess provides an indifferent meal and a cup of tea before performing a reading. These shamelessly commercial establishments have given tea-leaf reading a tawdry reputation. For example, the reputed psychic Eileen Garrett, who remained skeptical about most forms of fortune-telling, recounted in one of her books the tale of a lonely country schoolteacher who came to New York in the early part of

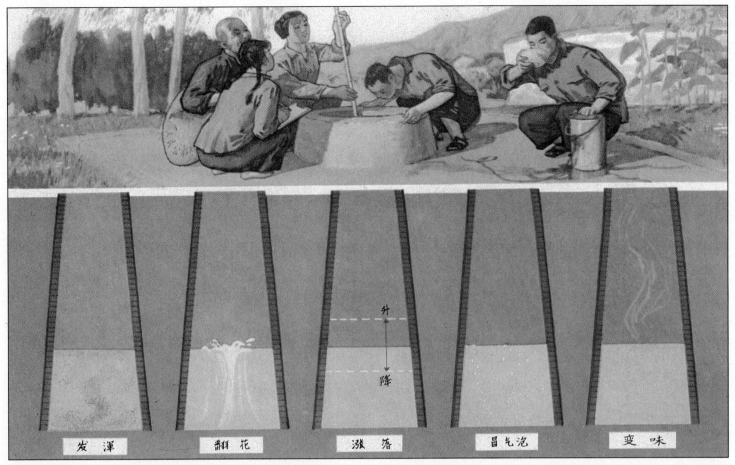

发渾　翻花　漲落　冒气泡　变味

Rearing horses, panicked pigs and fowl, and leaping fish may be harbingers of an earthquake, according to four scenes taken from a modern Chinese educational poster (opposite). Scientists there take heed of these and other natural omens, such as irregularities in well water (above), to help anticipate and prepare for major tremors.

this century and had her tea leaves read. During the sitting, the reader picked up clues that her client held a secret passion for her happily married local minister. Playing on the teacher's hidden desires, the reader hinted that the leaves indicated the minister's wife was engaged in an extramarital affair. This information apparently goaded the teacher into sending anonymous warning notes to the minister, thereby causing a great scandal. Eventually she was driven to confess what she had done and was forced to leave both her job and her community.

To be sure, would-be subjects of a tasseography session can avoid the risk of being thus manipulated by reading their own tea leaves. In a recent book on the subject, seasoned leaf reader Ian McKinnie—who practices his art in Santa Rosa, California—explained the technique. He recommends starting with the right sort of tea: English breakfast—loose tea, not tea bags. (In a pinch, coffee grounds can be substituted for tea leaves.) Brew the tea and pour it with some of the leaves into a plain bone-china cup. After drinking all but the last half-teaspoonful, swirl the cup around

several times and turn it upside down into its saucer. Wait a few moments for the liquid to drain out, then lift the cup, turn it over, and examine the pattern of leaves that should be clinging to the interior.

Look for the shapes of familiar images in the scattered leaves. Said to portend future events, the more obvious ones include an airplane (an imminent journey), an angel (good tidings), a beehive (prosperity), and a mountain (either an obstacle or great ambition). Some of the more obscure images are opera glasses (a quarrel), a kangaroo (domestic harmony), a saucepan (anxiety), and a steeple (a setback). Mice or rats mean danger or bad financial news, which grows worse with the length of their tails.

In addition to displaying such portents, McKinnie believes, the distribution of the leaves within the cup says something about the seeker's personality. Leaves spread evenly all around the cup denote an outgoing optimist; one large clump at the bottom indicates a stick-in-the-mud.

McKinnie claims much success in his tasseographical career. In one case, he says, the leaves enabled him to predict that a high-school friend of his daughter would become a flight attendant, marry her current boyfriend, and move to Australia—all three of which she eventually did.

Because its perceived omens are so subjective, tas-

*In 1935 a vision in the sacred lake of Lhamo Latso
reportedly guided a Tibetan council to their new spiritual ruler; the fourteenth
Dalai Lama (right) was only two years old at the time.*

seography is most often—and perhaps most appropriately—treated as entertainment rather than a serious attempt at divination. As a dubious Eileen Garrett once put it: "Have you ever really *looked* at wet tea leaves? . . . I must confess that to my jaundiced eye, they reveal very little . . . . What astute jurisdiction is to decide whether that wiggly line of leaves is a snake, the symbol of evil, or a serpentine line, the symbol of fortune? . . . To get any picture out of them at all requires a most abundantly fertile imagination."

Possibly the most pervasive form of natural divination is known as scrying, in which a practitioner presumes to plumb the depths of hidden knowledge by concentrating on a smooth, clear, or reflective surface. Derived from the old word *descry,* meaning to catch sight of, scrying takes many forms. Ancient Greeks practiced hydromancy, or scrying in the waters of a spring, such as the one in front of the goddess Demeter's sanctuary. To see the fate of a sick person, hydromancers lowered a mirror on a string to the water's surface, letting it graze the water. When they pulled the mirror back up and looked at it, they supposedly would see the image of the person as either dead or living.

Gastromancy was another form of scrying. According to the sixth-century philosopher Damascius, gastromancers "filled certain round glasses with fair water, about which they placed lighted torches, then invoked the question to be solved. At length, the demon answered by reflections from the water representing what should come to pass."

In ancient India, warriors often practiced cylicomancy, peering into a vessel of water before heading into battle. If they saw their reflections, they knew they would return. Tahitians claimed to use cylicomancy to track down robbers. After digging a hole in the earthen floor of a burglarized house, the cylicomancer would fill the space with water, pray to a deity, and wait for the image of the culprit to be revealed on the surface of the water.

Despite—or perhaps because of—scrying's widespread acceptance in ancient times, early Christian leaders were dead set against it. Saint Patrick declared that any Christians who believed demons could be seen in mirrors would be expelled from the Church until they repented. Even so, the Middle Ages continued to foster scrying of all sorts, and scryers used every aid from fingernails to swords.

Roger Bacon, the thirteenth-century British scholar and mystic, was reported to possess a glass "of excellent nature, that any man might beholde any thing that he desired to see, within the compass of fifty miles round about him." (Some historians now believe that this legend may have grown out of Bacon's studies of optics.) Later in his life, however, Bacon was imprisoned for some of his occult practices, as well as for his attacks on established theologians and scholars of the time. And in 1467, when one William Byg of Yorkshire confessed that he had used a crystal in order to find his neighbors' stolen property, he was forced to march to the Cathedral of Saint Peter at York, recant, and burn his books.

Virtually every kind of smooth or reflective object has been used for scrying, including the simple stone of Coinneach Odhar, the Brahan Seer. Others have claimed to use the back of a watch, a door lock, an eggshell, and soap bubbles. One contemporary scryer says he has employed a blank television screen, a radiator, the outside of a black coffee cup, and even his own highly polished shoes.

For sheer potency, however, no scrying tool outdoes the alleged powers of the familiar yet enigmatic crystal ball. And no crystal gazer has cut a more dramatic swath through history than the Englishman John Dee—mathematician, philosopher, and adviser to Queen Elizabeth I.

The son of a minor palace official in the court of Henry VIII, Dee was an exceptional student who entered Cambridge University when he was fifteen. Although he claimed to study a full eighteen hours a day, Dee once took time out to build an intricate prop for a school play: a high-flying beetle that carried the hero of a Greek drama up to the ceiling. The audience was reputedly so terrified by the spectacle that a number of them jumped up during the performance shouting, "Sorcerer!"

Dee excelled at Cambridge and was named Under-reader (junior faculty member) before taking his degree. After graduating he traveled to the Continent to continue his studies, achieving overnight fame in Paris at the age of twenty-three, when he delivered a series of lectures on the recently exhumed works of the Greek mathematician Euclid. Like other classical sciences, mathematics had languished in Europe during the Middle Ages, and it continued to possess an air of magic and forbidden knowledge in the sixteenth century. Dee's lectures caused a sensation, and thousands of students packed the lecture hall and scaled the outside walls in order to listen to them.

After returning to England in 1551, Dee met the future Queen Elizabeth while she was being held under house arrest by Queen Mary. The two developed a friendship that lasted for the rest of their lives. As queen, Elizabeth gave Dee money and eventually a royal assignment as warden of Christ's College in Manchester. More importantly, she protected him from those who accused him of witchcraft. She even set the date for her coronation in 1558 according to his astrological calculations.

Dee's house in Mortlake, near London, was for many years a major center of science in England. Dee salvaged many ancient scientific tomes that had been scattered when Roman Catholic churches and monasteries were ransacked during the Reformation, and his own library of more than 4,000 books may have been the largest of its kind in Europe at the time.

In the year 1581, however, John Dee's life swerved onto an entirely new path. He later wrote of how, as he knelt in prayer late one autumn evening, "there suddenly glowed a dazzling light, in the midst of which, in all his glory, stood the great angel, Uriel." The spirit reportedly handed Dee a crystal "most bright, most clear and glorious, of the bigness of an egg" and informed him that by gazing at it he could communicate with otherworldly spirits. John Dee was enraptured by this prospect, but in spite of the angel's promise, he had little luck at scrying with this "shew-stone." The scientist resorted to employing others to do the actual scrying, conversing directly with the spirits, while he kept scrupulous notes.

Unfortunately Dee's scryers were less scrupulous than he. The one with him the longest was Edward Kelley. A classic Renaissance scoundrel, Kelley was an erstwhile lawyer who had already had his ears cropped for counterfeiting before he met Dee. He also stood accused of necromancy—the practice of using dead bodies for divination.

Kelley was unquestionably a charlatan, but his attempts at scrying with Dee may well have been honest—at least at the beginning. Gazing into the glass, he reported to Dee that "in the middle of the stone seemeth to stand a little round thing like a spark of fire, and it increaseth, and it seemeth to be as a globe of twenty inches diameter, or there about." In this glowing central sphere, Kelley claimed to raise a host of spiritual beings who attempted, among other things, to teach Dee "Enochian," the language spoken by angels and the inhabitants of the Garden of Eden. In fact, Dee's alleged Enochian records are elaborate enough to have convinced some credulous readers that they represented a genuine pre-Hebraic language. But at least one researcher has suggested that Enochian was a code Dee used to transmit messages from overseas to Queen Elizabeth in his alleged capacity as a founding member of the English secret service.

Dee's avid interest in crystallomancy seems to have been merely part of his driving intellectual quest to understand the secrets of the natural world. To his restless mind, there was no distinction between magic and science—knowledge was knowledge, and who better than angels to provide it? The sly Kelley, on the other hand, was more interested in acquiring instant wealth through alchemy, espe-

*Catherine de Médicis watches in wonder as, in this idealized
1887 engraving, the famed prophet Nostradamus causes the royal destinies of her sons to
appear in a mirror. The Queen of France regularly consulted
the seer, who probably censored his forecasts to suit her expectations.*

cially by way of the long-sought secret of transforming base metal into gold. In pursuit of both ideals, Dee and Kelley eventually made their way to Poland in 1583 at the request of Count Albert Laski, who hoped they would help him master the alchemical sciences.

By this time, Edward Kelley seemed to have Dee firmly under his control, but one day he finally took things too far. On April 18, 1587, he announced that the crystal had ordered the pair to share their wives. So dependent was Dee on Kelley that he and his wife actually signed an agreement to do so. Whether the pact was ever consummated is unclear, but soon afterward the Dees returned—without Kelley—to England.

The irrepressible Kelley then moved on to Prague at the invitation of Holy Roman Emperor Rudolf II, who also

hoped to learn the secret of alchemy. When Kelley failed to provide it, he was thrown into prison on charges of sorcery and fraud. In 1593 he tried to escape by climbing down from a high window, but his improvised ladder of bedsheets gave way under his considerable bulk, and he fell, breaking many bones. He died the next day.

Dee's fortunes were not much better. His patron Elizabeth died in 1603. He tried two other scryers, both dishonest, and finally ended up, in the words of the biographer John Aubrey, as a beaten old man with "a long beard as white as milke, tall and slender, who wore a gowne with hanging sleeves." He earned a pittance telling fortunes and even sold his beloved books, one by one, in order to eat. Dee died in 1608, his dreams of sublime knowledge long since dashed. He did, however, gain a measure of immortal-

ity: Some believe he may have served as the model for Shakespeare's Prospero, the learned sorcerer of *The Tempest.*

Among all the means of scrying, crystallomancy has continued to hold center stage. And like so many other forms of the occult, it flourished in the late-nineteenth-century heyday of spiritualism. One of the more colorful crystal gazers of that era was Nell St. John Montague, an Englishwoman whose autobiography, *Revelations of a Society Clairvoyante,* shows a flair for the thrilling tale.

Montague was born in India not long before the turn of the century, the daughter of Major General C. B. Lucie-Smith. Her favorite childhood toy, she wrote, was a crystal ball given to her by her Indian nurse. One day when she was about five years old, Montague related, she was gazing into the ball when it suddenly seemed to move and become shapeless. "In its place," according to Montague, "came a thick black mist which seemed to spread, enveloping all the space before me. Then slowly in the blackness I saw reflected the interior of my mother's bedroom, and my eyes became focused upon the blue embroidered dressing-gown laid on the bed ready for her to put on. . . . My mother was approaching the bed, her hands outstretched to pick the garment up, when, almost paralysed with horror, I saw something uncoil itself from amongst the soft silkfolds. A wild shriek broke from me, and I dropped the ball, as the concealed cobra darted out and reared to strike."

The terrified young girl ran for comfort to her mother, who assumed that her child's screams resulted from a nightmare. Hoping to ease her fears, Mrs. Lucie-Smith summoned a sentry, and the three went to the bedroom to investigate. As Montague told the story, her mother told her to look and assure herself that there was no snake in the room. "Then to show the truth of her words she approached the bed. As she did so, a loud cry broke from the sentry's lips, and with wonderful courage he pushed her aside and sprang forward, his bayonet uplifted to strike the cobra which had suddenly darted out, and reared up with inflated hood."

From then on, according to Montague, her parents believed firmly in her powers, and she went on to a lifetime of successful scrying in Europe. Once, she claimed, while giving a reading for a naval officer, she peered into her crystal and saw several blood-spattered women, their clothes ripped from their bodies. Fearing that her client was or would be a murderer, she nonetheless told him of her vision. About a year later, he wrote to inform her that the vision had come true, that the women were in fact earthquake victims from Messina, Italy, taken aboard his vessel in a rescue effort. On another occasion, an Englishwoman living in India wrote and asked for a reading, enclosing a letter from her young son. Montague placed the letter against her crystal ball and saw an image of three boys being mistreated by a "vile-looking" clergyman. Informed of the vision, the woman expressed some surprise, noting that her son, a student at an English boarding school, had described in his letters the warm, loving care he was receiving. Not long afterward, according to Montague's account, she herself discovered the boarding school—conveniently located next door to a good friend of hers—and liberated the boy from the clutches of the abusive headmaster. Montague continued her readings until she was killed in a World War II London air raid—presumably having failed to foresee her violent end.

Nell Montague and other scryers of her era inspired many amateurs, who were further encouraged when the renowned English psychic researcher Frederic W. H. Myers estimated in the late 1800s that one in twenty people had scrying abilities. And a number of books published at the time drew on traditional sources to describe the proper techniques for those who wished to try crystal gazing.

The tract *Crystal Gazing and Clairvoyance,* published in 1896 by John Melville, prescribed an elaborate scrying ritual that required equally elaborate paraphernalia—including an ivory or ebony stand for the ball, inlaid with magic words in raised golden letters. In proper Victorian fashion, Melville insisted that the scryer must consecrate all of the implements and repeat a long and pious Christian invocation. He also issued a stern warning to any scryer with evil intentions: "When he or she uses the crystal . . . it will *react* upon the seer sooner or later *with terrible effect."*

Modern-day scryers are less formal and less fearful than Melville, but their recommendations for successful scrying are still complex. According to one author, the ball should be round or oval and about four inches in diameter. A natural crystal is preferred, although glass is less expensive and perfectly acceptable.

Ideally, the orb should be kept in the dark and always in the same place, to avoid extreme temperature changes and unwanted influences. It must also be spotless and unscratched so that imperfections will not distract the scryer. One age-old cleaning technique calls for boiling it in a five-to-one mixture of water and brandy for fifteen minutes and then drying it with a chamois cloth. For a few days before scrying, says another author, one should also purify one's thoughts through positive thinking, one's body through frequent baths, and one's insides by a judicious diet.

A dimly lit room is ideal for the reading. The orb should be surrounded by dark, heavy cloth—such as velvet—to cut down on distracting reflections, and it should be viewed from about a foot away. Some scryers recommend passing one's hands over the ball to increase its power and sensitivity. Others suggest trying to look at the crystal and through it at the same time in order to temporarily short-circuit normal eyesight and induce so-called inner vision.

Within about five minutes, if the scryer is successful, the ball will supposedly become opaque and milky, as if clouds are passing through it. When the clouds disperse, images may form. They might appear as a single static image, in a series like a slide show, or as a full-blown movie-like presentation.

If no images are forthcoming, one might be able to read portents in the clouds alone. According to Melville, whose interpretations are still widely accepted, white ones mean yes or good tidings, while black are, of course, bad news. Bright colors like red and yellow signal unpleasant surprises, while blue and green portend coming joy.

The solid images that appear in a crystal ball are said to be more difficult to interpret objectively, because they have different meanings for each person. Thus an airplane could mean either an impending journey or an unconscious desire to get away from an uncomfortable situation.

Most scryers emphasize that the ball acts not as a telescope into the unknown but as a means of focusing their attention and sharpening innate ability. As Miss Angus, a scryer of the late 1800s, explained, "The moment the *vision* comes the *ball* seems to disappear, so it is difficult for me to say if my pictures are actually seen *in* the crystal."

The Message of the Pendulum

The ancient practice of divining with pendulums is enjoying new popularity. Some modern mystics believe that the swinging motion of a pendant responding to gravity—and perhaps to more mysterious forces as well—can reveal inner truths and foretell the future.

A pendulum is any object suspended so that it can move freely. The weight itself, called a bob, may be made of almost anything. But some pendulum enthusiasts prefer using a quartz crystal, such as the one shown here, in the belief that crystals are keys to unlocking psychic potential.

To make a pendulum, simply attach a weight to a thread, string, or lightweight chain. There are no specific requirements for the thread's length or the bob's weight, but the pendulum should swing easily and be comfortable to hold.

Specialists claim numerous uses for pendulums. The objects purportedly can help diagnose disease, for instance, or help locate water, treasure, or even missing persons. For more general divination, however, the easiest and most widely practiced way to use a pendulum is this: Hold it perfectly still and concentrate on a question that can be answered yes or no. Theoretically the pendulum should move in response, prompted by some mysterious source of truth. The most common interpretation of its message is that rotation in a clockwise direction means yes, a counterclockwise motion no.

The experimenter should know that the slightest movement at the top of the string will be greatly magnified by the bob. Critics observe that pendulum power might therefore be no more than the amplification of the holder's own muscular movement. In other words, a subconscious hope for a particular answer may prompt the slightest inadvertent twitch, which will, in turn, deliver the desired response.

While occultists would argue that the crystal somehow helps its users harness paranormal powers, psychological theory offers another explanation for scrying, suggesting that it is a form of retrieving and projecting knowledge buried in the subconscious. The following experience, related by the English psychical researcher and scryer Ada Goodrich-Freer, seems to support this notion. "The crystal had nothing more attractive to show me than the combination 7694," she wrote of one of her sessions. "I laid aside the crystal and took up my banking-book, which I had certainly not seen for some months, and found, to my surprise, that the number on the cover was 7694."

In a somewhat similar vein, a number of children and some adults exhibit a capacity called eidetic imagery—the ability to stare at an object or scene and then mentally project it onto a wall or other suitable screen. This could account for the fact that in ancient cultures young children were often used as scryers. The images they saw in the mirror or the water may have been projections of images in their memories or imaginations.

In recent years, crystals and other stones have gained a considerable reputation as mystical objects, allegedly useful for healing and meditation as well as divination. Ursula Markham, a British medium, developed her own system of "gemology," employing many semiprecious stones instead of a single crystal orb.

For divination, Markham suggests collecting a wide variety of stones, at least forty. These include labradorite, signifying a place overseas; iron pyrite, or fool's gold, signifying mistrust or deception; purple agate, emblem of emotional sensitivity; green jasper, for unrequited love; and perhaps most important, aquamarine, warning of a cool, logical client who doubts the validity of crystal readings.

For her readings, Markham sits opposite the questioner with her collection of stones in a velvet tray between them. The questioner picks out nine stones, and Markham divines their portent according to the choice and the order in which they were chosen. For example, a tiger's eye (meaning independence) followed by a turritella agate (sig-nifying a change in employment) might indicate that the questioner is thinking of starting a business.

Diviners such as Ursula Markham can rarely provide solid evidence that their techniques actually work. In the final analysis, the efficacy of her stone readings and of tea-leaf readings and scrying must rely on faith: A questioner who believes that a certain form of divination works will be inclined to find evidence that it has. And as Eileen Garrett, a woman who claimed remarkable psychic abilities, once suggested, many diviners and other psychic readers are, if nothing else, at least willing to take the time to listen to their clients, something that physicians, the clergy, and even professional counselors frequently do not do.

Nevertheless she sounded a skeptical, cautionary note: "Modern man, like his primitive ancestors," she wrote, "still pays homage to the soothsayer who can offer a reassuring word and a bright future. And I am afraid that that is about all that most crystal gazers can supply, whether the bright future is there or not. . . . The lights are low, the price is high; the atmosphere is dim and the future is bright. But that future depends on what you do and not on the dazzling crystal."

On the other hand, the time-honored tradition of interpreting natural signs—observing the behavior of birds or the shape of clouds—can in fact yield scientifically valid information. Few today would deny that animals, plants, and the atmosphere itself form an interwoven ecological entity, of which one part may give clues to the whole. And the ancients, most of whom lived closer to the land than modern people, may have learned much about nature that we retain only as quaint nuggets of folklore.

In any case, we still exhibit a strong appetite for divination of many sorts. We may no longer inspect animal entrails for clues to what lies ahead, but many of us still attend crystal readings, stroll into Gypsy tearooms, or hang on every word of the long-range weather forecast. Like all mortals since the emergence of humankind, we fret about the future and yearn for signs of hope, for good things to come and for bad things to stay away.

Portents in the Palm

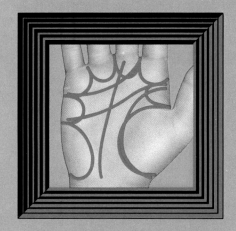

For thousands of years, in diverse cultures, people have believed that an individual's destiny is previewed in the hands, that every palm, from the time of birth, holds in its own unique network of mounts and valleys, lines and markings, the key to life's potential. It is also said that as the person matures, significant events in his or her life will be reflected in the palm. But these markers of the past and guideposts to the future are usually indecipherable to all but a few—those who can supposedly divine the course of someone's life through palm reading.

Palmistry has changed little over time. Its proponents claim that it enables people to understand themselves better. It may also reveal inherent strengths and weaknesses in character—useful knowledge when facing life's challenges—and provide clues as to how one's nature can affect health, career, and relationships. But most of all, many palmists contend, hand analysis enables people to make choices that will bring them pleasure and self-fulfillment.

In a reading, palmists usually compare the subject's right and left hands. The lines and overall form of the so-called passive hand are thought to reflect one's innate potential, while those of the dominant hand—typically the one used for writing—are said to reveal choices the individual has made and what may lie ahead. A thorough palmist generally discerns from the hand's shape and markings a likely life pattern, a set of tendencies, or particular events that may occur. Some of the features from which palmists gather information are examined on the next pages.

Observing the Hand

In palmistry, personality analysis is based on the appearance of the entire hand. Among the various factors taken into account in this overview, the basic form of the hand is particularly important.

Hands are often classified as one of four types, named by some practitioners of the art to correspond to the traditional four elements of nature—air, earth, water, and fire. The classifications are based on the shape of the palm and the length of the fingers in relation to it. Palms are typically rectangular or square, with either long or short fingers. Fingers are considered long if the middle finger (called the Saturn finger in palmistry) is at least as long as the palm itself, and short if that finger falls short of the palm's length.

Other factors that contribute to the hand's appearance are the shapes of the fingertips and the placement and flexibility of the thumb *(opposite page)*. To analyze the shape of your own hand, trace its outline on paper, then compare the drawing to those shown here.

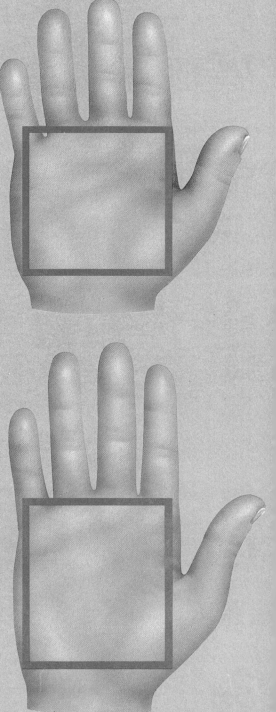

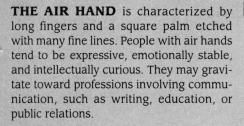

THE AIR HAND is characterized by long fingers and a square palm etched with many fine lines. People with air hands tend to be expressive, emotionally stable, and intellectually curious. They may gravitate toward professions involving communication, such as writing, education, or public relations.

THE EARTH HAND, signified by a deeply lined square palm and short fingers, may reflect a serious, practical person who delights in physical activity. These individuals tend to enjoy manual occupations, such as carpentry, farming, and working with machinery.

THE WATER HAND, with its long fingers extending from a finely lined rectangular palm, often reveals a sensitive, creative, quiet personality. Studious or relatively low-pressure occupations—such as research, office work, or retail sales—may appeal to these individuals.

THE FIRE HAND, recognized by its short fingers and rectangular palm filled with clear lines, denotes an energetic, impetuous person. People who have fire hands seem drawn to professions that involve challenge, risk, and creativity, such as medicine, law enforcement, or the arts.

A Variety of Fingertips

The shape of an individual's fingertips, palmists maintain, provides further insight into his or her character. There are four distinct fingertip shapes—conic, round, square, and spatulate.

Conic fingertips, which taper off almost to a point, imply a sensitive and impulsive nature, as well as a love of art and beauty. The individual may also be highly intuitive, relying more on that gift than on powers of reason.

A well-balanced disposition is usually denoted by round fingertips. This individual adapts easily to change, is receptive to new ideas, and reacts to situations with equal measures of mental and emotional reasoning.

People with square fingertips tend to thrive on order and regularity and to express themselves clearly and with confidence. They desire security and stability for themselves as well as for their loved ones.

Fingertips that are narrow at the first joint and then flare to a wide tip are known as spatulate. Individuals with spatulate fingertips are usually considered to be independent, energetic, and enthusiastic; they love action everywhere in their lives, even seeking it in the books and other materials they read. These generally down-to-earth personalities often make true and loyal friends.

Palmists observe that some fingertip shapes are typically associated with certain hand types. Individuals with water hands, for example, frequently possess conic fingertips, while square fingertips are commonly found on individuals with air hands.

A mixture of one or more fingertip shapes on an individual's hand is also common. These so-called mixed hands suggest a person who is versatile, adapts quite easily to new situations, and may excel in a variety of occupations.

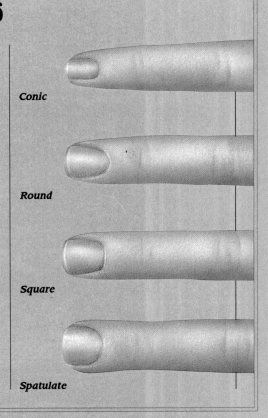

Conic

Round

Square

Spatulate

The Revealing Thumb

The thumb is regarded by some palmists as the key to personality. It is thought to reveal so much, in fact, that some Hindu palmists study only the thumb when analyzing an individual's character. Most practitioners of palmistry, however, insist on weighing the thumb's length, placement, and flexibility in relation to the entire hand.

In general, the thumb reveals an individual's energy level and strength of will. A long thumb, reaching past the knuckle of the index, or Jupiter, finger, may indicate a forceful personality and an abundance of energy. Someone with a short thumb may lack self-confidence and have little ability to complete projects.

The thumb's significance is also affected by its placement on the hand.

A low-set thumb, one that creates an angle of sixty to ninety degrees between the thumb and index finger, reveals a personality that is flexible, independent, logical, and well-directed. Someone with a high-set thumb, creating an angle of thirty degrees or less with the index finger, may be tense and self-contained.

Another indication of ego strength is in the thumb's tip. If the tip is flexible, bending back easily at the first joint, the person probably adapts easily and is generous, although not indiscriminately so. If the thumb is extremely flexible, the individual might be extravagant or show a lack of restraint.

A thumb that bends only slightly under pressure may indicate a practical personality and a strong will modified by open-mindedness. The owner of a rigid thumb may be stubborn and resistant to new ideas and experiences. However, this person is usually very reliable, stable, and responsible.

Minding the Mounts

The most thorough readings by professional palmists may include an analysis of the palm's mounts, the fleshy pads found at the base of the thumb and each finger and on the outer edges of the palm. The larger the mount and the more directly it is centered under the corresponding finger, the greater its supposed influence on the personality. Prominent bulges are considered strong or highly developed mounts, while those that are flat or only slightly raised are judged normal or well developed. A depression in the palm instead of a fleshy pad constitutes a weak mount.

MOUNT OF SATURN. Found at the base of the middle, or Saturn, finger, this mount governs the introspective aspect of the personality. A well-developed Saturn mount reveals an independent nature, that of a person who enjoys solitude as well as the company of others. Self-awareness and emotional balance are indicated, as are fidelity and prudence.

A highly developed mount may indicate an unhealthy tendency toward self-absorption. And lack of a Saturn mount may denote indecisiveness, a pessimistic tendency, and a poor sense of humor.

MOUNT OF APOLLO. This mount, located at the base of the Apollo, or ring, finger, is said to govern all forms of creativity. A well-developed mount implies strong artistic abilities and a love of beauty. These talents may not apply solely to the fine arts but may also include culinary expertise or other forms of expression. A prominent Apollo mount may signify a tendency toward extravagance and materialism as well as vanity and self-indulgence. Low physical energy, a lack of aesthetic values, and a disregard for creative pursuits may stem from a weak Apollo mount.

MOUNT OF JUPITER. At the base of the index finger, the mount of Jupiter reveals an individual's degree of self-confidence, social sense, and leadership ability. If the mount is well developed, healthy measures of assertiveness and ambition are indicated, as well as an even temper, generosity, and self-assurance.

An unusually strong mount may tip the scales toward vanity, narcissism, and an overbearing attitude. However, if the prominent mount is modified by factors in the lines and fingers, the individual may simply exhibit strong leadership skills. An underdeveloped mount may suggest a poor self-image, lack of respect for authority, and a tendency toward idleness.

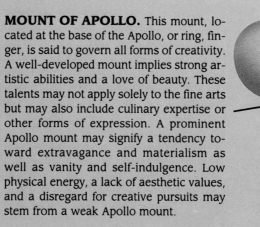

MOUNT OF MERCURY. Communication is ruled by the mount of Mercury, at the base of the pinkie. A well-developed mount implies a talent for self-expression and a lively disposition. A large mount has no negative connotations, but an underdeveloped one may mean a lack of business acumen and difficulty communicating. A mount with short, straight lines may denote a caring, compassionate nature.

LOWER MOUNT OF MARS. This fleshy area located just inside the thumb joint is considered a barometer of the individual's assertive nature and ability to overcome obstacles. A normal mount indicates courage and aggressiveness; an overdeveloped mount may indicate a hot temper as well as an abundance of sexual passion. A weak lower mount of Mars suggests a quiet, passive nature and timidity in the face of challenge.

MOUNT OF VENUS. A fleshy ball at the base of the thumb, the mount of Venus is considered by some to be the seat of basic emotions. This mount is said to indicate physical and sexual energy, an appreciation of beauty and the arts, and the ability to love and be loved.

A firm and rounded mount of Venus suggests compassion, sincerity, warmth, and vitality, as well as a love of the outdoors. An overdeveloped mount, especially one with reddish skin color, reveals physical energy and sexual passion, and a healthy appetite for food and drink. An individual with a small or weak Venus mount may suffer delicate health, a lack of exuberance and intensity, and perhaps a lack of sensitivity. Frequently, palmists say, a strong love relationship can cause this mount to increase in size.

UPPER MOUNT OF MARS. Located just beneath the Mercury mount, the upper mount of Mars reportedly measures an individual's determination and resistance. A firm, well-formed mount reveals courage, self-reliance, and a somewhat stubborn nature. An extremely large mount might indicate inflexibility and, perhaps, a tendency toward violence or cruelty. A weak mount may reflect a lack of assertiveness, the sign of an individual who is easily manipulated by others.

MOUNT OF LUNA. A well-developed mount of Luna, located opposite the Venus mount and just above the wrist, suggests a balance between imagination and reality and a love of peace and harmony. The more fully developed the mount, the greater the individual's gift of intuition and imagination and the stronger the nurturing instincts; for some, restlessness is also implied. A weak Luna mount may suggest a steadfastly realistic personality who seldom indulges in fantasy.

Looking at the Lines

The complex network of lines discernible in every palm is allegedly capable of steering each of us along life's course. Palmists analyze these lines not only to reflect the development of an individual's character traits as he or she matures but also to reveal insights into the future. And armed with this knowledge, the believers say, a person can actually affect future events. The lines of the palm are constantly changing: Old lines may fade or grow clearer and new ones may appear, sometimes in a matter of weeks. By modifying behavior and changing attitudes, palmists maintain, we can change our lines—and thus our lives—to achieve our predestined potential.

HEART LINE. An ideal heart line, indicating a warm and demonstrative nature, begins at the hand's outer edge, beneath the Mercury finger. It traverses the palm near the base of the finger mounts, curving upward slightly before ending between the Jupiter and Saturn mounts.

An upward curve implies a physical or instinctual sexuality, while a straight heart line suggests that romantic imagery is important in love. Two or three branches at the line's end are thought to indicate a balance between emotions, realism, and physical passion.

A wide space between the heart and head lines reflects extroversion and an unconventional outlook on life; a narrow space might imply some lack of self-confidence, difficulty expressing feelings, and a secretive nature. If the heart line is longer than the head line, the person could be ruled more by emotions than reason.

A chainlike heart line may signal a person who falls in love easily but fears commitment. Romantic upsets are suggested by short diagonal lines crossing the heart line; small islands—points where the line splits in two, then merges once more—especially near the Jupiter mount, could imply significant romantic disappointments, such as divorce.

HEAD LINE. The head line, reflecting intellectual capacity and potential, usually begins below the Jupiter mount and traverses the palm. An analytical nature is typified by a straight head line, while a downward-sloping line suggests creativity. A forked end indicates a balance between imagination and realism.

Average intelligence and good reasoning powers are symbolized by a head line stretching at least two-thirds of the way across the palm. A longer line is said to reveal keen insight and a range of intellectual interests. A wide gap between the head and life lines at their origin may reflect impulsivity and impatience; the closer the lines, the more tentative the person.

RELATIONSHIP LINES. On the outer edge of the hand, between the heart line and the base of the Mercury finger, one or more short, horizontal lines may be found. Called relationship or marriage lines, they supposedly indicate important commitments. The lines can signify deep friendships as well as intimate relationships. The stronger the line, it is said, the more potential for the union.

Lines denoting current or past relationships are usually indelibly etched in the palm, but those signaling future ones may change periodically. A line may become clearer to show deeper feelings, or new lines may appear. To estimate the age at which a relationship may occur, note the line's position between the heart line and the base of the Mercury finger; a point about midway may mean age thirty-five.

LIFE LINE. An indicator of disposition, physical energy, and well-being, the life line usually originates between the mounts of Jupiter and lower Mars and follows the curve of the mount of Venus. A broad arc around the Venus mount is thought to indicate a warm and emotionally responsive nature; a shallow arc, cutting into the mount, suggests an aloof, inhibited, or unresponsive individual. If the life line ends curving toward the Venus mount, the individual is said to be domestic, drawn to the comforts of home. A line curving toward the mount of Luna suggests a restless personality, one who loves adventure and travel.

The life line itself, if deep and clear, denotes a strong physical constitution, good health, and vitality. Any islands may signal periods of ill health or indecision. Breaks in the line are sometimes interpreted as an illness or accident or as a change in the individual's life-style.

While the length of the life line has often been used to predict a time of death, reputable palmists believe such predictions are virtually impossible—and irresponsible—to make. The line shows tendencies, they say, not facts, and the length of the life line is no guarantee against life's uncertainties.

FATE LINE. Also known as the career or destiny line, this line reveals an individual's level of satisfaction with a profession or other chosen task. Ideally, the fate line begins just above the wrist and moves upward toward the mount of Saturn. Generally, the higher in the palm the fate line begins, the later in life the person will find his or her true vocation.

If the fate line originates in the mount of Luna, it portends a career that depends on the decisions of other people—as in politics, for example—or the potential may exist for a number of careers and possible relocation. If the line arises from the mount of Venus, the family may play a part in the individual's profession.

The more content an individual is with his or her chosen path, the clearer the fate line may be; a weak, fragmented line may reveal a person who feels restless or unfulfilled. Breaks in the fate line are interpreted as a hiatus in one's career or a change of direction, and islands may reveal a temporary obstacle in the path. An additional vertical line running close to the fate line may suggest a second career or strong avocational interest.

A person will remain active throughout life, it is thought, if he or she possesses a long fate line. If the line comes to a stop at the heart line, however, the individual's ambition could be thwarted by emotions; if the line ends at the head line, his or her success may be stymied by some sort of intellectual blunder.

A Sampling of Readings

Palmistry is an art acquired through study and patience, and skillful observation is essential to a responsible reading. During a hand analysis, a reputable palmist will carefully examine the various features of the fingers and hands discussed on the previous pages. He or she will also observe the dozens of other markings of the palm, since even the most subtle striation may be imbued with special meaning. Each element is usually described separately, then discussed in the context of the entire hand.

Although most palmists agree on the significance of the palm's major markings, interpretations may vary somewhat from one reader to another. The palm prints of two men and two women, along with brief readings based on the most prominent features—all prepared by professional palmist Nathaniel Altman—appear on the following pages.

SENSITIVITY IN AN AIR HAND. The palm print of this twenty-six-year-old woman reveals a sensuous nature. The heart line is very long, indicating a person who is sensitive and humane. She tends to fall in love easily and may be guided more by her heart than her head in relationships with others. Lines at the base of the Mercury finger indicate three important relationships, one probably at an earlier age and two others that may lie in the future. These could also be close friendships.

A high level of physical and emotional energy is indicated by the firm, large mount of Venus. The life line is also fairly strong but has some overlappings; this could signal a need to pay more attention to health. The life line touches the head line at its origin, implying a high-strung nature. This is compounded by the large number of fine lines in the palm, suggesting a sensitivity to stress.

A balance between imagination and realism is indicated by the split at the end of the head line, and the downward slope of one branch toward the mount of Luna suggests good instinctual ability. The Luna mount is well developed, reinforcing both the imaginative and the intuitive traits.

Several career lines are visible in the palm. This could indicate literally more than one career, or a very important hobby or volunteer work in addition to a profession. The long fingers, typical of an air hand, show an ability to focus on details; the Jupiter finger is slightly longer than the Apollo, suggesting a take-charge personality. Although the Mercury finger is long, a mark of good communication, it is slightly twisted, signaling a need to be more direct with others. The thumb is rather rigid, showing a tendency to be stubborn but also responsible and reliable.

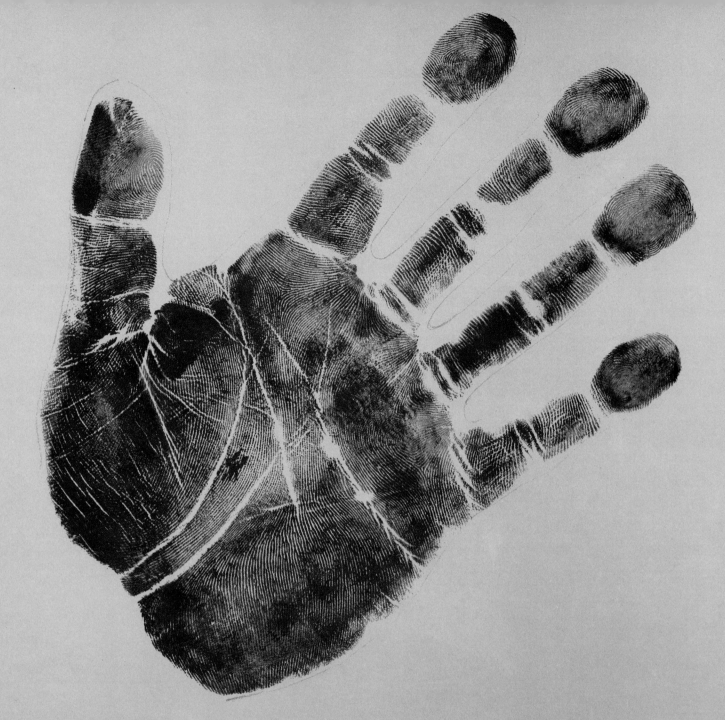

A SIMPLE DOWN-TO-EARTH HAND.

The square palm and short fingers of this earth hand suggest that this twenty-eight-year-old loves the outdoors and is physically oriented. The round fingertips signal a fairly even disposition, but the thumb is rather stiff, so he may tend to be stubborn. A long and straight Mercury finger indicates that he is a good communicator, while a Jupiter finger that is shorter than the Apollo finger may mean a lack of self-esteem.

The mount of Venus, at the base of the thumb, is large and well developed, signifying an abundance of physical energy and passion. A good measure of instinct and a protective nature are revealed in the large mount of Luna, and a strong upper mount of Mars suggests a lot of resistance but also a good deal of courage. The lower Mars mount is prominent, too, reflecting assertiveness and, possibly, a short temper.

The major lines of the hand are deep and well defined, and there is a lack of small, spidery lines. This suggests a simplified way of viewing things—a clear and direct approach, narrow in scope, rather than an all-encompassing philosophical view—and a lesser degree of sensitivity. But these characteristics are modified, in part, by a long heart line, which reveals a generous, loving nature. The small branches at the beginning of the line, under the Mercury finger, reflect some sensitivity in the personality, particularly in the younger years.

The head line, strong, clear, and of average length, shows a good ability to assess situations and a strong sense of purpose. The life line has no major breaks or islands, suggesting good health and vitality.

A particularly clear fate line indicates involvement in one career for a long time. The split in the line above the head line is a sign of dual careers—and indeed, in this case, the young man is an automobile mechanic who also sells automotive parts.

Just below the mount of Mercury is a fairly long relationship line, reflecting his happy marriage. Just below that line, barely visible in this hand print, is a line from an earlier union, which ended in divorce.

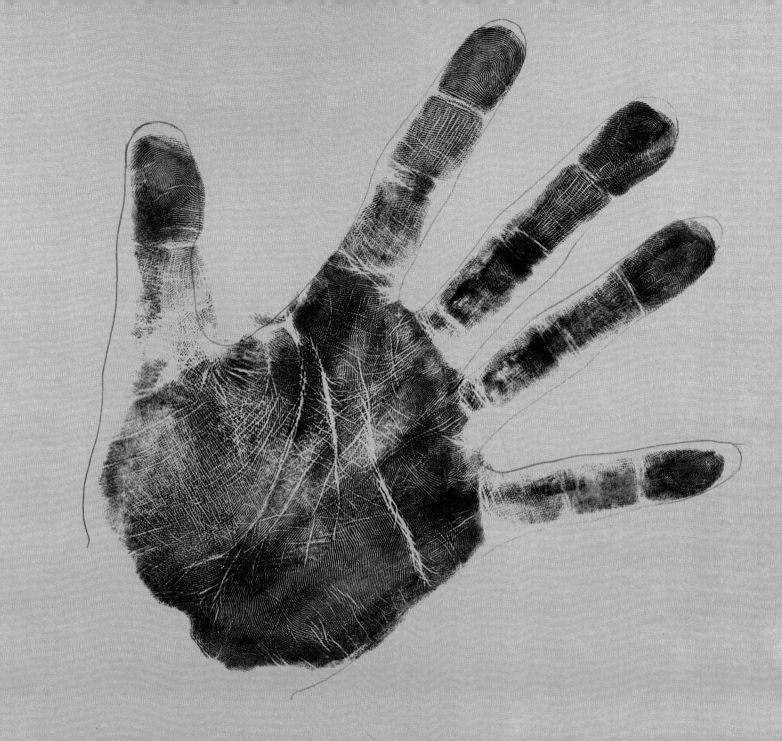

AN ARTIST'S WATER HAND. The long, thin fingers and rectangular palm of this woman, a thirty-five-year-old artist, reveal the patience, attention to detail, and intellectual nature typical of a water hand. The Mercury finger tapers to a point at the tip, reflecting sensitivity and a love of art and beauty. It is also very long and straight, indicating good communication, a trait that is underscored by a well-developed Mercury mount.

The head line is strong and forked at its end, denoting a balance between realism and imagination, and its downward slope toward the mount of Luna reveals a creative intellect. Good imagination and instinct are suggested by a prominent Luna mount, and those traits are strengthened by a skin ridge pattern that appears to connect the two branches at the end of the head line. Instinctual abilities are also seen in the small diagonal lines moving up from the Luna mount toward the center of the palm. A good measure of self-reliance is indicated by the space between the head and life lines, but there is also a tendency to be impulsive.

The life line itself is fairly long, but some islands appear about the time of middle age; this suggests a need to be mindful of health then. The line forms a wide arc around the mount of Venus, reflecting a warm and sensual nature. Near the life line's end, a branch moving toward the mount of Luna implies restlessness. This coincides with the short horizontal lines at the palm's outer edge, indicating the potential for travel.

The heart line, which ends between the Jupiter and Saturn fingers, suggests a generous, sympathetic spirit, but also a good balance between reason and emotions. The heart line is somewhat chained, revealing sensitivity, emotional intensity, and a vulnerability to hurt.

A DYNAMIC FIRE HAND. The independent, energetic nature of the fire hand is evident in the palm of this fifty-year-old writer and editor. The wide angle that is formed between his thumb and index finger reveals self-reliance and optimism, and the thumb itself is very flexible, suggesting that the man has a generous nature. The mount of Venus, which indicates physical and emotional exuberance, passion, and the ability to love, is quite well developed. The skin of the palm has a reddish color, which adds to the energy level in general. Moreover, the life line is long and clear, another indicator of vitality and a strong constitution.

The life line moves in a broad arc around the mount of Venus, revealing a warm, emotionally responsive individual. By curving toward the mount, this line also suggests a penchant for the comforts of home. Those traits are reinforced by a very long heart line—again, the sign of a sensitive, generous personality. The heart line ends under the mount of Jupiter, implying this individual tends to be idealistic and romantic. Since the line drops to touch the head line, strong conflicts may emerge between the head and heart. A very long relationship is suggested by the length of the horizontal line at the base of the Mercury finger. A shorter line beneath it may signal a previous bond, probably occurring in the man's early twenties.

A wide range of intellectual interests and mental and emotional flexibility are reflected in a very long head line. An exceptionally vivid imagination and good creative abilities are suggested by the downward slope of the line, toward the mount of Luna. This indicator is balanced by the thumb's square tip, which signals orderliness and organization. The Mercury finger is extremely long and straight, which signifies honesty and forthrightness in communication. And a large Luna mount, marked with upward-moving diagonal lines, indicates intuitiveness and some psychic ability.

Uncertainty about early career direction is suggested by a somewhat weak fate line. However, a new, clearer line takes over, revealing a straighter course and professional satisfaction.

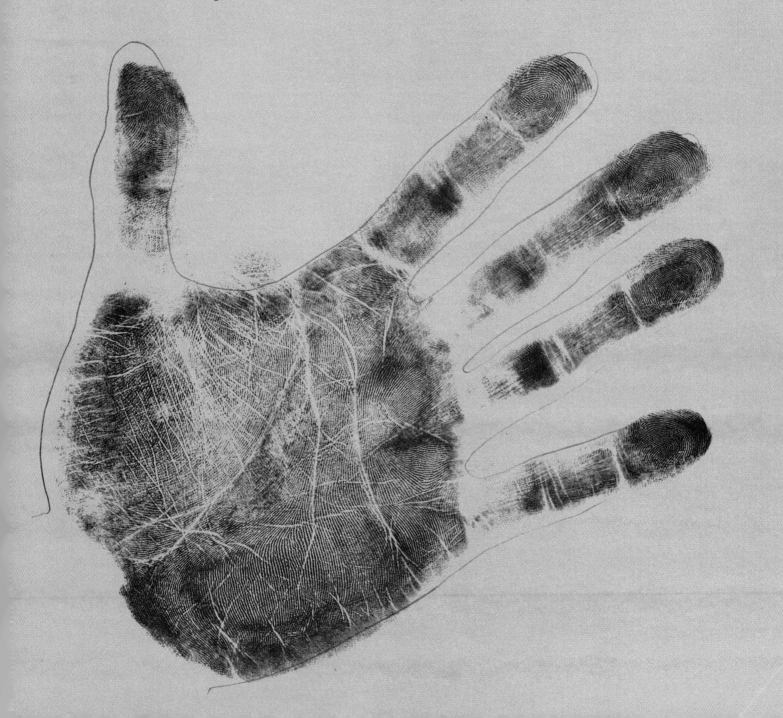

CHAPTER 3

Body Languages

**S**amuel Clemens was a troubled man as he made his way along the fashionable London street in the early 1890s. The source of his unease was not readily apparent. He was one of America's leading men of letters, world famous as a writer, humorist, and social commentator. His appearance at a podium was enough to bring an audience to delighted attention while they awaited his next barbed comment about their Victorian foibles. Although he was nearly sixty years old, he still enjoyed the vigorous health that had sustained a strenuous and varied life as a printer, roustabout, river pilot, and general hell-raiser.

Yet despite all this, Clemens was depressed. For one thing, he was just starting to feel his age, as he approached the last decade of his appointed three-score and ten years. And he was keenly aware that he had been forced to leave his native land and live in Europe in order to economize. Sam Clemens—Mark Twain—was, in fact, headed for financial ruin.

This master storyteller had proved once more that he was no businessman. The publishing firm of Charles L. Webster & Company, which he had founded and backed financially, was floundering. Another venture, into the manufacture of typesetting machinery, was going badly as well, taking thousands more of his dollars.

At last Clemens found the Bond Street address he had been looking for, and as he squinted at the small brass address plate by the door, his thoughts were no doubt edged with irony. Here he was, one of the world's foremost skeptics and debunkers, about to engage the services of the world's foremost reader of palms.

"Cheiro," read the brass plate. "Hours: 11-6." It was the understated announcement of a man who claimed nearly miraculous success in predicting the fates and fortunes of his well-known and wealthy clients. The consulting rooms inside were more consistent with the reputation—ornately furnished with oriental rugs, lush tapestries, and elaborate draperies. Exotic plants sprouted from tables and stands amid a collection of heavy, dark, Victorian chairs. A sphinxlike statue crouched in a corner.

Samuel Clemens was greeted by a powerful, handsome man in his twenties, whose Irish accent lent a friendly lilt to his confident voice. With little time wasted on preliminaries, Cheiro grasped his visitor's hands, looked at the palms, and began an insightful analysis of the famous American's character as well as a detailed cataloging of important events and dates in his life.

Clemens was impressed, and while it is unclear what, if anything, Cheiro said about his future, the author was fascinated and perplexed by the notion that the palmist might have it within his power to foresee what was to come. "The past may leave its mark, I admit," Clemens said, "and character may be told even down to its finest shades of expression; all that I might believe—but how the future may be foreshadowed, is what I cannot understand."

It was all in the hand, said Cheiro: The hand revealed a person's subconscious knowledge of future actions. As confirmation, he showed the writer the hand prints of a mother and daughter whose lives, he said, had been remarkably parallel; illness and marriage at the same ages, the same number of children, and even widowhood at the same time of life. Their hand prints were almost identical.

Clemens was enthralled by the palm reader. "He took notes of the various hands I showed him," Cheiro wrote later, "and we examined with a microscope the lines in the tips of the fingers of the mother and this one daughter, whose fate had been so nearly the same and we found that even the circles in the fingertips and thumbs also agreed."

As he paid his fee, Clemens already felt his own fortune—and his mood—changing. "The one humorous point in the situation," Cheiro quoted him as saying, "is that I came here expecting to lose money by my foolishness, but I have gained a plot for a story on which I shall certainly get back my money." Then he wrote in the palmist's visi-

tors' book: "Cheiro has exposed my character to me with humiliating accuracy. I ought not to confess this accuracy; still I am moved to do it."

The writer's financial fortunes did indeed change. A series of European lectures yielded the cash he needed, and royalty agreements with publishers gave him a secure income for the rest of his life, although he had already done his best writing. Some of those royalties were to come from sales of a book—*The Tragedy of Pudd'nhead Wilson*—in which the plot involved the uniqueness of fingerprints.

For all his mordant skepticism, Samuel Clemens apparently was not immune to the persistent human impulse to find quick answers to two of the most enduring questions that beset the thinking individual: Who am I? What will I become? Uncertain of their own impulses, confronting an unknown future, humans have always struggled to find the keys to the inner psyche and the distant moment.

In every era there have been seers who claim success in this struggle. They may use as their keys the innards of birds, the glimmer of crystal, or pure meditation. But many practitioners insist that the nature and destiny of humans can be read in their own flesh and bone. It once was thought, for example, that a person's fate could be determined by studying his or her face—considered the closest and most expressive adjunct of the mind. Other analysts devised a system for interpreting the meaning of the shape of the skull—which, after all, encloses and thus, in a sense, defines the mind.

These techniques wielded enormous influence for a time, and they have left an enduring imprint on the way we assess character: People are still described as having "strong jaws," "weak chins," or "intelligent foreheads." But other approaches, still linked to the human body but with a touch more of mystery and the occult, have proved longer lived. Among these is the technique that so intrigued Samuel Clemens—the art of gleaning information from the lines etched on the palm of the hand.

We live in a skeptical age, a time when it is far more fashionable to ridicule a palmist than consult one. Yet, like our forebears, we cannot escape the urge to seek a Rosetta stone that will reveal what we are and where we are going. We laugh at the phrenologists' maps of the head but eagerly read books that purport to interpret body language. We may have relegated the palmists to small cottages or storefronts in the questionable parts of town, but we occasionally invite graphologists—those who profess to know the secret implications of an individual's handwriting—into corporate boardrooms. Sam Clemens would surely make fun of all this, but he would understand.

Ancient Greece, that citadel of rationality, was fascinated by the notion that physical features might bespeak the inner self. As Greek scholars sought to comprehend human nature, they reasoned that since facial expressions revealed something of what a person was thinking, detailed analysis of facial features ought to yield details of a person's character. This practice came to be known as physiognomy. As an addendum to his exhaustive *History of Animals,* the philosopher Aristotle wrote that truths about a person can be deduced by observing his or her resemblance to certain animals. Those with small foreheads are likely to be ignorant, he said, since they resemble pigs; people with large, doglike foreheads, on the other hand, would tend to be flatterers. In this scheme of things, craftiness would be indicated by a red complexion reminiscent of the supposedly sly fox.

To physicians of that period, the face was the barometer of health. Hippocrates, the father of medicine and author of the oath that still epitomizes the ethics of the medical profession, used facial readings in order to diagnose the ailments of his patients.

Hippocrates also developed a variant of physiognomy called moleoscopy, the reading of body moles to assess a subject's personality and future prospects. According to Hippocrates' elaborate system, a mole between the elbow and wrist, for example, revealed a cheerful and placid disposition, while one on the left shoulder betrayed a quarrelsome and unruly nature. A mole on the left thigh foretold many sorrows in life, such as poverty, unfaithful friends, and imprisonment. But a mole on the right thigh indicated success early in life.

The art of reading moles attracted adherents for many centuries after Hippocrates' death. In 1670, an Englishman named Richard Saunders published a book that covered his studies of the subject, which had revealed to him relationships between moles on the face and those on the body. Little was heard about the subject thereafter, however, although the reading of the human face enjoyed something of a renaissance with the dawn, in the mid-eighteenth century, of the Age of Enlightenment.

This rebirth was hardly welcome in every quarter. In 1743, for example, the British Parliament declared physiognomists to be rogues and vagabonds and provided that they be publicly whipped or jailed. At times, though, physiognomy—even of a very amateurish kind—could produce startling results. It was recorded, for example, that in 1770, thirteen-year-old William Blake—later to be a renowned poet and artist—went with his father to visit an engraver. As they left the shop, the youth announced, "I don't like that man." When his surprised father asked for a reason, the younger Blake replied, "His face looks as if he will be hanged." Twelve years later, the man was convicted of forging bank notes, and he was eventually hanged. Later, the story was recounted less to illustrate Blake's prophetic genius than to confirm the persistent belief that an individual's

Writer and humorist Samuel Clemens was down on his luck and uncertain about the future when he visited renowned palmist Cheiro in the early 1890s. Cheiro is not known to have seen a change of fortune in his client's palm print (right), but Clemens praised Cheiro in the guest book, signing his pen name, Mark Twain.

face, properly scrutinized, would reveal the essence of character and future prospects.

The reputation of this divination method was given a boost in 1775 with the appearance of the first installment of *Essays on Physiognomy*, by Johann Kaspar Lavater, a pastor and poet in Zurich. Lavater's book surpassed by a large margin all earlier efforts to publicize the practice. For one thing, the quality of the printing was superb, and the book included scores of finely drawn portraits of the famous and powerful of the time. Even more important, however, was the seemingly rigorous nature of Lavater's approach. He attempted to do for physiognomy what his contemporary Carolus Linnaeus had done for botany—produce a system of classification that would lead to the formulation of hypotheses and eventually to scientific laws.

Take, for example, the case of the nose. "A beautiful nose denotes an extraordinary character," wrote Lavater. "It should have a length equal to that of the forehead. At the top there should be a gentle indenting. The button or end of the nose should be neither hard nor fleshy. Viewed in profile the bottom of the nose should not have been more than one-third of its length."

To be sure, Lavater acknowledged that it was possible for a person to rise above the character deficiencies dictated by a defective nose. He conceded, for example, that Socrates was a great man who nevertheless had an ugly nose. And the aristocratic arched noses of such figures as Jonathan Swift, Cesare Borgia, and Titian, while hardly perfect in Lavater's eyes, indicated a compensatory capacity for command and action found only in the "extraordinary" person.

On every front during the Age of Enlightenment, the secrets of nature were falling to scientific investigation, and Lavater's pretensions to science seemed to bode well for this venerable branch of knowledge. In 1810, the American poet Joseph Bartlett effused: "Had but LAVATER'S science then been known, / We had been happy, PARADISE our own; / EVE would have seen the craft, which lurk'd within, / Perceiv'd the DEVIL . . . / Then this our earth MILLENIUM had been, / Free from all death, from misery and sin."

Others were not quite so certain as Bartlett. Lavater had many critics, among them several who published in the *Gentleman's Magazine* satirical letters mocking his comparisons of human and animal faces. To be sure, some of Lavater's writings strayed far beyond the boundaries of scientific investigation and invited satire. One example of this tendency was his extravagant ex-

Cheiro has exposed my character to me with humiliating accuracy. I ought not to confess this accuracy, still I am moved to do it. Mark Twain

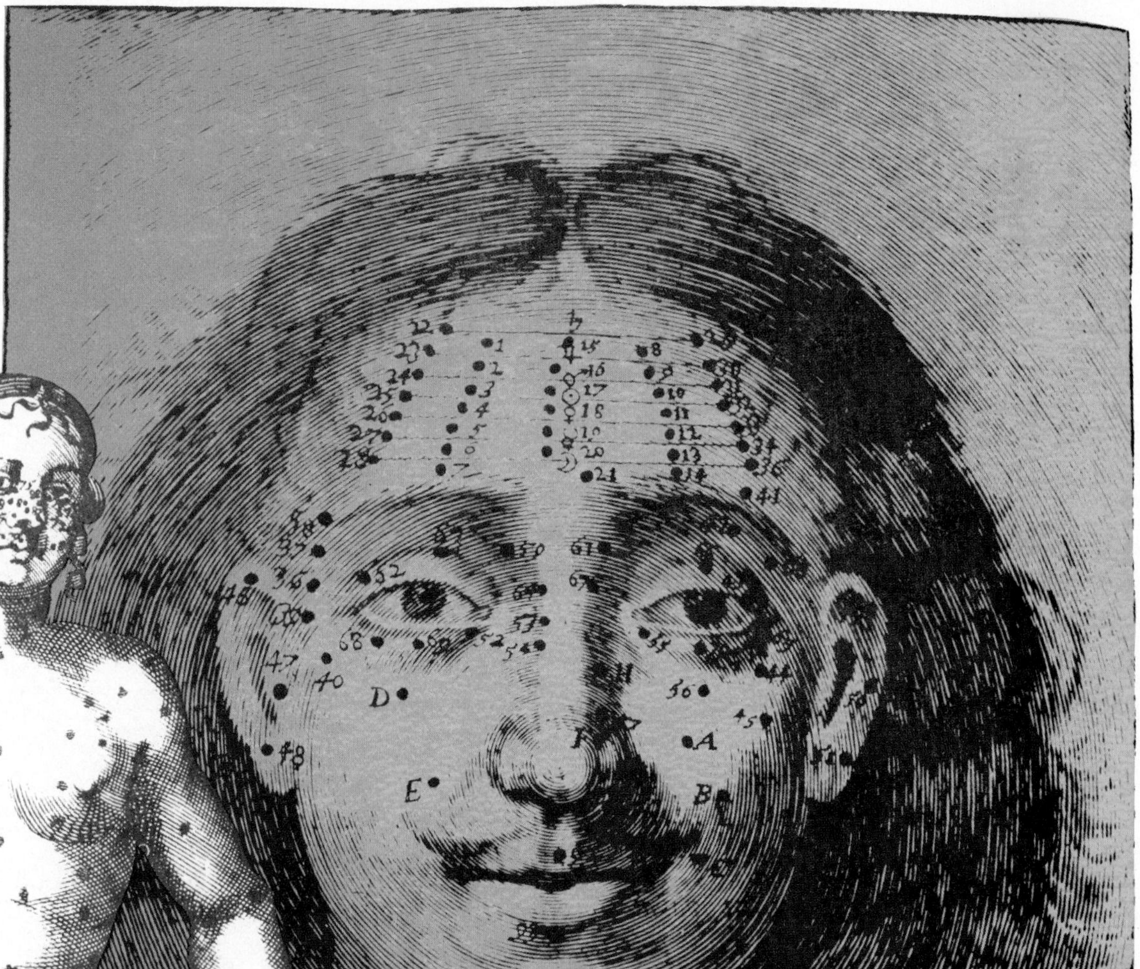

The study of moles, or moleoscopy, as an insight into character and the future peaked late in the 1600s with the publication of a treatise by Englishman Richard Saunders. He included the two engravings shown here—one showing the placement of moles most frequently found on the body (left), and the other suggesting their position on the face and neck may parallel the orbits of celestial bodies (above).

position on the subject of the mouth: "This part of the body is so sacred to me that I scarcely dare speak of it. What a subject of admiration! The mouth is the interpreter and organ of the mind and of the heart. . . . The woman whose eyes have awakened our love inspires us with enthusiasm, exalts us, throws us into intellectual ecstasy; but she whose mouth fascinates us twines us round, binds us, belongs to us already, at least in the irresponsible world of desires. The eye is the azure heaven to which none may attain; the mouth is the earth with its perfumes, its ardours, and the profound sensuality of its points."

Nor was Lavater alone in his excesses. One later enthusiast named Simms examined faces for the quality of what he called elevativeness. He advised those in whom he detected this trait that they would have the desire "to raise your body, mount a horse, climb trees, ascend church steeples, rise in a balloon and hope to go up, when done with this earthly form." The facial sign indicative of such lofty goals, Simms solemnized, was "a nose that stands well out and up at the point."

Despite the often farfetched ideas of its proponents and the resultant blasts of its critics, physiognomy continued to be widely regarded as valid. Employers consulted Lavater's book before hiring servants; some people ventured into the streets only after donning a mask to prevent strangers from detecting their true character.

A steady procession of the great and famous sought Lavater's assessment of their true nature and their likely fate. Emperor Joseph II of the Holy Roman Empire consulted him in 1777, and later visitors included the Grand Duke of Russia and Prince Edward of England, as well as many men of science and the arts.

By all accounts, Lavater was a good, generous, and uncommonly kind man. The full title of his book was *Essays on Physiognomy: Designed to Promote the Knowledge and the Love of Mankind.* Humanity, he reasoned, was inwardly beautiful by reason of God's creation; the face must therefore be the outward evidence of that beauty, if one could only know what to look for.

Lavater died in 1801, but his cherished physiognomy lived on. For more than a hundred years after his death, his book was regularly reprinted in Germany, France, the United States, Holland, Switzerland, and England, going through a total of 151 editions in many languages. Nonetheless, the would-be science steadily declined in popularity. People increasingly perceived it as subjective, imprecise, and threadbare. At the same time, however, a new system for interpreting clues to human character and destiny was gaining in influence.

As a German schoolboy in the 1760s, Franz Joseph Gall concluded that boys with good memories also shared another trait—bulging eyes. Exploring this concept further, he found support for such a connection among the notions of physiognomy current at the time, and he went on to make additional observations of his fellow students—and then to study medicine in Vienna.

But while he was learning the secrets of anatomy and disease, the question continued to plague him: What accounted for the differing abilities and propensities of different people? He reasoned that such things were the province of the brain, and that different portions of the brain must handle different capabilities and aspects of personality.

 all decided that there were thirty-seven such functions, each of which must be controlled by a corresponding area—or, as he put it, "organ"—of the brain. If only one could read the topography of the brain, Gall thought, one could read a person's character and determine his strengths and weaknesses. Size would be the controlling factor, he believed; the larger a particular organ of the brain, the better developed would be the traits governed by that organ. And surely the size of the brain would affect the dimensions and shape of the skull containing it.

He subjected his hypothesis to extensive testing. Visiting insane asylums, prisons, and schools, Gall interviewed people and measured their heads, looking for a connection between the skull shape and certain character traits. In ad-

The Face as a Mirror of Fate

The ancient art of physiognomy—the divining of character and fate through analyzing the face—has enjoyed periods of intense popularity throughout history and across the globe. But nowhere has it been elevated to a higher level of importance than among the Chinese.

While modern physiognomy is essentially a folk practice, the Chinese have studied and refined it to such a degree and over so many centuries that it is considered an adjunct of medicine. They believe that clues to the state of one's emotional and physical health are to be found in the shape and placement of the facial features as well as the texture and coloring of the skin. Further, physiognomists assert that the facial structure reveals personality traits and signals past events and ones yet to occur in the individual's life.

Chinese face-readers are exhaustively trained in ancient texts on the subject, including portions of the *I Ching,* and many are apprenticed to elderly practitioners of the art. They learn to interpret each facial sign according to prescribed rules. First the physiognomists observe the basic shape of the face; then they scrutinize the features for balance and proportion. No matter what size or form the features take, unity in the face indicates balance. And a balanced face suggests a strong character as well as a promising future.

From these initial observations, the physiognomist goes on to examine the face in depth. Physiognomy is based on a complex system of more than one hundred facial "positions" or areas, each thought to reveal an aspect of personality or fate. The positions are first examined independently, and then they are considered in relation to one another. During the course of a reading, the physiognomist is guided by a chart *(opposite)* that indicates each position on the face by number.

The major physiognomical positions are those extending down the center of the face and those relating to the eyes, eyebrows, nose, mouth, and ears. The area between the eyebrows, for example, indicates an individual's ability to attain an important post or a level of social prominence. A wide space between the brows signals great vitality and enormous intellectual power, as does a raised, fleshy bump marked with deep vertical lines.

Blemishes or disfigurement in this particular area of the face suggests that the person may have a reduced ability to achieve desired goals.

The face-reader interprets information from each facial position in turn, weighing and correlating the examination results before coming to any definite conclusions. While physiognomy is certainly far from being an exact science, the practice has withstood the test of time in Chinese culture, and the physiognomist's findings are thoughtfully rendered and accepted with genuine respect.

Hong Kong physiognomist Liang Songzeng examines the face of one of the dozen or more clients he sees each day. The 74-year-old Liang and about one hundred other fortune-tellers occupy booths located near the Wong Tai Sin Temple, a popular place of worship.

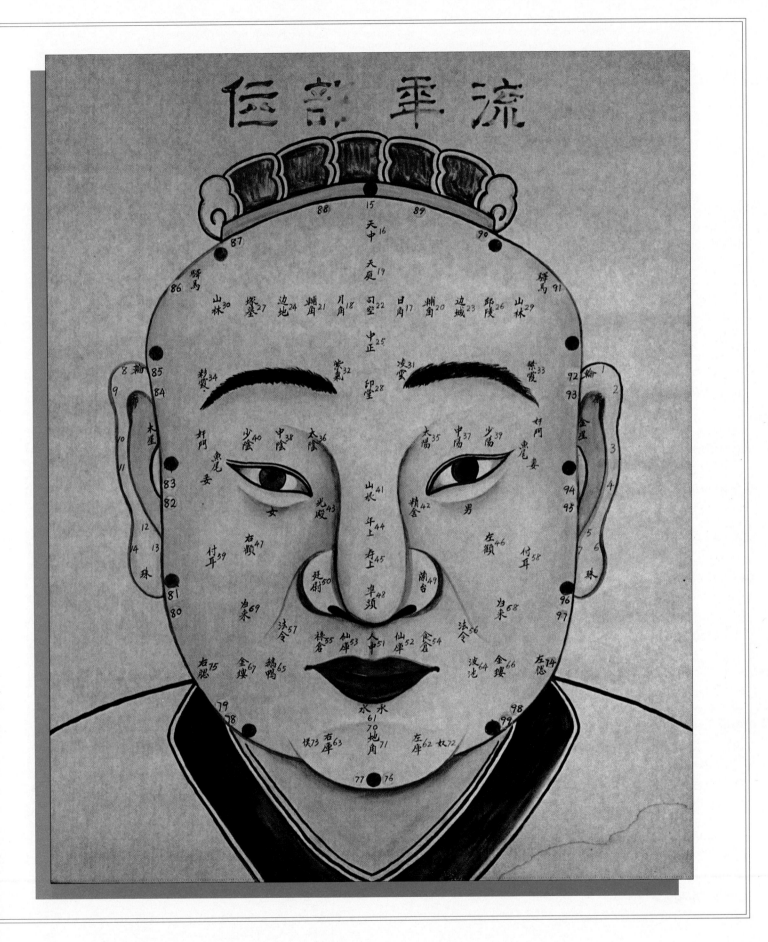

*A page from a 1777 treatise on physiogonomy (opposite) by Benedictine monk
Antoine Joseph Pernety illustrates the author's contention that long noses suggest heightened
sexuality. He also believed that a prominent and fleshy chin signifies
"solid judgment, a man of good counsel, liberal, decent and with a good appetite."*

dition, he performed many autopsies in an attempt to confirm his belief that the contours of the cranium conform to the enclosed brain. Citizens of Vienna began to stipulate in their wills that their heads be protected from the saws and scalpels of Dr. Gall.

Finally, in 1796, Gall was satisfied that the facts supported his hypothesis and that it could now be accepted as a theory and used in diagnosis. He began a series of lectures on the subject of what he called organology, later to be better known as phrenology, from the Greek for "science of the mind." As a result of his expositions, he soon had large numbers of supporters—among them a colleague, Dr. Johann Kaspar Spurzheim, who became a dedicated assistant—and also a good many detractors. Gall's admirers paid him the compliment of comparing him favorably with the trailblazing physiognomist Johann Lavater. The Austrian government, by contrast, decreed that Gall's lectures were "subversive of religion and morals" and ordered them stopped. As so often happens in such cases, though, the ban merely intensified interest in the work. After a successful tour of Europe, Gall and Spurzheim moved to Paris, where they continued to spread the gospel of organology among a Paris intelligentsia that was hungry to hear about this latest source of insights into human character.

For Swiss clergyman Johann Lavater, who attempted to raise physiognomy to the level of a science, the practice affirmed the link "between the external and internal man."

By then, people throughout the continent were memorizing the locations of what Gall identified as the organs of Amativeness, the ability to love; Philoprogenitiveness, or parental love; Constructiveness, an inclination to build; Inhabitiveness, a preference for a permanent residence. Guided by Gall, they also probed themselves and others for evidence of Benevolence, Veneration, Firmness, Hope, Wonder, Ideality, Acquisitiveness, and—above and forward of the temples—Ludicrousness. Destructiveness, it was known, lurked just above the ears; Order at the outside border of the eyelids; Self-esteem at the crown of the head; Firmness behind.

Gall included evil in his mapping of the brain's organs; he even designated one of them Murder. But Spurzheim came to believe that the brain was fundamentally good—and could be made better. Organology ought not to be content with merely identifying traits of character, he thought, but should work to improve them, and thus to improve the overall fortunes of the populace and society at large. Gall did not agree, and in 1813 the colleagues went their separate ways, Gall remaining in Europe while Spurzheim—having determined to change the name of the new science from organology to the more elegant phrenology—went on to proselytize in England and America.

His own tenacity and the yeoman support of the Scottish phrenologist George Combe helped Spurzheim overcome the initial indifference and hostility that greeted his message in the British Isles. The next two decades, indeed, saw the founding of at least twelve phrenological societies in Britain and also paved the way for a wave of enthusiasm in the United States. Medical professors from Harvard University and Bowdoin College had encouraged study of the new science in America after hearing Gall and Spurzheim lecture in Europe; by 1822, physicians and academics in Philadelphia had formed the Central Phrenological Society.

Ten years later, when Johann Spurzheim set out on an

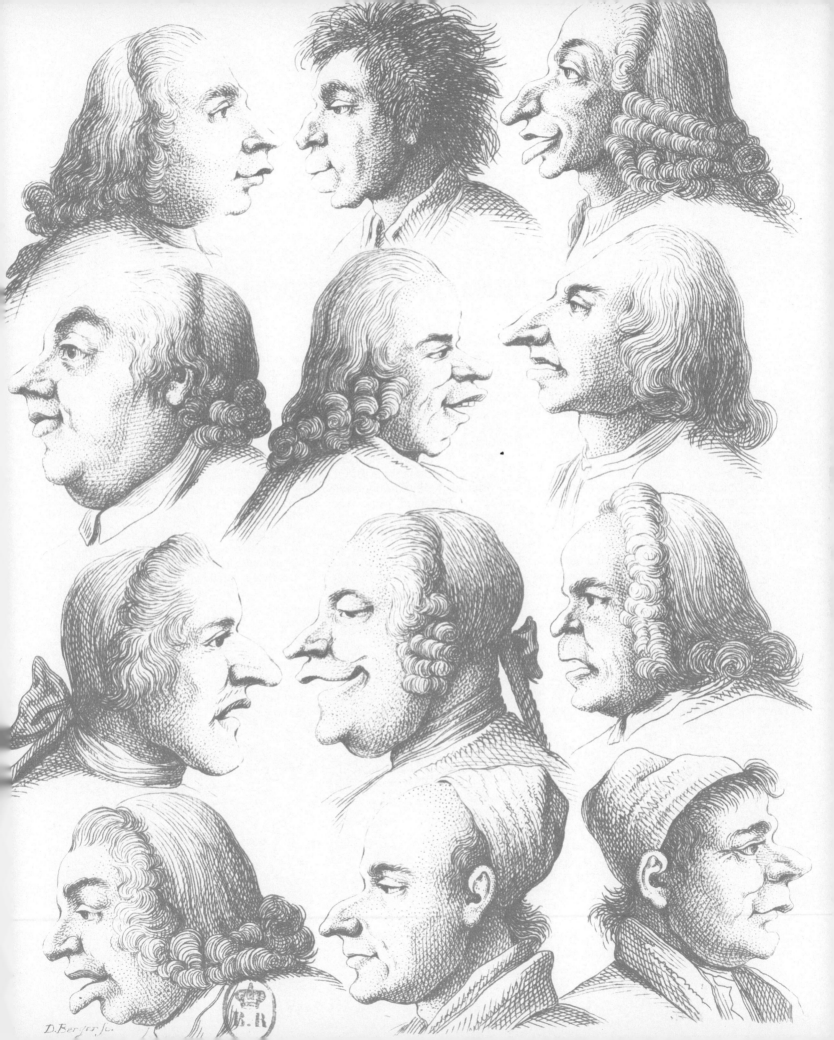

D. Berger sc.

Dr. Merton's Facial Prescriptions

By the turn of the century, popular interest in physiognomy had begun to wane in both the U.S. and Europe. But for Dr. Holmes Whittier Merton, face reading was becoming the basis of a life's work that would affect the lives and livelihoods of countless others.

Merton's interest in physiognomy had begun when he was a young man. He was particularly intrigued by the relationship between character, as revealed by facial features, and the type of occupation a person seemed best suited for. He spent twelve years observing hundreds of workers in many fields. After analyzing their facial topography and evaluating their levels of satisfaction and success, he came

up with a profile of the aptitudes and abilities necessary to excel in some 1,500 occupations. In addition, he devised a system by which others could learn to recognize the signs of those talents in potential employees.

In 1918 the Merton Institute for Vocational Guidance opened in New York City. There, personnel managers of some of the country's leading corporations were trained to analyze more than a hundred distinct facial features. These signs were rated in a variety of ways—by the firmness of the flesh, the distance between certain points, the prominence of an area, or its shape—as in the tip of the nose.

Using Merton's so-called facial

prescriptions, the managers also learned to recognize a number of job-specific attributes. For example, the prescription for an effective sales manager *(below)*, which illustrated a 1953 *Fortune* magazine article on Mertonian face reading, pinpointed the areas that supposedly govern such traits as enthusiasm, confidence, firmness, and judgment.

The Merton Institute flourished until the death of its founder in 1948. Thereafter, interest in Merton's methods faded, but those schooled in his system of vocational physiognomy undoubtedly continued to call upon it for years afterward when interviewing prospective employees.

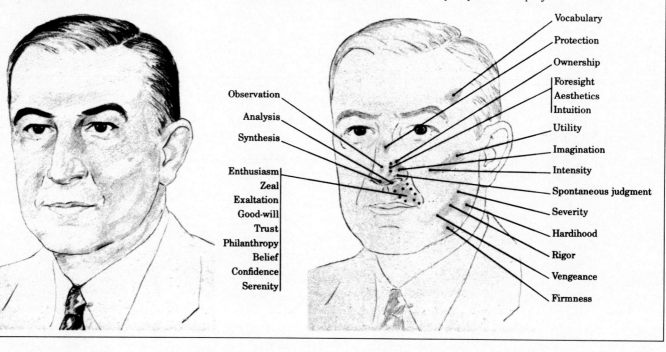

Observation
Analysis
Synthesis

Enthusiasm
Zeal
Exaltation
Good-will
Trust
Philanthropy
Belief
Confidence
Serenity

Vocabulary
Protection
Ownership
Foresight
Aesthetics
Intuition
Utility
Imagination
Intensity
Spontaneous judgment
Severity
Hardihood
Rigor
Vengeance
Firmness

American tour, enthusiasm for the man and his work had reached a feverish pitch. According to the Boston *Medical and Surgical Journal,* his lectures were attended by "our most distinguished physicians, lawyers, and divines, and citizens best known for their scientific and literary attainments." No less a luminary than the essayist Ralph Waldo Emerson hailed the phrenologist as one of the greatest minds in the world.

When Spurzheim died suddenly in Boston in 1832, the city treated him as a fallen hero. A public autopsy was performed on his body, preceded by a lecture on his teachings. It was noted with some wonder—but little real surprise—that Spurzheim's brain weighed fifty-seven ounces, 20 percent more than the average of forty-eight ounces. (Franz Joseph Gall had died four years earlier; his brain had weighed in at a scanty forty-two ounces.)

Artists sketched the late phrenologist's body as it lay in state. Members of the Boston Medical Society marched in his funeral procession, while the Handel and Haydn Society sang an "Ode to Spurzheim," written for the occasion by the Reverend John Pierpont and concluding thus: "Nature's priest, how true and fervent / Was thy worship at her shrine! / Friend of man,—of GOD the servant, / Advocate of truths divine,— / Taught and charmed as by no other, / We have been, and hoped to be; / But while waiting round thee, Brother, / For thy light—'tis dark with thee!" That same day the Boston Phrenological Society was formed, soon to be followed by some fifty other societies located around the country.

George Combe, the Scottish lawyer and disciple of Spurzheim, eagerly took up the torch of the phrenological movement in America. Between 1838 and 1840, Combe de-

Phrenology founder Franz Joseph Gall espoused the belief that personality was revealed in the contours of the skull.

livered no fewer than 158 lectures in the eastern United States, and he analyzed the heads and personalities of hundreds of people—among them President Martin Van Buren and Daniel Webster. Educator Horace Mann called phrenology "the guide of philosophy and the handmaid of Christianity." Rembrandt Peale did a portrait of Combe.

But as in Europe, phrenology encountered some strenuous opposition. John Quincy Adams—congressman, former president, and promoter of the Smithsonian Institution—wondered in print how two phrenologists could look each other in the face without laughing. Oliver Wendell Holmes, a writer and professor of anatomy at Harvard, called phrenology a pseudoscience in which "all positive evidence, or such as favors its doctrines, is admitted, and all negative evidence, or such as tells against it, is excluded."
Even supporters warned that the field was an inviting one for charlatans. The *American Monthly Review* of Boston, in a generally supportive article, cautioned that "shallow and self-sufficient pretenders . . . will eagerly snatch at phrenology as opening a royal road, easy and short, into the very depths of metaphysics and morals."

But phrenology's doubters were in the minority. Crowds of 500 people and more attended Combe's lectures, despite the fact that he was by all accounts an uninspiring orator. Most dissenting voices were drowned out in a general surge of delight with this new way to reveal a person's innermost secrets and possible fate.

And the intriguing science continued to gain influential converts. In 1833, for example, students at Amherst College arranged a formal debate on the merits of phrenology. A bright, enthusiastic young man named Alonzo Gray took

The Fowlers' Phrenological Empire

If there was a first family of American phrenology, the Fowlers of New York were undoubtedly it. Young Orson Fowler first became enamoured of the new "science" as a student at Amherst College in 1832, and his enthusiasm for phrenology proved contagious. After graduation, Orson and his younger brother Lorenzo spread their message throughout the country. In schoolhouses, churches, and town halls, the Fowler brothers expounded the principles of phrenology and performed examinations for only pennies per head.

Success came quickly to the Fowlers. In 1836 they opened a New York office from which they operated a publishing house and phrenology museum. They distributed their own essays on the subject as well as those penned by others and founded the monthly *American Phrenological Journal.* The journal, whose cover bore the motto Know Thyself *(right)*, carried news of phrenology and physiology, and it also covered other subjects, including science, agriculture, and home education.

Soon Orson's sister Charlotte and her husband, Samuel Wells, joined the burgeoning family business. One of Charlotte's tasks was to escort visitors through the Phrenological Cabinet, as the museum was known. On display were thousands of cranial reproductions of persons both living and dead, from all walks of life. Most visitors

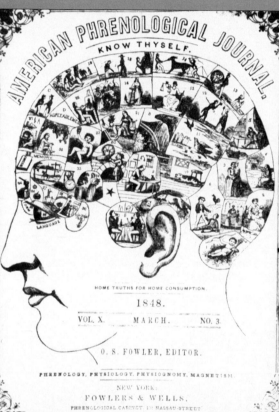

were also examined by a phrenologist, who palpated the "organs" of the skull for a small fee. Each subject then received a chart on which a number from one to seven, signifying size or degree of development, appeared next to an organ's supposed function.

The charts represented yet another branch of the Fowlers' business. Their success on the lecture circuit had spawned many followers and created a ready market for books, charts, and busts. And for those seeking a bit more realism in their props, human skulls

"imported from ancient battlefields" were available by mail order, as were those of "rare races" and animals.

The Fowlers did far more than supply itinerant phrenologists with the tools of their trade; by 1842, they were instructing them as well. Students came from as far as Europe and New Zealand for a nine-month course of study under a faculty mostly named Fowler. One grateful alumnus claimed that his diploma from the American Institute of Phrenology immediately elevated him by fifty percent in the estimation of those to whom he lectured.

Thus the Fowlers built an empire based on the phrenology fad. Their business continued to develop, entering the twentieth century under the leadership of yet another indefatigable Fowler, Lorenzo's daughter Jessie. Only the combined forces of the Great Depression and Jessie's death in 1932 ended the clan's century-long push to "phrenologize our nation."

The Fowler & Wells phrenological bust (right), which defined more than forty "organs" of the brain, was used to teach aspiring phrenologists. It was also sold to traveling practitioners, along with the charts (far right) that were a part of a reading. Phrenologists recorded each organ's size on the chart and listed functions to be cultivated or restrained. Expanded versions of the chart offered advice on nutrition, bathing, and treatment of minor ailments.

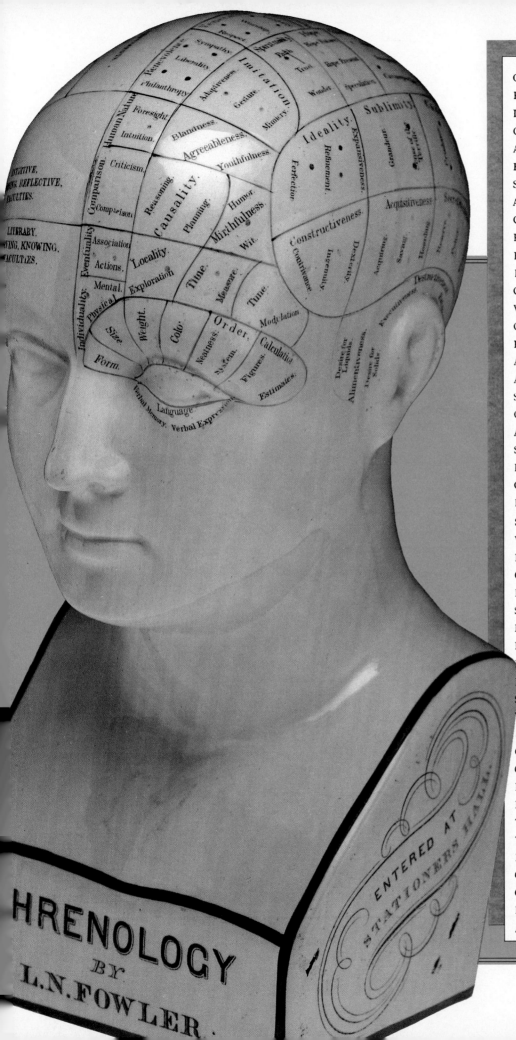

				CULTIVATE	RESTRAIN
Organic Quality 6.	...	...	...		✓
Health 6,5.	...	...	...	✓	
Digestion 5.	...	...	...	✓	
Circulation 5.	...	...	...	✓	
Activity 6.	...	...	...		
Excitability 6.	...	...	...		✓
Size of Brain 5.	...	...	...		
Amativeness 6.	...	...	...		✓
Conjugality 6.	...	...	...		
Parental Love 7.	...	...	...		
Friendship 7.	...	...	...		✓
Inhabitiveness 5.	...	...	...		
Continuity 5.	...	...	...		
Vitativeness 6.	...	...	...		
Combativeness 6.	...	...	...		✓
Destructiveness 6.	...	...	...		
Alimentiveness 5.	...	...	...		
Acquisitiveness 6.	...	...	...		
Secretiveness 5.	...	...	...	✓	
Caution 6.	...	...	✓		✓
Approbativeness 7.	...	...	...	✓	✓
Self-Esteem 5..4	...	...	...	✓	
Firmness 6.	...	...	...		
Conscientiousness 6.	...	...	✓		
Hope 5.4	...	...	...	✓	
Spirituality 5.	...	...	...	✓	
Veneration 5.	...	...	...	✓	
Benevolence 6.	...	...	...		
Constructiveness 6.	...	...	...		
Ideality 6.	...	...	...		
Sublimity 6.	...	...	...		✓
Imitation 7.	...	...	...		✓
Mirth 5.	...	...	...		
Individuality 7.	...	...	...		✓
Form 6.	...	...	...		
Size 5.	...	...	...	✓	
Weight 5.	...	...	...	✓	
Colour 6.	...	...	...		
Order 6.	...	...	...		
Calculation 5.	...	...	...		
Locality 7.	...	...	...		
Eventuality 7.	...	...	...		
Time 6.5.	...	...	...		
Tune 5.	...	...	✓		
Language 6.	...	...	...		
Causality 6.	...	...	...		✓
Comparison 7.	...	...	...		
Human Nature 6.	...	...	...		
Agreeableness 6.	...				

HRENOLOGY
BY
L.N.FOWLER

ENTERED AT STATIONERS HALL

accredited as a physician and the first woman to teach medicine. Charlotte's husband, Samuel Roberts Wells, contributed his business and managerial skills to the talented family.

Together, the Fowlers created a typically American organizational machine devoted to the propagation, practice, and development of phrenology as a means to a better way of life. They were tireless speakers and writers on a number of other subjects as well; the causes they embraced included temperance, educational reform, vegetarianism, women's rights, and the abolition of slavery. The family pressed for westward expansion and helped sponsor the Kansas abolitionist settlements of one of their followers, the firebrand John Brown.

The Fowlers derided the educational practices of their day, in which children were required to memorize passages from classical literature. Instead, they advocated giving children plenty of physical and mental exercise during shorter school days, then allowing them time to learn in their own creative ways. According to the Fowlers, the insane and the handicapped should not be isolated and consigned to the human scrap heap; instead, they should be examined to see which of their faculties were still strong, so they could be trained to use their talents for the good of themselves and society.

s a matter of fact, no aspect of nineteenth-century American life was considered off limits to the phrenologists. Theirs, they felt, was a science that touched on every dimension of human existence. Still, not all their reforms were welcomed by the American public. During an age of Victorian prudery, Lorenzo won no plaudits for his ironic call for sex education: "Is it not absurd for any one to advance the opinion that it is too *delicate* a subject? If it be *really too delicate* to discuss the principles necessary to be known and observed before one is qualified to enter upon the duties incumbent upon this change of condition—then it will most certainly be entirely *too delicate* to get married, and absolutely *shocking* to become parents."

the affirmative; Henry Ward Beecher, who would become one of the century's most famous preachers and abolitionists (and whose sister, Harriet Beecher Stowe, would write *Uncle Tom's Cabin*), was opposed.

The debate did not work out as planned. Beecher, who was already known as a formidable speaker, delivered a brilliant defense of phrenology rather than the expected ringing denunciation. He and another student and phrenology enthusiast, Orson Fowler, joined forces thereafter, with Beecher preaching the merits of the practice to fellow students and anyone else who would listen, and Fowler giving individual readings for two cents each.

After graduation, Beecher took up the ministry, as he had planned. Meanwhile, Fowler concentrated on phrenology, enlisting the support of his younger brother, Lorenzo, and sister, Charlotte. It was a remarkable family, in remarkable times. Orson was a true visionary, American style, who knew what he wanted to do and how to do it. Lorenzo was a master salesman. Charlotte was a champion of women's rights. They were soon joined by Lorenzo's wife, Lydia Folger, who was only the second woman in the nation to be

Even architecture became a part of the Fowler movement, and another fad—that of the octagonal house—was conceived. Having become convinced for some reason that eight-sided dwellings were more beneficial than conventional four-sided ones, Orson, in 1848, wrote a book entitled *A Home for All: Or a New Cheap, Convenient and Superior Mode of Building*. He put theory into practice by building a magnificent, if unusual, octagonal house in Fishkill, New York, fifty miles north of New York City. This dwelling became known as Fowler's Folly, but Orson's book went through at least seven printings in nine years, and more than a thousand octagonal houses were built in the United States during that time.

The family firm, Fowler & Wells, controlled a publishing empire that included several journals and periodicals, a large mail-order business, and even a popular phrenological museum in New York City. Most of the time, these endeavors produced substantial income, in addition to the large sums each Fowler earned lecturing.

In the mid-nineteenth century it would have been difficult to find a town or crossroads in America that was not affected by their teachings. As many Europeans of a generation earlier had insisted on a physiognomical examination of prospective employees, Americans now asked for an applicant's phrenological chart. The Fowlers' *American Phrenological Journal* became one of the largest magazines in the country, with a circulation of more than 50,000. In addition to information and advice on a variety of topics, subscribers of the magazine were treated to phrenological readings of the famous and infamous, often based on a photograph rather than an actual sitting. In fact, many were pompted to use this correspondence character analysis to check up on their friends, relatives, and co-workers, and worried parents sent in photographs of prospective sons-in-law to learn of their true intentions.

One such long-distance subject of a phrenological examination was Lizzie Borden, whose widely reported trial for the ax murder of her parents in Fall River, Massachusetts, in 1892, captured the public imagination. After she was accused of the crime, Nelson Sizer, the president of the American Institute of

When Orson Fowler set out to build his octagonal house in 1850, he was undaunted by his lack of training—a well-developed "organ of Constructiveness" meant he was phrenologically suited for the task.

Godly Phrenology

Throughout his life, Henry Ward Beecher, renowned nineteenth-century orator, author, and Congregational minister, was an advocate of controversial causes. From his pulpit in Brooklyn's Plymouth Church, where he presided for forty years from 1847 until his death in 1887, the fiery Beecher championed abolition, women's suffrage, the theory of evolution, and the principles of phrenology.

Beecher was initially introduced to phrenology in 1832 by Amherst College classmate Orson Fowler. After some study of the practice, Beecher enthusiastically embraced the fledgling "science," believing it would bring him closer to God. The young man felt that an expansive knowledge of the natural world and its workings would strengthen his faith and that phrenology would lead the way to a new conception of the laws of nature.

Beecher also believed that phrenology made it possible for the individual to alter—in the hope of perfecting—his or her mental capacity, and the minister remained devoted to the practice for the rest of his life. Phrenology, he maintained, "brings new aid to the statesman, the lawyer, the physician and the minister of Christ in their benevolent efforts to benefit society, and gives them a new power over the intellect and the will."

A Poet's Reading

By 1849 thirty-year-old Walt Whitman had plied various trades, traveled extensively, and was writing the words that would break new ground in American poetry. Yet he was unsure of himself, seeking direction and an affirmation of purpose, when he ventured into the office of Fowler & Wells for a phrenological reading.

As a newspaper editor, Whitman had reviewed books on phrenology and declared that it "has at last gained a position, and a firm one, among the sciences." Convinced that his destiny would be revealed, Whitman paid Lorenzo Fowler three dollars to palpate the bumps on his head.

The analysis described an independent thinker who had "a good command of language" and would "choose to fight with tongue and pen." Whitman published the results of his reading several times in later years, perhaps as proof that he was living up to his phrenological potential. The chart appeared in his controversial book of poems *Leaves of Grass,* which was first published in 1855 and distributed by Fowler & Wells. In the preface, Whitman credited the role phrenology had played in shaping his life and work. Phrenologists "are not poets," he wrote, "but they are the lawgivers of poets."

A Life Transformed

Clara Barton's encounter with phrenology changed her life. The youngest of five children, Barton grew up on a prosperous farm in Oxford, Massachusetts. She was a painfully shy girl, who, she later recalled, "would do without the most needed article rather than ask for it." Instead of overcoming her bashfulness as she grew older, she became even more timid and was plagued by loneliness.

Fortunately for Clara, in 1836 Lorenzo Fowler came to lecture in Oxford and boarded with her family for nearly a month. During that time Clara's mother spoke at length with Fowler about her daughter, and the fifteen-year-old girl submitted to a phrenological examination. As Clara later wrote, Fowler predicted her "sensitive nature will always remain. She will never assert herself for herself—she will suffer wrong first—but for others she will be perfectly fearless." His prescription for Clara was to "throw responsibility upon her. She has all the qualities of a teacher."

Clara Barton followed that advice. She successfully taught school for almost twenty years and fought to establish the first free public school in the state of New Jersey. She went on to nurse wounded Union soldiers during the Civil War and to organize the American National Red Cross.

Phrenology, was sent her photograph for review without being told the identity of the sitter. His "analysis and criticism," published later in the Chicago *Evening News*, included the observation that "the face indicates power . . . and the tendency to be thorough and severe." Lizzie Borden was ultimately acquitted, but to this day many people remain unconvinced of her innocence. Could her temperament, as divined from the shape of her head, have allowed her to kill so brutally her mother and father?

By the time Lizzie Borden's analysis made headlines, phrenology was long past its prime. During the second half of the century, people who sought to plumb the recesses of the human condition were more interested in Charles Darwin's work on evolution, Paul Broca's brain research, and as the century drew to a close, Sigmund Freud's new ideas about psychology.

In such glittering company, phrenology looked shopworn. Orson Fowler moved to Boston, where he continued to lecture until his death in 1887; Lorenzo and Lydia went to London, where Lorenzo remained with his phrenologist daughter after Lydia's death in 1879; he died a week after returning to the United States in 1896. What he had taught for so many years was virtually forgotten. Americans and Europeans were now more interested in a different guidepost to the depths of their personality and the far reaches of their future.

On a bright July day in 1894, a young Irishman strode confidently through the corridors of the British War Office. He had been summoned there by General Horatio Herbert Kitchener, whose victories in Egypt and the Sudan had already won public admiration and, from officialdom, a few frowns that may have been tinged with jealousy. Although Kitchener's name would soon become nearly synonymous with the golden age of the British Empire, his high reputation was by no means assured on this day.

In fact, concern about his future may well have prompted Kitchener to summon the twenty-seven-year-old self-styled Count Louis le Warner de Hamon—born William

Warner of County Wicklow, Ireland, but better known simply as Cheiro, a professional name taken from the Greek word for hand. Corporals snapped to attention and ushered the young man into the imposing presence of the British general. And then, just as the American writer Samuel Clemens had done only a year or two before, Kitchener offered his palm for a reading.

That the commander of the British Empire's military forces in Egypt should consult such a person was not at all unusual in the London of the 1890s. Palmistry had a wide following. And for those who linked lineage and respectability, it could claim long bloodlines indeed. Little is known about its origins (ancient adepts kept their knowledge secret from the uninitiated), but palm reading was certainly practiced in India almost 4,000 years ago and was a respected art from China to Greece by the fourth century BC. Aristotle, Hippocrates, Plato, and Galen are all reported to have been practitioners of palmistry; they referred to the technique as chiromancy.

anuscripts on the subject of reading palms began to appear in Europe in the fourteenth century, and in 1475 a German writer, Johann Hortlich, published the first textbook on the art: *Die Kunst Chiromantie.* But for a long time there was no Lavater to attempt to reconcile palmistry with the scientific method; while other disciplines of various stripes were being reorganized and reinterpreted in terms of the new way of understanding the world, palmistry remained shrouded in secrecy and superstition.

Finally, in 1889, a group of practitioners founded the English Chirological Society for the purpose of "firstly, raising the study of the hand to the level of scientific research; secondly, for promoting the study of Palmistry in all its branches; thirdly, as a safeguard to the public against charlatans and imposters." At just about the same time, Cheiro arrived in London, after what was—according to his own account—a long and exotic journey.

The flamboyant Cheiro was hardly the person to adapt palmistry to the modern, scientific age; nor would he create

the equivalent of the Fowlers' phrenological empire. But with his dark good looks and extravagant showmanship—a continually cultivated air of mystery and alliance with the occult—he seemed to personify the enduring appeal of the art of palmistry.

Cheiro's odyssey began, he said, when he was forced to leave school after his father fell on hard times. Lacking a complete education but amply equipped with intelligence and ambition, young William Warner followed in the footsteps of many a hard-pressed Irishman before him: He headed for London. It was on the train from Liverpool to London, as he told it later in his book *Confessions*, that the first of many fateful coincidences occurred.

Warner, who had long been interested in palmistry and the occult, was reading an English translation of *Die Kunst Chiromantie* when his companion in the compartment commented that this was "an odd kind of study." Warner defended and explained palmistry with such fervor that the skeptic allowed him to perform a reading. Peering closely at his companion's palm, Warner discovered "a well-marked line of fate that . . . would cause him to stand out as a leader above the common herd of humanity." But the line stopped, meaning, as Warner explained it, "rest for you; another Napoleon sent to St. Helena."

The cause of the sudden retirement, Warner remembered predicting, would be a woman. At this, the subject laughed, dismissing the prophecy by saying, "A man with my life has no time for women." According to Cheiro's later account, the man was Charles Stewart Parnell, at the time an outspoken proponent of Irish home rule. Several years afterward, Parnell's political career was destroyed and his cause crippled when he was named a corespondent in a divorce suit.

Warner stayed in London only briefly, then traveled to India, where he was befriended by a Hindu priest who offered to help him develop his gift for palmistry. This education, as Warner recounted it, involved fasting, inducing trances, seeking out mystical experiences, and studying a book about palmistry that had been written on human skin. After relating a series of other adventures—including reading about a murder in Britain and solving it while touring the monuments of ancient Egypt—Warner told how he returned to London, took the name of Cheiro, and opened for business at 108 New Bond Street.

Happily, Cheiro's first client was the influential and well-connected Arthur Balfour, who later would become president of the Society for Psychical Research and prime minister of England. Balfour was apparently impressed. Thereafter, the noble and notable flocked to see the charismatic palmist. And a remarkable succession of seemingly accurate predictions bolstered the confidence placed in him by his clients. Indeed, when Cheiro informed the shah of Persia that an attempt would be made on his life during an upcoming visit to the Paris Exposition of 1900, the warning was taken so seriously that security was reportedly tightened and an assassination attempt was foiled within a short time after the prediction.

Some readings, though, were played out over a longer time span. In 1894, for example, Cheiro told General Kitchener he would achieve his greatest success in 1914; in that year Kitchener was made an earl and was named as England's secretary of state for war. But during the same interview, Cheiro warned Kitchener not to travel by sea in his 66th year—and in that fateful year of 1916, a mission to the court of Czar Nicholas II impelled the general to board the HMS *Hampshire*. The vessel sank after striking a German mine off the Orkney Islands, costing the lives of Kitchener and many others.

Among Cheiro's other influential clients—in addition to Samuel Clemens—were King Leopold of Belgium; Edward VII, Queen Alexandra, and Edward VIII of England; American president Grover Cleveland; explorer Sir Ernest Shackleton; and Oscar Wilde, whom the palmist supposedly warned that unless he reformed his ways, he would be ruined. Seven years later, Wilde was convicted and imprisoned for his notorious homosexual practices.

Despite the demands of seeing as many as six thou-

The introduction in 1907 of the Lavery Electric Automatic Phrenometer—a metal device, resembling a lampshade, that mechanically measured cranial bumps—was an attempt to standardize phrenology readings. The machines later proved to be popular attractions in department stores and theater lobbies.

The dashing young palmist known as Cheiro performed readings for the great and famous in his opulent London salon (below). According to Cheiro, the lines of his patrons' palms did not directly provide him with the answers he sought but acted as a catalyst upon his "occult consciousness" to generate the needed information.

sand clients in one year, Cheiro traveled extensively—to the United States, France, Italy, and Asia. In 1904 he went to Russia, where, by his account, he foretold the demise of the Romanoff dynasty and engaged in a battle of wills with the baleful monk Grigori Rasputin. As Cheiro told it, the two men tried unsuccessfully to hypnotize each other, and the palmist's "last word" on the matter was the grimly accurate prediction that Rasputin would die in the Neva River of poison, stab wounds, and gunshots.

According to one account, Cheiro worked with the British intelligence services during World War I and numbered among his many paramours the legendary spy Mata Hari. Yet for all his self-described fame and success, Cheiro's later years were marked by misfortune and depression; it is said his powers began to fail him around 1930. He died in 1936 in Hollywood, where he had hoped to make a movie about his hero, the eighteenth-century Italian alchemist and mountebank Cagliostro.

Cheiro's contribution to palmistry was to bring the art to the attention of the multitudes in the best possible light. He neither innovated, as the Fowlers did in the field of phrenology, nor systematized, as Lavater did in physiognomy.

84

He was a brilliant publicist who stuck close to methods that had been around for millennia.

According to Cheiro and palmist tradition, the left hand of a right-handed person reveals inborn nature; the right shows how that nature has been applied to the circumstances of the person's life. The reverse would be true for a left-handed individual. A rounded hand with tapering fingers—such as those of Sarah Bernhardt, for example—"must necessarily be used in some artistic emotional career," as Cheiro wrote of the actress. A blunted, square-shaped hand indicates a person possessing more practical or scientific talents.

Palmists examine the shape of the fingers and the fingernails; the prominence of the joints; the relative size of the fingers and palm; and the size and shape of the hand's mounts—the fleshy cushions at the heel of the hand and at the base of the thumb and fingers. And, especially, palmists consider the length, definition, and prominence of the lines that crisscross the hand in predictable patterns but with individual variations of detail. Of these, the major and best known are the Life line, which circles the base of the thumb; the Head and Heart lines, which traverse the upper half of the palm; and the Fate line, which rises from the wrist to the middle finger *(pages 53-63)*.

Having made the obvious observations—the length of the Life line, for instance, and the prominence of the Heart—the palmist goes on to consider other, less obvious markings. Some lines, such as Intuition, relate to the individual's character. Others, including Marriage and Health, are interpreted as a record of the person's past and an indication of the future. Still others—the lines of Venus, Mars, and the Sun, and especially the various mounts and the individual fingers—are scrutinized for their relationship with astrological signs.

Some palmists insist that their art cannot be reduced

This series of French postcards from the early twentieth century illustrates personality traits thought to be revealed in the palm. From left, a fleshy hand indicates a passion for country life; a double Heart line suggests ideal love; well-defined lines in the palm reflect a utopian outlook; and a fine Life line signifies athletic prowess.

to memorizing the placement and meaning of various lines. What the palmist is really doing, they maintain, is setting up a subliminal, telepathic contact that permits the plumbing of the subject's inner nature, worries, and potential. This mental contact requires conscious concentration on the part of both reader and subject, and it is enhanced by physical contact. Thus, while chatter about the various lines engages the conscious mind, the holding of hands establishes a physical bond and the reader's subconscious is unleashed to probe for secrets.

In fact, a palmist's accuracy can seem uncanny. Some critics feel, however, that a palm reader's talent does not lie in any sort of psychic gift or interpretation of the lines of the hand, but in the ability to respond almost intuitively to nonverbal clues supplied unwittingly by the subject. Often, readers may learn much from a sitter's hairstyle or mode of dress, for example, or from some nervous habit, and convince even themselves that psychic powers are involved.

Diehard skeptics, of course, insist that palmists' readings are nothing more than recitations of stock phrases tailored to flatter and beguile a subject. This is made easier, they claim, by the human inclination to accept broad generalizations as amazing revelations. For example, researchers at one university asked students to assess the accuracy of a character analysis purportedly written for each individual. In fact, all the students participating in the experiment were given the same paragraph, which read: "You are a person who is very normal in his attitudes, behavior and relationships with people. You get along well without effort. People naturally like you and you are not overly critical of them or yourself. . . . Your prevailing mood is one of optimism and constructive effort, and you are not troubled by periods of depression, psychosomatic illness or nervous symptoms." The students gave it a near-perfect score as a unique description of their own personalities.

Most modern sophisticates place little stock in palmistry—and none whatsoever in physiognomy or phrenology. But even so, there remains an urge to believe that the body is somehow able to provide a set of clues that, properly read, will untangle the complicated psyche, simplify the business of relating to the world, and perhaps disclose what the future might bring.

And even those who have turned their backs on the occult may rely at times on seers of another sort, on people who go beyond inspecting palms and fingers and seek instead to find meaning in characteristics of the pen strokes made by the hand. These practitioners are called graphologists, analysts of handwriting—which one has described as "gestures frozen in time." Many of them do their work for hardheaded business corporations, both large and small.

Hundreds of companies in the United States have used handwriting analysis to screen applicants for employment and to help make decisions about promotions. In Europe and Israel, the practice is even more common, with many companies employing full-time graphologists to reveal to the employer things the employee will not tell and may not even be aware of.

A typical story was related in a business magazine by the general manager of Ohio's Phillips Supply Company. The firm's president recommended hiring an impressive young man he had met socially. Several company executives agreed, but the graphologist they consulted examined a sample of the prospective employee's handwriting and reported: "His integrity is not intact. He'll steal everything that is not nailed down." Phillips decided not to hire the young man, who was later reported to have stolen trade secrets from another company.

This and other such stories illustrate a dramatic shift in American attitudes toward graphology, which was long regarded as little more than an amusing parlor trick. During the nineteenth century, handwriting analysis never captured the public fancy as did phrenology, although it did attract the interest of such patrons as the writers Nathaniel Hawthorne and Edgar Allan Poe.

In fact, in November of 1841, Poe went so far as to publish the first of three articles in the popular *Graham's Lady's and Gentleman's Magazine,* in which he analyzed the

Gypsy Arts

Divination and prophecy have long been considered the special province of gypsies, a nomadic people whose folklore is replete with tales of secret powers and magical rites. And like the ancient arts they practice, the origins and ways of gypsies themselves have remained shrouded in mystery, entangled in legends and traditions.

Gypsies are thought to have lived originally in India. But sometime during the ninth century they began slowly moving westward. By the early fifteenth century, large groups of dark-skinned, exotically dressed people, claiming to be religious pilgrims from a country called Little Egypt, began appearing in Europe. These "Egyptians," or "gypsies," as they came to be known, were at first welcomed by sympathetic villagers. But some wandering tribes soon gained reputations as petty thieves and tricksters who displayed no obvious religious convictions.

The gypsies were, in fact, deeply religious. But their beliefs and practices were heavily influenced by magic. Regarded as authorities in matters of the occult, gypsies were often credited with supernatural talents beyond even their own beliefs, and many eagerly peddled their alleged powers to local townspeople. Usually just a few coins could purchase anything from herbal remedies for aches and pains to love potions and aphrodisiacs. But it was for their practice of the prophetic arts—reading tarot cards or tea leaves, a crystal ball or the lines on a palm—that gypsies became best known.

Gypsy men typically worked as horse traders or metalsmiths; the women told fortunes, often in the wagons or small tents in which they lived. Palm reading, shown here and on the following pages, was the favored method. And it has remained so today; palmistry shops operated by gypsies still flourish in cities and towns all over the world. And although complaints of unscrupulous practices have at times been leveled against them, customers keep coming to hear their fortunes told. Nothing, it seems, can dispel the romantic image of the brooding gypsy, whose dark, piercing eyes gaze intently into the palms—and, perhaps, the futures—of the hopeful and the curious.

Palm reading is a practice that is well suited to the footloose ways of gypsies. No props are required, and fortunes can be told quickly and from just about any location—the back of a wagon or in a gaudily decorated tent, apartment, or shop.

The eternal allure of the gypsy fortune-teller may stem from the ancient belief that gypsy seers had magical powers. These powers were thought to be inherited, signaled by a peculiar physical appearance, or bestowed upon a young girl by a water or earth spirit.

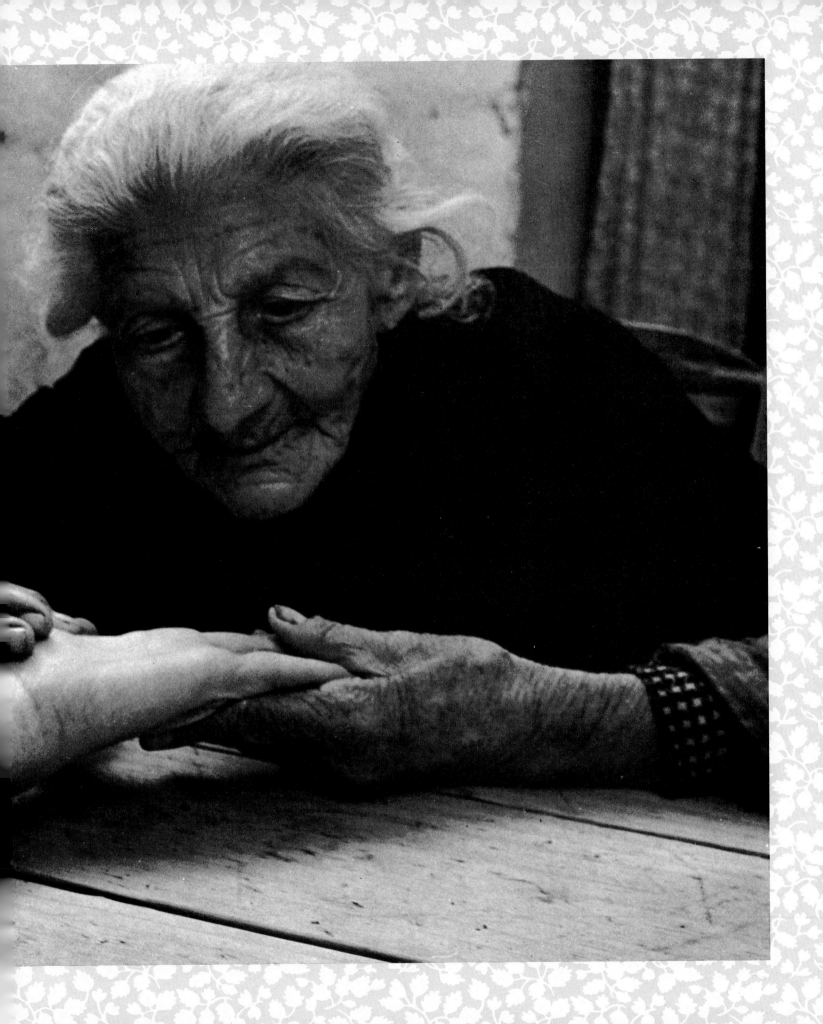

characters of noted authors by examining their signatures. Whether Poe believed he had stumbled upon a remarkable and reliable method for revealing the human soul or was merely using the signatures as a vehicle for critiquing his peers will never be known. Certainly, his approach seems to have lacked the vaunted exactitude of modern handwriting analysis. It is difficult to believe, for example, that Poe wrote with complete objectivity when he described Ralph Waldo Emerson as belonging "to a class of gentlemen with whom we have no patience whatsoever—the mystics for mysticism's sake. . . . His MS [signature] is bad, sprawling, illegible and irregular—although sufficiently bold."

Europeans, however, greeted graphology far more warmly than did Americans. Serious studies of the relationship between handwriting and character had been published from the seventeenth century onward. These studies reached a peak when a French pastor and graphology advocate named Jean-Hippolyte Michon persuaded the eminent psychologist Alfred Binet to test graphological findings. Binet's research had already established the validity of tests for intelligence and personality traits; when he published in 1906 the results of work that seemed to confirm a relationship between handwriting characteristics and personality, graphology gained considerable respectability.

Michon and Binet considered their craft a science. But another branch of handwriting analysis, called psychographology, was an allegedly psychic phenomenon that was practiced exclusively by one man, Raphael Schermann. Born in 1879 in Krakow, Schermann was indifferent to the peculiarities of an individual's handwriting; he did not analyze the slant of the line or the slope of the letters. Rather, he would hold a handwritten letter or envelope in his hand, close his eyes, and then describe the writer's appearance, temperament, past, and—if the spirit moved him—future. Schermann, who allegedly applied his talents on one occasion to help New York City police officers solve a murder case, does appear to have possessed remarkable talents of some sort. In tests conducted by a professor at the University of Prague, Schermann was reported to have had a success rate of 65 percent, a performance that self-styled psychics have attempted but thus far have not been capable of duplicating.

In recent years, most graphologists who offer their services to corporations have made only limited claims for their craft. Handwriting analysis is not presented as a broad window to the future, but as a valuable tool that can help assess an individual's intelligence, aptitudes, and character, and perhaps provide some clues to his or her prospective performance. Another thing that endears the graphologist to business managers is that an analysis of a handwritten note is cheaper, quicker, and more readily understood than a psychiatric evaluation or the results of a battery of aptitude tests.

The formation and ornamentation of individual letters, how they are slanted, and how lightly or heavily they have been applied to the page are among many supposed signposts to character examined by handwriting analysis. But serious graphologists maintain that while these factors can be clues, they are not valid indicators of personality when considered alone; they should be confirmed and modified by other observations, such as the shape and size of the letters, the speed of writing, the general shape of lines and paragraphs, as well as the way in which letters and words are connected.

Like palmistry, graphology is ancient. Aristotle, for example, believed that a person's soul could be defined by the way he or she wrote; a Chinese philosopher noted much the same thing in the eleventh century AD. But the age-old practice has changed considerably with the advent of modern times. At least one enthusiast has even combined the principles of graphology with the speed and data-processing capacity of a computer to produce faster and presumably more accurate analyses of the psychic signals embedded in handwriting. And so the search for the Rosetta stone of character and fate continues, with mysticism appealing to science for assistance in unlocking the secrets of inner space and future time.

Penmanship and Personality

Most handwriting analysts wince when their work is compared with divination. They practice a science and an art, they say; they are psychologists, not psychics. And indeed, forensic graphology—used, among other things, to detect forgery and establish authenticity of manuscripts—is widely recognized as legitimate science. More questionable, however, is the contention of many graphologists that they can deduce character traits from a sample of script. And it is in this nebulous area that they share with many diviners at least one aim: Both bend their labors toward extracting the essence of personality.

Graphologists emphasize that character reveals itself in handwriting by way of innumerable small clues, each one of which must be considered in conjunction with all the others. With proper attention to detail, they say, graphology can assess more than 300 personality characteristics, among them sociability or introversion, egocentricity, imagination, ambition, and enthusiasm.

Nevertheless, experts warn that graphology can yield only clues, not certainties, about character. But the same could be said of more traditional psychological yardsticks. Psychologist David Lester, who did an extensive study pitting graphology against standard tests such as the Minnesota Multiphasic Personality Inventory and the Rorschach inkblot, found that graphology was just as accurate as its more orthodox competition in assessing personality.

Some of the basic principles of graphology, along with an analysis of two writing samples, appear on the following pages.

Different Slants

Lincoln's Gettysburg Address

Four score and seven years ago our fathers brought forth on this continent, a new nation, conceived in liberty, and dedicated to the proposition that all men are created equal.

Most people learned as schoolchildren to write according to the Palmer Method, shown above in an exerpt from the Gettysburg Address. This standard, devised by educator Austin N. Palmer in the nineteenth century, is still used by handwriting experts as a control against which other scripts are measured.

No one mimics for long the tedious perfection prescribed by Palmer. Each individual adapts, embellishes, and eliminates until a handwriting style emerges that is as distinctive and specific as a fingerprint. Graphologists attribute this diversity to the uniqueness of each human brain. The brain, they say, does the writing; the hands are only the tools. Therefore, each person's writing can be seen as a kind of psychological logbook.

To read it, experts prefer to work from writing that is spontaneous—not copied—and inscribed on unlined paper. They look first at general characteristics, including the slant of the letters, their height and depth, the slope of the line, and the way words are spaced.

Script that slants to the right supposedly denotes a person pulled toward others, an individual who wants and needs human contact. The greater the slant, the greater the need for approval. A negative aspect of the forward slant is that its owner may be overly emotional, especially under stress. A backward slant reveals a loner, an introspective person who may overcontrol emotions. An erratic slant—letters leaning first one way, then another—connotes versatility, but also moodiness and instability.

Graphologists divide lines of script horizontally into three zones, illustrated by the heavy lines in the sample above. The proportional distribution of the letters within the zones can be telling. The upper zone governs intellect, spirituality, idealism, and imagination. The middle zone pertains to practical functions related to work and family and social interactions. The lower zone shows attitudes about physicality, sex, and material matters. Letters apportioned evenly through all three zones reveal inner harmony. If upper loops on such letters as *f, h, k,* and *l* show outsized height, the writer is apt to be idealistic and prone to daydream. Writing dominated by the middle zone purportedly implies a self-involved person who lives for the moment. Deep stretches into the lower zone denote strong physical and material drives.

The slope of a line of script is also said to be significant. Writing that marches directly from left margin to right reveals someone self-contained, even-tempered, and goal-directed. Writing rising toward the end of a line purportedly suggests optimism or exhilaration. And a sample that slopes downward shows pessimism, depression, or fatigue.

Spacing between words can reveal certain social and emotional tendencies. Narrow spacing implies a need for social contact, possibly leading to a certain lack of discrimination in choosing friends. Wide spacing reflects reserve and caution; the writer is metaphorically distancing himself or herself from others. Moderate spacing indicates a happy medium, a person who is both self-sufficient and sociable.

Another big-picture item the graphologist might address is the size of the writing. Large script denotes an expansive ego; medium-size writing a balanced, reasonable, and adaptable person; small writing a rationalist, possibly a scientist or academic. Very small writing that tends to flatten into a line denotes feelings of inferiority, while script that varies in size indicates moodiness and extreme sensitivity.

d Ee F Ff Gg Hh Ii Jj K

Different Strokes

After assessing the overall character of a handwriting style, the graphologist proceeds to the wealth of minutiae yielded by individual letters and strokes.

Capital letters are said to be clues to one's ego, the face one presents to the world. Large, overblown capitals, for instance, reveal a need for attention and admiration, while small ones suggest excessive modesty and a lack of self-assurance. Scroll-like, much-embellished capitals denote vulgarity; simple printed capitals good taste. The capital personal pronoun *I* is a particularly important benchmark of one's self-assessment. An *I* much larger than other capitals indicates self-interest and a confident facade that may mask uncertainty. A small, badly shaped *I* bespeaks self-consciousness and weak will. A very round *I* is self-protective and introverted, but an *I* that is large and angular shows an abrasive egotism.

I is also significant in the lower case, where its dot supposedly presents innumerable clues to character. For example, if the *i* has an elongated dot, the writer is probably highly sensitive with an acute critical sense. A thick, heavy dot indicates bad temper, possibly to the point of brutality. A light dot riding high above the *i*'s stem shows refinement and imagination.

A few more of the multitudinous clues that a good graphologist pursues are depicted on this page.

For all of graphology's breadth and attention to detail, however, there are two basic characteristics that the practice chronically fails to detect with any certainty: age and sex. It seems that maturity does not always parallel chronology, and most people have characteristics of both genders within their psychological makeup.

STARTS AND FINISHES

Long approach strokes to first letters can show attachment to the past. The small initial hook and long sweep into the f—significantly, in the word father—show someone seeking to retrieve the past.

Contrasting with the previous f, this one is without preamble. When there is no approach stroke at all, the writer is probably a direct, forward-looking, and efficient person.

The little upward flourish on the r indicates generosity, along with a possible interest in such matters as religion, theoretical reasoning, or abstract thinking.

The slight inward hook on the final y is tiny, but telling. It betokens a certain tenacity and persistence. The writer is probably also goal oriented and somewhat acquisitive.

THE LETTER *T*

On writing that slants to the left, a single long t-bar that crosses two stems shows willpower, mental agility, and possible executive ability.

The t-bar that loops backward to cross the stem reveals guilt feelings, though they might well be groundless.

Crossing a t above the stem bespeaks goals that may be too lofty. The bar's position left of the stem signals hesitancy or procrastination.

A t crossed low on the stem denotes a pedestrian thinker, one who sets safe, easy goals and takes refuge in the tried and tested.

A t-bar that slants upward, like a whole line of script edging upward, suggests an optimistic outlook on life.

The abrupt downward slant of this t-bar indicates a writer who is stubborn and willful and inclined to be overly critical.

Revelations in Script

The handwriting samples shown here were analyzed by Gloria Weiss, a forensic graphologist and graphology teacher based in Washington, D.C. The sample below was provided by a young mother and professional woman, the one on the facing page by a man who became a novelist after retiring from government.

Lincoln's Gettysburg Address

Four score and seven years ago our fathers brought forth upon this continent a new ~~so~~ nation, conceived in liberty, and dedicated to this proposition that all men are created equal.

The slant and fluidity of this sample give the overall impression of spontaneity, enthusiasm, versatility, imagination, directness, and efficiency. A variability in the size and shape of the writing suggests occasional moodiness and indicates the writer is often pressed for time.

The slightly arched t-bars denote concerted mental effort to control concentration that tends to be scattered; but on the positive side, a small flourish to the bars bespeaks a good sense of humor. The word spacing varies from close to comparatively wide. This means the writer knows how to be close to people without being intrusive. Innate good taste and quiet self-confidence show in the capital letters, which are sizable, but also simple, direct, and unassuming. The upward slope of the writing reveals an optimistic nature. Varied interests show in the way the writing balances fairly evenly across the three zones. But the middle zone is a little small, and projections into the upper and lower zones vary. These factors suggest the writer may have trouble with priorities and focus as she tries to juggle the diverse concerns in her life.

In the words *conceived, liberty,* and *proposition,* Weiss notes the script's tendency to begin large and taper down toward the end of a word. This is a habit that implies diplomacy and tact. In writing that is more thready and less defined, these virtues might change to hypocrisy, Weiss says.

However, the tapering here must be balanced against the ovals of the small *a*'s and *o*'s. The ovals are clearly formed and usually fully closed at the top, showing honesty and directness. Weiss concludes the writer is neither insincere nor manipulative, but she tends to temporize with the truth a bit to avoid hurting other people's feelings.

r r S s T T t U u V v W w X x Y y

In his Gettysburg Address

Four score and seven years ago our fathers brought forth upon this continent a new nation, conceived in liberty, and dedicated to the proposition that all men are created equal.

This writing shows a slight leftward slant, a singular regularity, and very straight alignment, marching left to right with precision and purpose. The writer is exceptionally goal directed, Weiss says. He is single-minded and tenacious in his aims; once he plots a course he will not deviate from it. He finishes what he starts, and he finishes on time.

This general observation is confirmed by smaller details, such as the writer's formation of the small letter *f*. The lowercase *f* is especially important to graphologists in what it reveals about organizational ability. According to Weiss, a well-balanced *f* whose upper and lower extensions are fairly equal—as those in the novelist's *f*'s are—almost guarantees that the writer has a strong sense of organization. Moreover, he is judicious. Wide spacing between his lines betokens a man who weighs and considers carefully before deciding or acting.

The upper zone dominates his script; the lowercase *l*'s and *b*'s have upward extensions that soar well out of proportion to the small middle zone. Here is a man of theory and intellect, more at home in the realm of ideas than with practical, mundane matters.

Nevertheless, certain clues imply the writer is not quite as rigid as an overall reading suggests. The odd reversal in the lower arm of his *f* shows flexibility, and the rightward t-bars indicate considerable enthusiasm and some spontaneity. Despite a certain standoffishness in the script's leftward slant, long final strokes on some of the letters show a degree of extroversion, a reaching out toward others. The simplicity of the capitals says the writer is no egotist. His good taste precludes presumption.

Still, he wants and expects a lot from life. Where the young mother writes with rather light pressure, the man bears down on his words. This shows strong drive and a will to achieve.

1 2 3 4 5 6 7 8 9 0

Charting the Four Basic Numbers

In the ancient practice of numerology, a person's birth chart consists of four basic numbers—three drawn from the name given at birth and one from the birth date. Numerologists analyze these numbers to discover clues about the individual's character, destiny, and life cycles. A personal chart reading, similar to those performed by professionals, can be done by simply calculating these four numbers and checking the capsule descriptions on the following pages. Although people are the usual subjects, the process can be applied to anything that has a name and date of birth or origin—a cat, a business, a nation, or even an idea.

The first step in this intriguing exercise is to translate the name into its numerical equivalent, using the number-letter conversion table shown on the opposite page. Each letter is assigned a single-digit number based on its sequential place in the alphabet: The letters *A* through *I* are numbered one through nine, with the remaining letters reduced to one of those digits through simple addition. For example, *J* as the tenth letter reduces to a one (10=1+0=1), and *U* as the twenty-first letter reduces to a three (21=2+1=3).

The three birth-name numbers are determined by adding the numerical values of three different sets of letters in the name: first, all the vowels that occur; then, all the consonants; and finally, the total of all the letters. The numerical total of the vowels—*a, e, i, o,* and *u*—in the name is called the Soul Number. This is thought to reflect the person's true inner self, encompassing ambitions and motivations, judgment and attitudes, and feelings. The total of the consonants, on the other hand, produces the Outer Personality Number, which relates to physical appearance, health, and the impression the person makes on others through dress and behavior.

The total of the entire birth name is known as the Path of Destiny Number. It indicates the sum of the individual's capabilities and achievements and how he or she will affect others. The Path of Destiny Number also influences the course a person will take to attain career goals—whether the career involves raising a family or running a corporation—and describes the types of people who will be encountered along the way.

Numerologists believe that although the birth name remains the foundation of nature and destiny throughout life, a name change can dramatically alter the mix of letters and numbers and thus expand the person's experiences, attitudes, and role in society. A woman who changes her last name at marriage, for example, may become more adaptable and flexible in her new circumstances because she is taking on a new set of numbers that will be used along with her birth name. Numerology points to a shift in personal numbers as a factor in such transformations. Similarly, movie stars and writers may take on new public identities—and private personalities—through name changes they hope will provide a certain image. Archibald Leach and Joyce Frankenburg certainly have a different ring from Cary Grant and Jane Seymour, the stage names these two performers chose.

Although a person's name may change over the course of a lifetime, the birth date is constant. And it is the sum of numbers in this date that produces the fourth and most important number in a numerology chart—the Life Lesson Number. This number reveals the lessons and truths a person is meant to learn during his lifetime; it signals the essential purpose of his existence.

The Life Lesson Number is obtained by writing the birth date in numbers and totaling them until they reduce to a single digit. If your birth date is November 4, 1947, for example, you would figure your Life Lesson Number by writing the date as 11-4-1947—making sure to use the full year, not the abbreviation '47—and then adding the digits until they reduce to a nine (1+1+4+1+9+4+7=27=2+7=9).

The birth-date number is also the key to interpreting what numerologists call "personal-year cycles"—a set of reigning patterns and influences such as assertiveness, harmony, security, resignation, and the like. These patterns are said to be set in motion on the day a person is born and continue in nine-year cycles for as long as he or she lives. The personal-year cycle explains where energy should be focused during any given twelve-month period—a kind of psychic homework assignment for the year.

A simple method of determining the current personal-year cycle is to go back to the person's last birthday and add the numbers in that date, as demonstrated above. The patterns associated with this number will prevail from that birthday up to the next birthday, and then the cycle will move forward one number; at the end of year nine in the cycle, the person begins again with year one.

Whatever Life Lesson Number is determined on the day of birth, that number is repeated in the person's ninth year—and every nine years thereafter. For this reason, the birth year and the ages of 9, 18, 27, 36, 45, 54, and so on are important years—periods when events occur that underscore the major theme of a person's life and remind him again of the lessons he is here to learn.

Once the four numbers in a personal birth chart are determined, the final step is to look up their interpretations. Each of the numerical descriptions on the following pages begins with the number's supposed essence, followed by its influence as a personal number in one of the four categories. If you are examining your Soul Number, for example, the definition describes your inner nature. If it is your Outer Personality Number, the description represents how others see you. If you are looking up your Path of Destiny Number, the influence applies to your career course. And if it is your Life Lesson Number, the definition suggests the lessons you need to learn. And finally, the personal-year cycle describes the prevailing pattern of events and attitudes for any year—past, present, or future.

1	2	3	4	5	6	7	8	9
A	B	C	D	E	F	G	H	I
J	K	L	M	N	O	P	Q	R
S	T	U	V	W	X	Y	Z	

Essence of One: Activation. One is the seed, the beginning, when the life force is self-compelled to move out to explore and confront newness. It is original and individualistic because it is uninfluenced by previous experience. Because it does not know that things cannot be done, it proceeds with complete faith to do them. One is the pioneer, facing the unknown with an innocent courage. It draws upon its own creative well to solve any problems that arise.

Personal Number One: You are an extreme individualist and a self-motivator, and therefore feel comfortable following your own ideas and instincts. Your individuality is the drive behind your need for freedom and independence. You express leadership creatively and with originality. Not wanting to take a secondary position, you handle the entire operation and leave the details to others. You learn more from experience than from instruction and advice, which you dislike. Your ardent nature can cause swings in your emotional behavior. Yet the intensity of your focus, together with your courage and intelligence, make you

a tower of inspiration in difficult times. You should avoid becoming arrogant, selfish, and stubborn.

Personal-Year-Cycle One: This is the beginning of a new nine-year cycle in your life. Major changes have occurred and you are still in the process of sorting them out physically and emotionally. You feel compelled to center on yourself, which may be a difficult mental transition if you have been trained to think of others first. However, your needs should come first now—the decisions you make during this cycle will influence your life for the next four to nine years. Even if there are people around you, you may feel isolated and alone. Do not let this be a concern, because your sense of separation allows you to make important decisions uninfluenced by others. People may offer advice, but you will not take it. You feel more independent, assertive, and willing to take chances. This is the year to express your individuality, to attempt those things you have only dreamed of to this point. One important person, attracted by your new attitude, may come into your life.

Essence of Two: Attraction. In its dynamic advancement, One is attracted to another One, and they become Two. Two is the gestation period where the seed from One is collected and assimilated, and things begin to form. It is the mirror of illumination where knowledge comes from opposites: night and day, female and male. Two is the principle of marriage between two distinct entities.

Personal Number Two: You are a diplomat with a strong desire for peace and harmony. Since you are so strongly tuned in to the moods and feelings of others, you collect and assimilate their ideas, which can make it difficult for you to make decisions. You are so sensitive that you naturally interact with others gently while staying in the background and remaining unobtrusive. The subtle forces of nature stir you deeply; music and other soothing art forms fulfill your deep sense of rhythm and harmony. You have an expansive imagination that creates a magic mirror in which you can see every detail. Your cooperative and patient nature, along with your sincerity and your ability to see both sides of things, makes you the perfect partner. Avoid oversensitivity, indecision, and feelings of inferiority.

Personal-Year-Cycle Two: This year requires a calm, receptive attitude on your part. Because you have the ability to see opposing points of view now, you become the peacemaker or mediator. You become aware of the needs of others and are willing to settle any differences that may have arisen as a result of last year's assertiveness. You may find it hard to make decisions now, preferring to remain more in the background. This is a good period for partnerships because of your sensitivity. Marriage may occur during this cycle. Your subconscious is very active, so you should explore and develop your intuitive abilities. Flashes of insight and understanding will aid you in solving difficult situations. Sudden recognition is possible for some act or work you are presently doing or perhaps have long forgotten. Legal dealings, sales agreements, legacies, and claims may occur now. It is a curious year, when life flows along quietly—until sudden, exciting events occur that can require overnight decisions. Your motto this year should be: Expect the unexpected. And listen to your inner self. Creative magic lies waiting to be explored.

Essence of Three: Expansion. The marriage of Two results in growth and unfoldment in Three. The most imaginative and creative of the numbers, Three is the mother-father-child. This family unit is symbolized by the triangle, known as the first perfect shape in mathematics—that is, the first closed plane that can be constructed with straight lines. The triangle represents the three-fold nature of divinity in most cultures.

Personal Number Three: You are an extremely expressive individual who can influence others with your ability to communicate in a flamboyant style. Somewhere there is a stage waiting for you. Whether you are speaking, writing, or acting, your bright, warm nature draws others who bask in your enthusiasm and energy. You are aware of your appearance because performing depends upon the impression you make on others. You dream big, and your faith is often rewarded because positive thinking produces positive results. Because of your expansive nature, you meet people from different cultures and social strata, increasing your already broad and all-encompassing thinking. Do not scatter your energies, and avoid exaggeration, self-indulgence, and foolish optimism.

Personal-Year-Cycle Three: This is your year of activity, expansion, travel, and luck. You need room to move and express yourself, to experience life, freedom, and the joy of living. You may travel to another part of this land or to another country and meet people who enlarge your idea of the world. Some of the individuals you meet now can be important business contacts in the future. You are aware of your appearance and may indulge in a new wardrobe, hairstyle, or other beauty improvements. Since this is often called a lucky cycle, your one ticket may win the prize. But do not overindulge. Overexpansion leads to bankruptcy. If you use good judgment, however, this is a fertile cycle that could include the birth of a child, a creation of the mind, or an expansion of your bank account. In the midst of this social cycle, you will be invited to parties and functions where you suddenly become the center of attention. People respond to you positively, which feeds a growing feeling of well-being within you. You have more faith in yourself and your abilities.

Essence of Four: Security. Four symbolizes the boundaries that provide security for the Three. As the square, the second perfect shape in mathematics, it suggests solid foundations and perimeters that contain and protect. The determined and conservative Four works hard to provide strong fences and square meals for the nourishment of the Three family.

Personal Number Four: You are practical, cautious, and reliable, the salt of the earth. You feel responsible for building solid foundations upon which the future depends. That is why you respect law and order. It also explains why your cupboard is never bare and you have something saved for that rainy day. You can be depended upon to be at the job every day and to finish any task assigned to you; you exemplify Kahlil Gibran's line from *The Prophet*, "Work is love made visible." You take pride in your work because it is an expression of yourself. You are concerned with the land and need to be connected in some manner, through a garden, nature trips, or environmental issues. Financial matters are of concern to you as well; they are another expression of the worth of your talents. You should avoid stubbornness, overwork, and hoarding.

Personal-Year-Cycle Four: The emphasis this year is on work, order, budgeting, foundations, close physical relationships, the body. You have an urge to organize all areas of your life, so you begin cleaning the attic, cellar, closets, the garage, the office. This action is a symbolic gesture indicative of your subconscious need to build an orderly and strong foundation in your life. Material things become important now because they add to your sense of security and satisfy your heightened physical needs. You may purchase goods or property, or decide to build or remodel. Exercise good judgment and organize your funds carefully. Your body is a physical possession, and since you may have put on a few pounds last year, now is the time to bring out the sweat suits, the diet book, and the bathroom scales. Health can be a concern, so rest, eat well, exercise properly, and have a physical examination. This can be a money cycle, but funds that come in are in direct proportion to the amount of work you do. Work well and you will be rewarded.

Essence of Five: Experience. Four, firmly entrenched in its home, now begins to explore the environment. The Five needs freedom and independence so that it can indulge its senses in the experiences of life. It has an insatiable curiosity through which it filters its encounters and ultimately makes choices that will influence its future.

Personal Number Five: You are a communicator. Impulsive and restless, you need the freedom to move freely through your life so that you can gather experience and information to feed your curiosity. You promote ideas and like change for the learning opportunity it provides. Mental stimulation is essential for your well-being. Your mind moves quickly, imitating and adapting to immediate influences so that you are able to blend in with any group. You can talk on most subjects with ease because of your vast experience, and you are a natural mimic, delighting others with your impish actions. Versatile and adaptable, you are the super salesperson and life of the party. You are efficient but dislike monotony and routine jobs. Because you have the power to communicate effectively, you should remain sincere and truthful.

Personal-Year-Cycle Five: You are restless and ready for change. Life suddenly becomes so busy that you feel as if you are on a merry-go-round, attending meetings and parties, running errands, answering mail and the telephone, and generally being available for others who suddenly need you. Communication is a key word this year. Get involved and meet people, because from these experiences you will gather the information you need to make important decisions that can affect your life for the next four years. If you are dissatisfied with your life, you can make changes more easily now. This is a turning point. Opportunities will arise in which you can find solutions to any current impasses. Because your mind is so active, this is a good time to take courses to satisfy your need for more experience. Your romantic desires increase, sending out magnetic waves that attract the opposite sex. Various love interests become possible. Your nervous system is in high gear, so avoid alcohol and drugs, and be careful of accidents. This is your year for fun, excitement, romantic encounters, decisions, and change.

Essence of Six: Harmony. After tasting experience through its five senses, Six realizes the importance of love, compassion, and social responsibility. The home, built in the Four, must now be filled with love and meaningful relationships. Home also becomes part of the community in which law and order are established to ensure social harmony.

Personal Number Six: You are an artistic individual whose sense of harmony may express itself in the home, the arts, or community service. You need and show love in your home, where family is all-important. Your sense of beauty may be evident in the way you decorate your home, or in crafts and cooking. Your innate ability to go right to the crux of the matter makes you the counselor to whom others go for answers to their problems as well as for the nurturing compassion you provide. If your profession is outside the home, you seek to bring harmonious order to the world through beautifying the environment, counseling, the arts, or through the legal system, which seeks balance in justice. You love people and are concerned,

generous, and tolerant. Be careful to avoid becoming a recluse or a doormat for others, playing the martyr.

Personal-Year-Cycle Six: This is the nesting phase where the emphasis is on home and family. In the natural order of things, after last year's possible romantic encounters, marriage and the birth of children are possible. Even if this does not apply to you, your attention shifts to the domestic front, and changes occur, such as family members moving in or out, children going to school or marrying, relatives wanting financial or emotional support. Responsibility for the family increases. Because your sense of justice is heightened, people may tell you their problems and ask your advice. Court decisions that restore balance are possible. Beauty and harmony become important in your life, so you may redecorate your home, surround yourself with works of art, and enjoy attending museums or the ballet. Community projects can satisfy your social sensibilities now. And close relationships with your partner, family, and friends are possible if you extend love and compassion.

Essence of Seven: Analysis. Now that the physical is taken care of, Seven goes within itself to contemplate its place in the universe. It begins to think and to analyze past experiences and present situations, and it wonders what lies ahead. Seven realizes that the skills it has developed must be perfected in preparation for the future. Seven is physical rest and mental work.

Personal Number Seven: You are a thinker, an idealist who thoroughly analyzes knowledge from many sources before accepting any premises. Noises and crowds disrupt your meditative nature; therefore, you spend time by yourself so your creative imagination can roam freely seeking perfection. Your intuitive abilities combined with your naturally analytic nature make you a prophet, able to anticipate future needs and events. You understand human nature and are not easily fooled by external appearances, and thus can make others uneasy. Because of your introspective demeanor, you are a puzzle to many. As a rule, you will not accept orthodox beliefs but will search for your own—although you may find these within the walls of

conventional educational or spiritual institutions. Try to listen to other ideas and do not allow your naturally aloof manner to alienate you from those you love.

Personal-Year-Cycle Seven: It is time to rest. You feel more tired and less social than usual and want to be alone to think about where you have been, where you are now, where you are headed. You may spend time with one or two friends who complement your contemplative mood. This cycle says it is time to go within and think. You have to maintain your everyday routine to some extent, but do not push your affairs aggressively—if you persist in scurrying about in the outside world, you may become ill. You can set your material worries aside; the things you have been worrying about for the past six years will take care of themselves. Your mind is keenly alert, and you should perfect any skills that you have; they will be useful next year. But for now, study, read, and take courses in philosophy, religion, numerology, astrology, or other metaphysical subjects to help you understand your place in life. Your intuitions are keen, and dreams, visions, and telepathic experiences are all possible.

Essence of Eight: Reward. The strength and skills gathered in the past seven numbers are now put to the test. Well grounded physically, emotionally, and mentally, the Eight reaches out into the world to establish its authority in positions of material power. The rewards for its past efforts come in equal proportion to the wisdom of past choices. This is the karmic period where Eight reaps what it has sown.

Personal Number Eight: You are the executive type in whichever sphere you move. Sensing your organizational and managerial abilities, people automatically look to you for leadershp. You know the value of a dollar, so your sound fiscal judgment can place you in positions of financial management. By working hard and exercising discipline and caution, you can achieve positions of great power. You do not rely on luck; you depend upon your own resourcefulness and perseverance. You know no halfway measures; your ambition drives you to achieve success. You must accept responsibility and handle it fairly because your actions have obvious repercussions in the world around you. As a steward of material re-sources, you must handle them wisely and with respect. Scheming and ruthless actions and personal advancement without regard for others lead to defeat.

Personal-Year-Cycle Eight: This year you will get what you have earned. Pursue your career goals with confidence and determination, because now you will be noticed. If you have planned well, you will get that promotion, raise, or recognition. Honors, awards, and legacies are also possible. You are finding out how effective you are in the material world. It is a year of pressure and responsibility in career and in finances. Depending upon your past actions, the reins of power can be placed in your hands—and possibly large sums of money. Personal relationships are also intense. To fulfill the needs of this cycle—as opposed to your Five Cycle, where romantic activities were for the purpose of experience—your relationships now must embody respect and equality, the physical and the spiritual, body and mind. You can find wholeness here, but whatever this cycle presents to you, an examination of your behavior during the past seven cycles will reveal how you arrived at this point.

Essence of Nine: Release. After experiencing the world of material power in the Eight, Nine now knows that physical things are transitory and must be returned to the giver. Having learned that life is c▊▊▊l, Nine gives back freely and with▊▊r those things it has gained so that the universe will be richer. Nine is the humanitarian carrying the light of wisdom.

Personal Number Nine: You are the humanitarian who feels compassion and love for others regardless of social, economic, or racial barriers. Because you understand that you are part of a greater whole, you give generously of your time and resources. You seek wisdom rather than mere knowledge, desiring to make the world a more loving place in which to live. Because you belong to the universal family, you know that you have to live impersonally and let go of things when it is time. People are drawn to you because of your tolerance, inner wisdom, and breadth of vision, which is often prophet-i▊ You must live your own philosophy because you are an example for others. The necessities of life may come easily so that you are free to follow your humanitarian impulses. Avoid self-serving interests, which can only lead to a lack of faith in life's bounty.

Personal-Year-Cycle Nine: This is the final year in your nine-year cycle, a cleansing period in which those things no longer necessary in your life must be discarded to make room for a new round of experience in next year's Personal-Year-Cycle One. Major changes occur now. People may leave your life, you may change jobs or have to relocate, and things you have grown used to may have to be given up. Your attitude changes dramatically. Use some of your energy in charitable deeds. Give back to life some of what you have been given so that you can experience firsthand the joy of giving. These acts are integral to the transition process. Old friendships become especially meaningful now; new ones can develop. You may receive gifts for your past efforts. Many goals have been accomplished, and you should tie up loose ends. The past eight years have added to your pool of wisdom. Sprinkle others with your sympathy, compassion, and understanding, and be open to the cleansing wash of change. An exciting new year lies ahead, beginning with your next birthday.

CHAPTER 4

Symbolic Guides to Fate

ccording to a traditional Hebrew system of deriving divinatory numerals from letters and words, the woman's name equaled two, identifying her as a paragon of femininity. The consonants in her name added up to eight, indicating the powerful influence in her life of money, power, and fame. The vowels, said to be clues to the inner self, yielded the number three, suggesting charm and luck, internal fire, and artistic talent. The most frequently recurring number in her name was five, an indication of a versatile personality driven by nervous energy. Next came one, the number of insatiable ambition. But not a single six—the number of peace and tranquility—appeared in her adoptive name, which was Marilyn Monroe.

In her brief and troubled life, cut short by suicide, this glamorous blond movie star seemed to have fulfilled the destiny foretold by the age-old art of numerology, one of several symbolic systems that have been devised to interpret the present and predict the future. Underlying all such systems is a persistent belief in the orderliness of the universe; our science and our religions are built on that conviction. It is only a small further leap of faith to believe that the same order that governs the course of the stars, the movement of the clouds, and the flow of the tides extends to human affairs as well. And if that order is all-pervasive, the reasoning goes, then surely it can be seen in small things as well as large.

What is revealed to some by the heavens may be discerned by others in, say, a sequence of cards or numbers, or in the fall of a set of sticks or coins. And if the eternal order of the universe is established and complete, as some believe, then there can be no accident or chance; the fall or sequence or pattern results from the confluence of all the forces of order at the instant of inquiry.

All cultures have sought the key to the workings of the universe. The search for the truths hidden in symbols continues today in three main currents. Some seekers rely on the ancient Chinese method called the *I Ching,* which derives complex meaning not from numbers but from combinations of lines selected by chance. Others consult the ornate pack of cards known as the Tarot, believing that fate governs the shuffle and the deal and will reveal itself in the symbols on the cards and their relationship with each other. Still others turn to numerology, which assigns numbers to the letters of the alphabet and derives from names and statements a quantity that corresponds to a special meaning.

No one knows for certain where or when the art of numerology began, but references to it date back many thousands of years. The ancient Maya were known to believe in the mystical significance of numbers, as were Mesopotamian astrologers and conjurers, who are sometimes credited with originating the concept that numbers explain the structure of the universe. The Cabala—a Jewish system of religious and mystical interpretation—maintained that God created the universe using letters and numbers for building materials. And some enthusiasts even believe that the Egyptian and Mexican pyramids incorporate dimensions that were dictated not by architects or engineers but by numerologists who designed the structures in order to express certain secret knowledge.

Early Jewish mystics used the association between letters and numbers to discover hidden meanings in scriptural texts. In their system of interpretation, called gematria, words or sentences whose numbers yielded identical totals were deemed to be identical in meaning or truth. The system that has been the most popular in the West, and the one that provides believers with an intriguing rationale for the whole notion of numerolo-

gy, however, is derived primarily from the work of an ancient Greek philosopher who is probably better known—and more revered—among hardheaded mathematicians than he is in occult circles.

By some accounts, he won the heavyweight boxing championship at the forty-eighth Olympian games. He studied with the best minds of his native Greece, and it is likely that he traveled to Egypt and Babylon to plumb the mysteries of geometry and astronomy. He achieved high honor as a teacher and leader of a philosophical brotherhood in the city of Crotona in Italy. But it is said that no thrill this merchant's son had ever experienced could compare with the stunning revelation of the lyre.

The setting was Asia Minor, the time about 530 BC. The man, whose name would be known to students of geometry for millennia to come, was Pythagoras, and his passion was mathematics. What his investigations into the tuning of the lyre might ultimately lead to was at the onset not entirely clear, even to him. But Pythagoras persisted, studying the octave, inquiring into the nature of harmony, probably measuring on a special single-stringed instrument called a monochord what length of string produced which note. And in time a discovery burst upon him that was to have a profound influence on subsequent human thought.

Pythagoras and his followers venerated numbers with all the enthusiasm and devotion reserved by their contemporaries for the numerous deities of the Hellenic world. During a period of unprecedented inquiry into the nature of things, an era that would later be known as the classical age, contemplating the significance of numbers was a novel and pleasurable pursuit. And these exercises involved far more than the flawless logic of mathematics. To Pythagoreans, numbers also possessed an abstract, even mystical, dimension; members of this trailblazing brotherhood were entranced by such notions as the elemental similarity between, for instance, three elephants and three fleas—their identical *threeness*.

To be sure, such reflections by the Pythagoreans were somewhat limited by the fact that their method of representing numbers was literal rather than symbolic. The number one was depicted with a single dot, two with a pair, three with a triangular arrangement, and so on. Numbers were employed for counting things, nothing else; in a sense, they were chained to what was being enumerated. But Pythagoras with his lyre and monochord was about to set them free, opening up whole new worlds for the system of numerology as well as for mathematics.

His catalytic finding was that musical harmony depended upon the relative length—measured, of course, in numbers—of the strings being played. When, for example, one string was twice as long as the other, establishing a ratio of 2:1, their notes were an octave apart and thus harmonious. Ratios of 3:2 and 4:3 yielded similarly pleasing chords, as did multiples of those ratios. All other arrangements produced ear-grating discords.

The Pythagoreans were intrigued by the fact that the harmonious ratios in music could be expressed by the numbers one through four. Set down in the manner of the time, in dots, the numbers could also be combined in the form of a logical triangular pattern, called the *tetractys,* that fairly

The Mystical Three

"Third time's a charm" is among the many casual superstitions that have survived from ancient times. Godhead as well as hell-sign, three has been regarded as a magical number in widely diverse cultures for millennia.

The classical Greeks had some 120 mythical triads, or groups of three. Some of them were beneficent, some were not. The good ones included the Three Graces, handmaidens of Apollo, shown below in a detail from Botticelli's *Primavera.* But there were also such triads as the three snake-haired Furies, goddesses of retribution, and the three grim Fates.

Norse mythology also had three Fates, and it divided the cosmos into three distinct parts. Even certain elements of Christianity, the Trinity and Holy Family, have rough counterparts in ancient Egypt's Osiris, Isis, and Horus, as well as in the Hindu trinity of Brahma, Vishnu, and Siva.

In numerology, three denotes both spiritual harmony and sexual energy, the transcendent and generative forces.

glowed with symmetry and meaning. It looked like this:

.

. .

. . .

. . . .

In this seemingly simple arrangement of ten dots, the Pythagoreans found all the ratios of musical harmony and encountered symmetry from every angle. They discovered enshrined in the center the number one, which they regarded as an absolute, and perceived a small triangle at the base—a mystical trinity—overarched by dots representing the seven notes of the musical octave. The Pythagoreans were also struck by the notion that the numbers one through four were the most important of all numbers: Added together, they equaled ten; all other numbers could be derived from them. Endlessly fascinated with the tetractys, they made it a holy icon of their order.

The connection with harmony and music served to convince Pythagoras and his followers that numbers signified far more than a mere quantitative description of things; they were in fact the essence of things, the expression of the fundamental laws of the universe. "Were it not for number and its nature," said the Pythagorean philosopher Philolaus in the fifth century BC, "nothing that exists would be clear to anybody either in itself or in relation to other things. You can observe the power of number not only in the affairs of demons and gods but in all the acts and thoughts of men."

The ideal was harmony—not merely in music but in the cosmos, and not only in the material world but in the spiritual as well. Just as numbers pointed the way to musical harmony, so, properly understood, they led to cosmic and spiritual harmony—a kind of music of the universe in which the individual notes or phenomena vibrated at different rates and produced harmonies and discords according to their ratios.

As worked out by the Pythagoreans, the lessons were manifold, and each number had its various parts to play.

The Significant Seven

Folklore has it that seventh sons of seventh sons have uncanny powers—one legend among many that reflect the number seven's mystical connections. The legends may be related to human knowledge of the heavens. The astronomy of antiquity knew only seven "planets," whose movements were thought to bear on human destiny. As an illumination (above) from a manuscript of the 1300s shows, astronomers studied a solar system in which the sun, the moon, Mars, Mercury, Venus, Jupiter, and Saturn revolved around Earth. It was also deemed mystically noteworthy that the moon's four phases lasted some seven days each.

The Bible abounds with significant sevens, from Genesis's precept of a seventh-day sabbath to the seven-headed Great Beast of Revelation. Pythagoreans apportioned life itself into ten periods of seven years each. The ancient Assyrians divided their gods into groups of seven, and Sanskrit lore has seven sages, seven castes, seven worlds. The Chaldeans thought seven was a holy number, and it was sacred to two ancient sun-gods, the Greek Apollo and the Persian Mithras.

The number one represented the primordial unity—omnipotent, whole, male, and good—separated into component parts by the creation of the physical universe. Two, the first result of that division, was regarded as quintessentially female, divided, and bad. (Bowing to changing times, modern numerologists tend to downplay such sex-based classifications.) Everything in creation was deemed to be divided into ten pairs of opposing categories, such as good and evil, light and darkness, and male and female.

None of these attributes was more important than whether the thing was associated with an odd or an even number. Odd numbers, containing as they did the number one (which always stood out prominently in the dot arrangements used to represent these numerals), were associated with unity, goodness, and masculinity. Three, for example, was creative and brilliant—it made one and two harmonious by combining them. Even numbers, on the other hand, signified divisiveness, evil, and femininity. Four, the first of the numbers whose depiction in dots appeared to enclose space, was prosaic as well as stable; in addition, it represented justice.

Five was seen as a number in motion, with an affinity for adventure, and since it was the first combination of an odd and even number (one being regarded as an absolute, not a number), it stood for marriage. Six was at rest in domestic tranquility. Seven turned away from earthly matters toward introspective mysteries, while eight enjoyed the material world and all its goods. Nine stood apart and symbolized perfection of mind and spirit.

How much of all this can be attributed to Pythagoras himself is uncertain, since he left no written records. Myths about him have multiplied over the centuries: He has been

The Ominous Thirteen

So persistent is the superstition surrounding the number thirteen that many hotels continue to omit a thirteenth floor. Some local jurisdictions never designate thirteen as a street-address number, and wary hosts avoid having a dinner party consisting of thirteen guests.

It is widely believed that the fear of thirteen—or triskaidekaphobia—originated with the Last Supper, depicted at right in an Andrea del Castagno fresco. The traitor Judas was the insidious thirteenth participant in that portentous Passover meal. It may also be that Friday the Thirteenth is deemed particularly unlucky because Christ was crucified on a Friday. Another source of triskaidekaphobia, less well known but probably valid, has to do with the Norse goddess Freya, after whom Friday is named. Both Friday and the number thirteen were sacred to her.

For early Christian missionaries bent on stamping out paganism—particularly paganism rooted in a matriarchal tradition—the greatest of the Norse goddesses was especially odious, and so were her day and number.

In fact, however, the aversion to thirteen is not confined to Christian cultures. Even the Norse were ambivalent: There is a Norse myth about twelve gods holding a banquet and neglecting to invite Loki, god of mischief. The malicious god —the thirteenth guest—crashed the party and played a trick that resulted in the death of one of the other deities. In a remarkably similar Greek myth, the twelve Olympians held a feast and did not include Eris, goddess of discord. For spite, she threw into the deities' midst a golden apple that was inscribed For the Fairest. According to legend, contention over which of the goddesses deserved the prize eventually led to the Trojan War.

Numerologists of antiquity had a certain contempt for thirteen because it exceeded the number twelve, which was associated with completion. Thirteen was thus the number no one needed or wanted, the one that signified a breach of proper limits. Ancient Romans believed thirteen to be unlucky, as did some sects in India.

Nevertheless, thirteen's bad repute is not universal. The number is a rather propitious one in Hebrew lore, and it had divine importance for certain Indian tribes of Central America. Moreover, a few Christian numerologists were kindly disposed to it, pointing out that the Trinity and the Ten Commandments added up to thirteen, as did Christ and his twelve apostles.

cited variously as a magician, a poet, and even as creator of the Cabala. Apparently, toward the end of the philosopher's life, citizens of Crotona became suspicious and frightened of the school and its heretical teachings—not to mention its growing political influence. A mob drove Pythagoras and his followers away, then destroyed the school and all its records. Another story maintains that political infighting among the various members resulted in the eventual dissolution of the school.

In any event, their ideas would be revived and expanded by later generations of scholars. In the sixth century AD, the Roman statesman and philosopher Boethius introduced Pythagorean doctrine into a world that had been transformed by Christianity, and the study of numbers began to flourish anew. The perfection of the number one, for example, came to be associated with God,

and the divisiveness of two with separation from God.

Poring over the Scriptures, numerologists found a wealth of new meanings. In the book of Revelation they discovered what they considered to be an example of their art: The Beast from the Sea—the Antichrist—was given a number, "six hundred threescore and six." Thenceforward, every person or thing whose name could be represented as 666 would be suspected by some of being an emissary of the devil. (By various applications of numerological technique, that number can be discovered in the names of the imperial city of Rome, the emperors Nero and Caligula, and Germany's Adolf Hitler.)

The Christian doctrine of the Trinity was a natural for further commentary from numerologists. To the nineteenth-century French occultist Éliphas Lévi, for example, it was obvious why God chose the number three: "Were God only

Casting Your Fate

"The die is cast," said Shakespeare's Julius Caesar as he crossed the Rubicon in the great gamble of his career. The expression was new, but the linkage of dice and destiny was a very ancient idea.

Forerunners of dice, made of bone, probably existed tens of thousand of years ago. They were almost surely used for gambling and quite likely for fortune-telling as well. It appears that primitive man concocted divinatory games as avenues through which gods could send omens concerning the future.

Among the first dice, much used by the Greeks and Romans but far older, were those carved from the four-sided knuckle-bones of sheep. They were called astragali. The decorations on their faces, though not necessarily dots, had designated values for use in gaming and augury. For centuries, astragali existed alongside cube dice bearing the pattern they have today—the spots on opposite sides always totaling seven. These came into use around 1400 BC.

Other dice existed in Egypt at least as early as 3500 BC. How they served for divination is lost to history, but certain gambling uses are clear. Excavations of Egyptian tombs have turned up loaded dice, made specifically for cheating.

Several methods of telling your fortune with dice have evolved over the years. Unlike numerology, the *I Ching,* or the Tarot, they require little expertise and so are easy to try at home.

Perhaps the simplest system involves questions and answers. You invent the questions, depending on what you want to know. Will I be married soon? could be asked, or Will I be rich? or Should I change jobs at this time? Then devise a list of possible answers, numbered from four to twenty-four. Some examples are: Yes, definitely, Yes, if you work hard, Not at this time, or Only if you persist. With a particular question in mind, throw two dice and add their numbers. Then throw again and add the second total to the first.

With that result, consult your answers list for the corresponding response to your question. More formal methods require a little ritual preparation and—according to tradition—attention to circumstances. Friday and Sunday are said to be unauspicious for divination. Cool weather is considered best for dice casting, and a tranquil atmosphere is essential. Be absolutely silent as you throw the dice.

Draw a circle about a foot in diameter and put it on a table or some other flat surface. This will be your target in throwing, and you must take care to hit it. To have the dice fall outside the circle or on the floor is unlucky. Use three dice. If all three of the dice land outside the circle on your first cast, try again. If this happens once more, the time is not auspicious, and you should abandon the experiment for the present.

The total face value of the three dice in one throw yields the number for a divinatory message, such as those found in the following list derived from traditional sources:

Three. Unexpected good news, a

gift, the beginning of a lucky time.

Four. Disappointment, unpleasantness, or bad luck; exercise some caution.

Five. A wish fulfilled, a stranger bringing happiness, a new and lasting friend.

Six. Financial loss, dishonest friends or loved ones.

Seven. Setbacks, unhappiness, scandal or gossip; guard your secrets.

Eight. Strong outside forces; blame, fair or unfair, headed your way.

Nine. Luck in love or in marriage, reconciliation, a wedding or some other kind of festivity.

Ten. A birth, domestic happiness; a business promotion.

Eleven. A parting, possible illness, unhappiness for you or someone close.

Twelve. Good news, maybe by letter or telephone, but get advice before replying.

Thirteen. Grief and sorrow, depression and worry.

Fourteen. Help from a friend, a new friend or admirer.

Fifteen. Caution—guard against temptation toward dishonesty, avoid arguments and gossip.

Sixteen. Travel, a good journey.

Seventeen. A change caused by someone from afar, a move, cheerful industriousness.

Eighteen. The luckiest number of all, boding success, wealth, advancement, and happiness.

For more specific revelations about your future, a third method may yield more complete meanings. Divide your circle into twelve equal parts and assign letters to each one. Each section will pertain to a particular aspect of your life, as follows:

A The next year
B Finances
C Travel
D Domestic affairs
E The present
F Health
G Love and marriage
H Legal matters
I Your current emotional state
J Career
K Friends
L Enemies

Again, use three dice. But with this system, the dice are not totaled after they are thrown. Rather, the number that turns up on the die landing in a particular segment is the one to conjure with. Thus you are dealing only with numbers one through six. Their meanings are as follows:

One. Favorable aspects, but they should be related to the reading as a whole.

Two. Success depends on your friends.

Three. Signs are excellent for success.

Four. Disappointment and difficulties.

Five. Auspicious indications.

Six. Uncertainty.

Say, for example, you throw your three dice and turn up a four on letter *F*, a six on *E*, and a two on *A*. The *F*/four combination might mean health problems are in the offing, and therefore a medical checkup could be advisable. The *E*/six takes up the theme, indicating a degree of uncertainty in your life at the moment. Combining the two divinations, you might conclude that less than optimum health at the present time is the cause of doubt and unease. But the *A*/two augurs a favorable outcome, indicating that the year to come will bring good things, provided you take care to get along with people.

Like most divination systems, dice casting permits—even encourages—you to read your own meanings into the fall of the cubes. And, as is generally the case with augury, there is no empirical evidence whatever to prove the dice are accurate. Yet tales of truth-telling dice do exist, as one might expect with a divinatory system that predates history itself.

Dominoes and Destiny

While nowhere near as old as dice, dominoes are nevertheless respectably antique. The first record of them comes from twelfth-century China, where they were probably used for divination rather than gaming. In fact, some antiquarians believe dominoes evolved as an early form of dice, a variety that was employed exclusively for occult practices.

They are still widely used for fortune-telling in Korea and India; and in both India and China there are domino games that combine gambling and augury. Certain tiles are thought to be lucky for a player, regardless of the outcome of the game.

Dominoes apparently made their way to Europe by way of China, and in the West the tiles took on their current name and a more modern form. By the end of the eighteenth century, they were in use in Italy, France, and England. They probably were named after a black-and-white masquerade costume called the domino—popular in Europe at the time—that matched the color combination of the common ebony-and-ivory tiles.

Modern dominoes are usually made of wood, ivory, or plastic. Standard sets in the West consist of twenty-eight rectangular tiles, one of them completely blank and the others marked on one side with dots. Each tile is bisected, and the halves that are not blank bear dots numbering one to six. Thus they represent all of the possible number combinations, ranging from double blank to double six.

In their occidental incarnation, dominoes have tended to be far more popular as a game than as a tool for divination. Even so, Western methods for telling fortunes with them have evolved over the centuries and still persist.

To begin your domino reading, place all the tiles face down and then shuffle them. Three tiles will be used for the reading, and they may be selected in either of two ways. You may pick all three at once, or you may choose them one at a time, reading the chosen domino and divining its message and then returning it to the pile to be shuffled again. The second method offers the possibility that the same tile could be drawn twice. If this happens, an immediate fulfillment of the message is indicated.

However the tiles are drawn, only three may be used at a sitting. Moreover, it is said that you should not divine with dominoes more than once a week, lest the results lose all meaning.

Here are the traditional meanings of the various number combinations to be found on a single tile:

Six/six. The luckiest domino of them all, forecasting happiness, success, and prosperity in all aspects of life.

Six/five. Enhanced status, the presence of a close friend or patron, a sign that any kindness will bring you esteem, a caution toward patience and tenacity.

Six/four. A quarrel, perhaps even an unsuccessful lawsuit.

Six/three. Travel, enjoyment, a happy holiday; a gift.

Six/two. Good luck and improved circumstances but only for those who are honest.

Six/one. A wedding; an end to problems, possibly as a result of the intervention of a good friend.

Six/blank. Beware of false friends, for their malicious gossip could cause suffering for you.

Five/five. Change bringing success, a beneficial move, money that results from a new idea.

Five/four. Financial luck, possibly unexpected, but avoid making investments at this time.

Five/three. Calm, serenity; a guest; good news or helpful advice given to you by your boss or a visitor.

Five/two. Birth, influence from a true and patient friend, sociability and enjoyment.

Five/one. A love affair or new friend, possible unhappy endings for those who are in love.

Five/blank. Sadness, the necessity of comforting a friend in trouble but with tact and caution.

Four/four. Happiness, celebration, relaxation, fun.

Four/three. Happiness and success instead of expected disappointments but possible domestic problems.

Four/two. An unhappy change, setbacks, loss, possibly a theft. Beware of a deceitful acquaintance.

Four/one. Financial problems ahead, pay outstanding debts.

Four/blank. Bad news; disappointment in love, temporarily thwarted goals. Reconcile disagreements.

Three/three. Emotional obstacles, jealousy, but beneficial financial indications; a wedding.

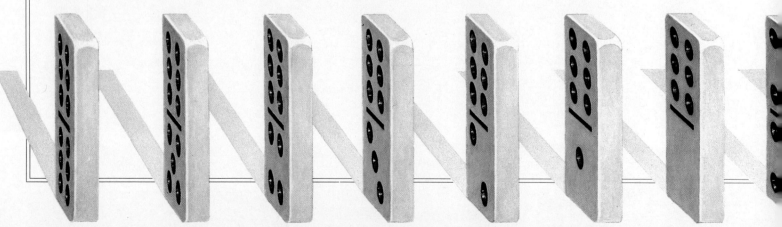

Three/two. Pleasant changes, but be cautious—particularly where monetary matters are concerned.

Three/one. The answer to your question is no, unexpected useful news, outsiders could cause problems.

Three/blank. Unexpected problems at home and work.

Two/two. Success and happiness, in spite of the efforts your enemies may be making against you.

Two/one. Loss of money or property, but old friends and a happy social life.

Two/blank. Travel and new friends, but also anxiety. Someone could cause serious difficulties.

One/one. Pleasure, harmony, and affection; a stranger; avoid delaying an important decision.

One/blank. Be careful; do not let yourself be overly trusting, even though a stranger could bring you news that seems to promise financial gain.

Blank/blank. Direst omens, negative indications in all areas of life.

one, He would never be Creator or Father. Were He two, there would be antagonism or division in the infinite. He is therefore three for the creation by Himself and in His image of the infinite multitude of all things."

Today's numerologists are more interested in reading character and predicting the future than in musing upon theological issues. Much as Pythagoras taught that number is all, they believe that a name—or the numbers associated with it—is everything, not merely a description, but the essence of the individual. Names may be identical, of course, but when the numerologist combines name with date of birth, the result is distinctive. One numerologist has calculated that the chances of duplicating all the number patterns generated by such a combination are an astronomical 10 billion to one.

In modern practice, a person's name is reduced to a single-digit number by assigning each letter its numerical value and then combining the values. The numbers in any two-digit quantity are added until the result is a single number. Thus, in numerology, eight plus eight does not equal sixteen, but seven—the sum of one and six.

There are two generally accepted ways in which names are converted to numbers. The simpler and more popular method is the modern one, which assigns to the letters of the alphabet the numbers one through nine in repeating cycles. The other procedure involves a chart derived from the Greek and Hebrew alphabets that assigns the numbers one through eight to the letters of the alphabet, in no particular order.

The absence of the number nine from this system is deliberate. In Hebrew tradition, nine was the number that represented God, whose name was sacred and unutterable; it could not be used for such purposes as numerology. Cu-

riously enough, in the peculiar way numerologists arrive at their sums, nine is invisible: Adding it to a string of numbers does not have any effect on the numerological total. But many modern practitioners claim that omitting nine means missing some interim results and failing to identify certain patterns that served as the very foundation of the Pythagorean system of numerology.

This sum of all the letters in a person's name reveals to the numerologist the qualities and traits the subject has developed most fully. Other numbers, derived from the birth date as well as from the vowels and consonants in the name, are said to yield clues to personality, character, and destiny *(pages 98-103)*.

People turn to numerology for advice and guidance in all manner of things, most of them having to do with their personal lives. A person might, for example, consult the charts to find out whether a potential mate is compatible or to determine whether a job change or a move to a new city would prove advantageous. Of course, no objective evidence has proved that such counsel is valid, and it is also highly likely that the Pythagoreans and other early numerologists, who viewed numbers as guideposts to cosmic truths, would consider these common applications of their art to be quite frivolous.

With its emphasis on the occult, the subjective, and the mysterious, numerology would seem to have little in common with science, apart from working chiefly in the language of numbers. Yet certain parallels between the two can be discerned.

In science, numbers have often been used in an almost divinatory way. So it was with the researches of the nineteenth-century Russian chemist Dmitri Mendeléev. When Mendeléev ranked the known chemical elements according to their identifying numbers—their atomic weights—he noted that strong and distinct patterns emerged. Not only did all known elements fit neatly into this periodic table, as it is now called, but gaps in the table indicated to Mendeléev the existence of elements that had not even been guessed at.

Mendeléev had discovered a kind of harmony, based on numbers, that no doubt would have pleased Pythagoras greatly. Later scientists predicted the existence of planets and subatomic particles by applying mathematical principles, and today's theorists sometimes speak in terms of parallel universes and multiple dimensions—concepts that can sound no less mystical than many of the pronouncements of numerologists.

What science and the mystical analyses of numerology share, underlying their manipulations of numbers, is a commitment to the notion of order in the universe. Indeed, all humanity seems compelled to seek out the nature and consequences of that order. While Western thought has progressed on somewhat mechanical lines, however, stressing mathematics and the so-called hard sciences, the thinkers of the Orient have generally preferred a subtler approach, a way of looking at things that has led to what surely must be the world's most complex system for using symbols to probe the unknown.

In 1962 a British author and scholar named John Blofeld, for years a resident of the Orient, turned to this venerable technique of divination in hopes of foreseeing the outcome of a long-simmering border dispute between India and China. Toward the end of that year, swarms of Chinese soldiers suddenly and surprisingly advanced down from Tibet against India, whose ill-equipped forces were routed in the first clashes along the Tibetan border. Its allies were unable to offer timely assistance, and India stood shocked and virtually defenseless in the path of the attackers.

In Bangkok, Thailand, where he was living at the time, Blofeld read the daily newspaper reports in growing dismay and apprehension. During his years in China, Blofeld had become familiar with the fabled *I Ching,* or *Book of Changes.* This cryptic summation of the wisdom of the Orient, purportedly the oldest book in the world, was intended as a diviner's tool, and Blofeld possessed a translation; he decided to use it in seeking an answer to the urgent question of what would happen to India.

It is unlikely that Blofeld performed the traditional ceremony in consulting the *I Ching,* beginning with the lengthy sorting and re-sorting of bunches of dried yarrow stalks. Since he was from the West, he probably employed the simpler method of tossing three coins to arrive at a series of six numbers. Guided by the precepts of the *Book of Changes,* he went on to convert the numbers into a sequence of straight and broken lines.

The result was a column of six short lines arranged vertically into a configuration called a hexagram. There are sixty-four such hexagrams possible in the *I Ching,* and each is the subject of an enigmatic essay.

But the diviner's task does not stop there. Each of the hexagram's component trigrams, or three-line groups, has an identity that also must be considered, in conjunction with the subtleties of the relationships between the two trigrams. Moreover, if the hexagram contains what the infinitely complex *Book of Changes* designates as moving lines, then a second hexagram, one containing the opposite of the moving lines, must be drawn and taken into account along with the first.

The figure produced by Blofeld's number conversion was Hexagram 48, which contains two moving lines; his requisite second figure was Hexagram 63. He proceeded to meditate on the appropriate texts in the *I Ching.* "Hexagram 48 signifies a well," he wrote years later. "My knowledge of the Indo-Tibetan borderland, where the mighty Himalayas slope sharply down to the flat dead plain of North India, led me promptly to equate India with the well and to think of the Chinese as looking down into it from above.

"Of the two component trigrams, one has 'bland' or 'mild' among its meanings, while the other means 'water'. Taking water, the contents of the well, to be the people of India, I found it easy to think of bland or mild as representing their declared policy of non-violence and neutrality."

Amid the epigrammatic sentences

A Chinese fortune-teller sorts yarrow stalks to be cast for an I Ching augury. He uses fifty stalks, one of them a spare that does not figure in the reading. The highly complex yarrow method is preferred by traditional I Ching oracles.

of the commentaries, Blofeld found other thoughts that seemed to relate to his question. Of the first hexagram, he read that the well "suffers no increase or decrease" and that those who dipped into it would find their rope too short and see their pitcher broken.

One of the moving lines indicated lack of success, a time to "give up," while the other suggested that there were definite advantages to be gained by giving up before being forced to do so. And the main commentary for the second hexagram, which Blofeld believed represented the Chinese, stated in part, "It is clear that good fortune will accompany the start; but ultimately, affairs will be halted amidst disorder because the way peters out."

Thus Blofeld derived from his reading of the *I Ching* an answer that contradicted the Thai newspaper reports that portrayed an India about to be overrun by an overwhelmingly superior force. Blofeld now told his friends that China would halt its incursion before descending to the plain. Several weeks later, the prophecy was confirmed when China agreed to an end to the hostilities.

n assessing the situation in India, Blofeld had drawn upon a compendium of knowledge that has long been revered. Its origins are mythic, its language laconic, its divinatory symbols deceptively simple. The web of relationships that is created by the pairing of various trigrams and hexagrams is in fact so complicated and abstract that it may defy mortal comprehension. Toward the end of his life, the Chinese philosopher Confucius remarked that if he could live another fifty years, he would spend the time studying the *I Ching*.

Little is known for certain about how the *Book of Changes* came into being, but for some reason it gradually replaced oracle bone divination in ancient China. In this older method, priests inscribed symbols on a polished tortoise shell or the carefully prepared shoulder blade of an ox, then applied heat to the shell or bone until it cracked. The diviners found the answer to the question being asked in the patterns formed by the cracks. Since tortoises were rare and oxen

expensive, only the rich could afford to have such readings performed. Some historians speculate that the *I Ching* gained acceptance and grew in popularity because it was a cheap and accessible alternative.

According to one legend, the *Book of Changes* was written by the Chinese Emperor Fu Hsi, who is said to have lived perhaps 4,500 years ago. Some accounts hold that Fu Hsi divined the symbols from patterns he found in nature, while others claim the trigrams were revealed to him on the back of a sacred tortoise.

Another story has it that a military commander named Wen Weng wrote the explanatory texts, or commentaries, for each trigram and hexagram while serving a prison term in about 1000 BC. Wen later became king, and after his death, his son, the duke of Chou, added commentaries on the individual lines and the meaning of each position within the trigrams and hexagrams.

In later years, other commentaries were added, including several by Confucius. Most scholars seem to agree that the *I Ching* was first widely used—by priests, as an aid to divining the future—between 1000 and 500 BC, during the Bronze Age in China. But the practice did not acquire its philosophical overtones until the third century AD, when a Chinese sage named Wang Pi declared that the *I Ching* should be used not merely for fortune-telling but also for seeking wisdom and spiritual harmony.

The West knew virtually nothing about the *Book of Changes* until the British scholar James Legge translated it into English in 1882. Unfortunately, Western knowledge of the ancient Chinese languages was limited at the time, and the translation suffered accordingly. In the early 1920s a

The mythical first emperor of China, Fu Hsi, draws inspiration from a tortoise in this thirteenth-century Chinese painting on silk. Legend says the emperor derived the eight basic trigrams of the I Ching (lower left in the painting) from studying lines on the tortoise's shell.

German scholar and missionary named Richard Wilhelm, who lived for many years in Beijing, translated the *I Ching* into German. Wilhelm's translation received a great deal of attention, partly because of the introduction written by the noted Swiss psychologist Carl Jung, who had been experimenting with the *I Ching*. Although numerous translations have since followed, Wilhelm's version is still considered to be one of the best.

Consulting the *Book of Changes* in the old way required complete attention and a lengthy ritual. An inquirer would not have asked the question personally, as Blofeld did, but would have sought out an experienced diviner. According to the earliest accounts of the method, dating to a few centuries before Christ, practitioners would first light incense, then retrieve the revered book from its storage place—which was supposed to be at least shoulder-height above the floor.

Removing the book from its protective wrapping—silk was the preferred material—the diviner would place it on a table and sit to the south of it. In a container within reach would be fifty dried stalks of the milfoil plant, which is more commonly known as yarrow. Interpretation could begin only after a painstaking procedure involving sorting and re-sorting the stalks in order to arrive at numbers denoting the nature of each line of the hexagram. Since the sixth century or so, however, flipping coins has been considered to be an acceptable alternative to sorting yarrow sticks. Each toss of three coins yields a number designating the type of line that goes into the hexagram next.

There are two basic kinds of lines in the *I Ching* system of divination—Yin lines, consisting of two dashes, and solid Yang lines—representing the two fundamental, eternally contesting forces of the universe. According to the precepts of a philosophy that arose not long after the dawn of Chinese civilization (and that infuses such successors as Taoism and Confucianism), everything in existence is thought to be a combination of Yin—the negative, female, weak component of the universe—and Yang, the positive, male, strong force.

All such combinations, hence all things in creation, are in a state of endless change, with first one and then the other influence dominating. The purpose of the *I Ching* ceremony is to identify the Yin and Yang influences at play in the individual or situation being asked about. The objective of the commentaries is to show the way toward harmony with the great, rhythmic tides of cyclical change that underlie the universe as well as everything that happens in it. The *I Ching* does not make flat predictions; it suggests possibilities. Then it speculates cryptically on how a "superior

Tortoise breastplates preceded yarrow stalks in I Ching divination. Cracks in this Shang dynasty shell were read by the oracle Bin, who inscribed on it his name and that of the inquirer, one Chu Hua, along with the date and the question. Chu Hua sought guidance on whether to harm an enemy, X.

A World of Yin and Yang

In the West, fortune-telling has generally implied no volition and therefore no morality. A certain immutable fate is foretold, and there is no question of the choices that one might make in order to fulfill its promise or minimize its pitfalls.

But divination with the *I Ching,* or *Book of Changes,* is different. To the question, What will befall me? it adds, What am I to do about it? Response is possible, so moral choices are to be made. Thus divination takes on moral weight; fortune-telling becomes philosophy.

Arguably, a difference between Eastern and Western mainstream thought explains the extra dimension of the *I Ching.* To some degree, the occidental mind has tended to see creation as a finished act, fixed and static. Past, present, and future cannot be changed. What is, is. What will be, will be.

But at the core of traditional Chinese philosophy is the notion of a universe in flux, a continuing, eternal creative act. What is, is becoming. What may be, may be. The future is not fact but potential, and anyone who seeks to know the future is obliged also to seek the proper way to shape it.

The symbol of this central thought of shifting potentials is depicted at right on an antique Chinese door plaque once used to ward off devils. At the center of a circle bearing the *I Ching*'s eight basic trigrams is the dual embryo of the Yin Yang—dark and light, female and male, earth and heaven, corporeal and spiritual—apparent opposites that are in fact complementary, different phases of an essential unity.

Each is necessary to the other, and as the circles inside each embryo indicate, each bears within it the seed of the other. Contending, yet in harmony, the two parts forever flow into one another in stately cosmic rhythm.

As a moral system, the *I Ching* teaches how to align oneself with the rhythm. It elucidates fate as continually changing tendencies and possibilities that mandate moral attitudes and actions if they are to be realized to one's benefit.

YANG

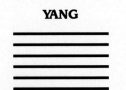

Western prophecies are often straightforward; the prophecies of the *I Ching*, in contrast, are always oblique. They are couched in symbols that, in turn, are wrapped in parables. It is the task of the questioner to adapt the parables to the circumstances of his or her own life.

The bases of *I Ching* divination are sixty-four vertical, six-line columns called hexagrams. The Yin-Yang principle that underlies the system is expressed by the two kinds of lines composing the hexagrams—the solid Yang line and the broken Yin. The Yang denotes heaven, light, primal force, maleness, energy, aggression, strength, spirit.

Hexagrams are read from bottom to top. All have numbers and names. The first, which is made up of six Yang lines *(above)*, is called *Ch'ien*, the Creative. According to the *I Ching* as translated by Richard Wilhelm and Cary F. Baynes, the presence of Ch'ien in a reading yields the following message: "Hidden dragon. Do not act. / Dragon appearing in the field. It furthers one to see the great man. / All day long the superior man is creatively active. At nightfall his mind is still beset with cares. Danger. No blame. / Wavering flight over the depths. No blame. / Flying dragon in the heavens. It furthers one to see the great man. / Arrogant dragon will have cause to repent."

In Chinese lore, the dragon is the traditional symbol of dynamic force. Thus the hexagram's first line is said to mean a great man who, although he is as yet unrecognized by the world at large, stays true to himself. Unswayed by worldly success or failure, he awaits his time. In the second line, he enters his destined field and begins to distinguish himself. His great influence means that it is advantageous to see him. The third line shows the man in the process of gaining more fame and authority. His energies are equal to his station, but in his rise there is the ever-present danger that ambition will outstrip integrity. He must be very cautious if he is to remain without blame.

In the fourth line of the hexagram, the questioner reaches a transition point where he must make a choice between a great role in the world, or withdrawal and solitude for the purpose of self-development. The man attains worldwide influence, as well as the sphere of heaven itself, in the fifth line. Simply to see him is to be blessed. But in the sixth and final line, exalted heights have removed the man from his fellows. He learns that great ambition can presage failure.

The oracular judgment that is given to someone who receives this hexagram is, "The Creative works sublime success, / Furthering through perseverance." It means that the inquirer will be the recipient of success from the very depths of the universe, provided he perseveres in doing what is right.

YIN

True to the notion of eternal flux, the six Yang lines of Ch'ien are changing even as they appear. The hexagram is metamorphosing into its complementary opposite, *K'un*, the Receptive.

K'un, the second hexagram of the *I Ching*, is made up of six Yin lines *(above)*. Yin represents the universe's primal feminine power—dark, yielding, passive—the Receptive that completes the Creative. The two are equally important, but the Receptive is a power for good only as long as it accepts its subordinate place in the cosmic hierarchy. Yang is heavenly and spiritual, Yin earthy and sensual. Each one requires the other, but only one can be primary.

K'un's oracular message is: "When the hoarfrost is underfoot, solid ice is not far off. / Straight, square, great. Without purpose, yet nothing remains unfurthered. / Hidden lines. One is able to remain persevering. If by chance you are in the service of a king, seek not works, but bring to completion. / A tied-up sack. No blame, no praise. / A yellow lower garment brings supreme good fortune. / Dragons fight in the meadow. Their blood is black and yellow."

The first line evokes the inevitability of death, but it also reminds that proper precautions can impede decay. A mathematical metaphor for earth (the square) and the creative principle (the straight) emerges in the second line. It denotes the unerring logic of creation, whose greatness lies in its capacity to tolerate all creatures equally. Humans should follow the example that nature sets.

The third line advises that the wise man should eschew fame and conceal his talents while they mature. The fourth counsels restraint and solitude, lest one invite harm from strong enemies. In the fifth line, yellow symbolizes the earth and genuine, trustworthy things, while the lower garment stands for noble reserve. The message here is that true refinement relies on discretion and restraint. The black and yellow blood in the last line reveals unnatural contention between heaven and earth, which is damaging to both parties.

K'un's advice is that one's task is not to lead but to achieve as a subordinate. Accept guidance and attune oneself to one's fate, using as a guide the balance and symmetry of nature.

Critics of the *I Ching* make the argument that it is possible to read practically any meaning into its cryptic hexagrams. Proponents, however, say that this inherent ambiguity is also its strength.

man" might affect circumstances in his favor by wise and ethical conduct.

But a modern-age believer need not refer only to the ancient, mystical concepts of Yin and Yang for explanations of the *I Ching's* workings. Psychologist Carl Jung, who wrote so enthusiastically of the *I Ching* in his introduction to Wilhelm's classic translation, provided a theory that underpins the time-honored Chinese system in another way.

During the 1920s and 1930s, Jung developed his theory of the collective unconscious, a universal psyche that he believed to be a repository for certain images—or archetypes, as he referred to them—that are common to all human thought. He believed that these primordial images have the power to affect human circumstances according to a principle he called synchronicity—the coincidence of events that are similar but have no apparent cause-and-effect relationship.

Jung cited as an example the time one of his patients, a young woman, described a dream she had had about a golden scarab, a beetle that is also an important symbol in ancient Egyptian mythology. She had not finished talking when a beetle almost identical to the scarab flew in the window. The event had a powerful effect on her therapy and was ascribed by Jung to synchronicity.

Similarly, Jung regarded the *I Ching* hexagrams and the elemental concepts they represent, such as birth, death, fire, and water, to be closely related to the universal images of the collective unconscious. The relationship between the hexagrams and real events, like the relationship between the dream scarab and the real one, was governed by synchronicity. To put his ideas to the test, Jung experimented with the *Book of Changes*—"sitting for hours on the ground, the *I Ching* beside me," he wrote, asking questions and frequently receiving "undeniably remarkable, meaningful connections."

As in the case with numerology, modern consultation of the *I Ching*, while widespread, tends toward the frivolous. Requests for advice about career paths and love relationships are far more frequent than are such larger questions

as those addressed by Blofeld and Jung. Detractors say the answers are hopelessly obscure and generalized, couched in flowery language with little objective meaning. And the critics point to direct contradictions among the various translations from the ancient Chinese. But as is so often evident when it comes to the occult, none of this criticism deters those who believe. Princeton University Press reports that its version of the *Book of Changes* (the Wilhelm translation) is its all-time best seller.

Among many believers in the power of symbols to provide guides to the future, the *I Ching* is rivaled by another popular system, the Tarot. It is perhaps not so ancient as the *I Ching,* but it is almost as complex.

In using the Tarot, a would-be diviner consults a deck of seventy-eight elaborately illustrated cards of enduring popularity and tantalizing mystery. Unlike practitioners of numerology and the *I Ching,* Tarot readers do not rely on numbers or images that have been selected for the situation; instead, meaning is derived from the particular arrangement of the cards.

Interpreting the cards is no simple matter. Those

wishing to learn the art are advised to spend long periods meditating on the individual cards of the deck and on their multiplicity of interrelationships. According to one authority on the subject, such study helps to build a bridge of intuition between the reader's unconscious mind and the symbolism found in the cards.

A good deal of ritual is involved as well. When not using their Tarot decks, dedicated diviners keep them wrapped in a square of purple or black silk and placed in a covered wooden box. For optimal results, the box should be out of sight and facing eastward—which is thought to be the direction of enlightenment. Moreover, the deck should never be handled by the idly curious or the mocking, for it is said the Tarot responds to such people with unpleasant, if not dire, predictions.

In current practice—little changed from older ways—the reader usually begins by having the inquirer select a card from the deck's so-called Major Arcana—made up of twenty-two cards bearing strange and ominous images such as a magician gesturing oddly with his arm or a skeleton wielding a scythe. The card selected, called the significator, influences the entire reading.

Next the inquirer shuffles the remaining cards—often, but not always, including the fifty-six cards that make up the part of the deck known as the Minor Arcana—and cuts them. After retrieving the deck, the reader lays out a specific number of cards in a traditional pattern for study.

One common layout, called the Celtic cross, has the top card from the deck placed atop the significator, the next card laid lengthwise across the first, and then four more cards placed above, below, and to the right and left of the first group. Together, these cards define the inquirer's situation and the forces acting upon him or her. Four more cards are then turned over and placed in a column to the right of the central group of cards. These final four contain the divinatory message, which the reader delivers after careful consideration of the supposed significance of each card *(pages 146-149)*.

Stories abound about those whose fates have been foretold by the mysterious cards. One such tale concerns Henry Cuffe, the sixteenth-century author, scholar, and secretary to England's Robert Devereux, second earl of Essex. According to some accounts, when he wanted to learn about his future, he consulted a reader of the Tarot, and when told that the cards predicted he would suffer an unnatural death, he demanded details. The reader responded by telling him to draw three cards from the Tarot deck and to place them on the table, face down. Then if Cuffe still wanted more information, all he had to do was turn the cards over, one after another.

The first card depicted a man in the custody of guards. The second portrayed a scene of judgment in a tribunal. The third bore the images of a gallows and hangman. Cuffe apparently found the last card amusing, for he reportedly laughed out loud. Whether he saw a joke or an irony, no one knows. But on March 13, 1601, Cuffe was found guilty of helping the earl of Essex plot against Queen Elizabeth I. Later that same day, he was taken to the gallows and hanged.

Like so many tales of the mysterious and occult, the account of Cuffe's consultation with a Tarot reader may well be apocryphal. As a matter of fact, the cards may not have been used for divination until a considerable time after Cuffe was put to death. Nevertheless, such stories about the eerie accuracy of the predictions of the Tarot cards, particularly in connection with unusual death, have circulated for centuries.

No one knows for certain the beginnings of the Tarot, or for that matter those of standard playing cards—which are also used in cartomancy, or divining the future with cards. Playing cards are believed to have originated in China or Korea sometime in the tenth or eleventh century AD, perhaps evolving from the first paper money, whose designs seem to be similar to those on some of the cards. Within a few hundred years, they made their way to Europe. A German monk writing in a Swiss monastery in 1377 referred to a new game that "came to us this year"—the first known reference to playing cards in the West.

The eminent psychologist Carl Jung lent legitimacy to both the Tarot and the I Ching. He believed both systems activated images existing in all unconscious minds. He also thought the two systems of divination could help elucidate certain coincidences in life that seem to defy the ordinary course of cause and effect.

Tarot cards do not appear in recorded history until the mid-fifteenth century, when a hand-painted Tarot pack was presented to the young duke of Milan. Although no mention was made of where the cards came from, it is clear that they were not considered new at the time. This observation has caused some to speculate that Italy is the true home of the Tarot, a conclusion strengthened by the fact that two medieval Italian card decks—*tarrochi* and *minchiate*—are strikingly similar to the Tarot, in their numbered cards as well as in their trumps.

In recent times, various researchers have attempted to trace the Tarot etymologically, examining various languages for word clues. Some have claimed that the Tarot comes from the ancient Hindustani *taru,* for "pack of cards," while others have said it comes from *tarotee,* a French word supposedly referring to a design on the back of the cards. It has also been proposed that the Tarot got its name from the first place where it is known to have appeared—the northern Italian region near the Taro River. As for the original purpose of the cards, there is evidence that they may have descended from a perfectly mundane medieval instructional card game that used elaborate picture cards for memory training. No one knows, however, and those with an interest in the occult are attracted to some much more exotic possibilities.

Some have proposed that the Tarot originated with the Gnostics, a heretical Christian sect that flourished in the second century and virtually died out in the third century, but whose ideas survived long afterward. The Gnostics—who took their name from the Greek word *gnosis,* for "knowledge"—believed that material things were the creation of the devil and that the human soul, or Godhead, was imprisoned in the body and could be liberated only through a process of enlightenment. Taken in sequence, the cards of the Tarot's Major Arcana have been interpreted as a representation of the major principles of Gnosticism, beginning with the Fool card as a symbol of human ignorance of the divine power within, and ending with spiritual ascension into the heavens of the World card.

*This World trump was part of a
Tarot owned by the Visconti-Sforza family,
Renaissance rulers of Milan.*

Whatever their origins, Tarot cards incorporate images that have resonated down through the ages. Christian, Islamic, Norse, and Celtic ideas can be found in them. The Judgment card, for example, suggests the biblical Apocalypse, while the Tower Struck by Lightning card can be seen as reminiscent of the hammer of Thor, the Norse god of thunder. Indeed, such are the universality of the symbols that practitioners always seem able to find in them whatever they want to see.

The Tarot remained relatively popular throughout the Renaissance. And then, in the eighteenth century, scholars became fascinated with the putative wisdom of the ancient Egyptians. The hieroglyphs had yet to be deciphered, and speculation about their meaning was unrestrained. It was perhaps inevitable that someone would propose links between the Tarot and Egypt, thus spurring new interest in the colorful cards.

In 1781 Antoine Court de Gébelin, French author and theologian, took note of the odd-looking deck of cards some friends were playing with. Examining the exotic cards of the Tarot with increasing fascination, he immediately declared them to be of Egyptian origin. The four suits of the Minor Arcana, de Gébelin said, represented the four classes of Egyptian society. The name for the deck he believed to be a combination of two Egyptian words: *Tar,* or "roadway," and *Ro,* or "king"—hence, the "Royal Road." Considering the prevailing ideas of the time, the theory seemed to be perfectly plausible.

Not long after de Gébelin published his work, a Parisian by the name of Alliette, a wigmaker turned fortuneteller, enlarged upon the Egyptian connection. Using the pseudonym Etteilla—his own name spelled backwards—Alliette claimed that the Major Arcana was the work of seventeen magi in service to Hermes Trismegistus, or Thoth, the Egyptian god of wisdom and magic. Thoth had wished that all his secret knowledge be written down on leaves of gold.

The magi encoded the knowledge into pictures and then assembled them into a complete book whose original name, Alliette claimed, was the *Book of Thoth.* Although Al-

liette's method of Tarot reading spread rapidly and was widely accepted, later occultists would ridicule the French fortune-teller for the fanciful notions he espoused concerning the origins of the cards.

thers, however, updated the Egyptian theme, theorizing that the cards originated in Egypt during the Crusades, when Christian armies made their way eastward from Europe, laying waste to the countryside and besieging cities in hopes of wresting control of the Holy Land from the infidels. Egyptian priests, determined to preserve their libraries of occult lore, allegedly seized on a desperate stratagem. They translated their secret wisdom into images and symbols, inscribed them on playing cards, and then gave the deck to a passing gambler who, being accomplished in deceit, would doubtlessly elude the enemy. It is believed that the ancient knowledge survived, as a result accessible in future generations to those who were wise enough to decipher the symbols of the Tarot.

By the mid-nineteenth century, interest in the Egyptians had waned somewhat among students of the arcane. But fascination with the Hebrew Cabala was growing, and the remarkably adaptable Tarot cards were soon applied to yet another system of belief.

In 1856, the Frenchman Éliphas Lévi produced a work in which he traced each of the Tarot's four suits to one of the four letters in *YHWH*, the unutterable name for God in the Old Testament. Combining this system with a sprinkling of numerology, he derived additional significance from the fact that there are twenty-two cards in the Tarot's Major Arcana just as there are twenty-two letters in the Hebrew alphabet.

The letter aleph, for example, was the first in the alphabet and also stood for the number one. As Lévi wrote, aleph was associated with being, mind, man, God, and "the unity mother of numbers." He claimed that all of these were symbolized in the card of the Juggler, whose posture resembled aleph's shape. Similarly, he implied that just as the Cabala comprised secret knowledge of the whole world, the Tarot was a synthesis of everything humankind could ever hope to learn.

Despite a complete lack of confirming evidence—no factual connection between the Cabala and the Tarot has ever been established—Éliphas Lévi's interpretation gained adherents among occultists throughout Europe. For almost twenty years after he passed away in 1875, his home city of Paris remained a major center of occult activity, frequented by the likes of poet, magician, and drug user Stanislas de Guaita and his friend Gerard Encausse, who was better known as Papus. The two men were heavily influenced by Lévi, especially Papus, who described the Tarot as "the book of the primitive Revelation of ancient civilizations, the most ancient book in the world" and suggested that it "condenses in a few very simple laws the whole of acquired knowledge."

Lévi's influence spread to England as well. In London in 1888, S. L. MacGregor Mathers founded an occultist society called the Hermetic Order of the Golden Dawn, whose numerous members included the poet W. B. Yeats and author Bram Stoker, who would achieve immortality of a sort with his best-selling Gothic novel, *Dracula.*

The Golden Dawn expanded Lévi's theories into a comprehensive system that studied and taught the Tarot as an integral part of several other occult practices such as ritual magic, alchemy, and numerology. Mathers presided over the society until its members expelled him in 1900 for his autocratic leadership. When he made his exit, he called down curses upon them.

At least one member of the Golden Dawn, a historian of the occult named Arthur Edward Waite, was more of a realist than his colleagues, dismissing most ruminations on the Tarot's mysterious origins as sheer fantasy. "The chief point regarding the history of the Tarot cards," he wrote, "is that such history does not exist." But while dismissing the cards' use in divining as "fortune-telling rubbish," he did believe that they might well be the carriers of some ancient lore. He wrote a book connecting the four symbols of the Holy Grail legend—cup, lance, dish, and sword—to the Ta-

rot's four suits. He also designed one of the more famous Tarot packs *(pages 142-143)*.

By far the most controversial member of the Hermetic Order of the Golden Dawn was the irrepressible Aleister Crowley, a practitioner of demonology as well as various kinds of ritual magic. An imposing figure who was frequently photographed wearing exotic headdresses, Crowley was once dubbed by the English press "the wickedest man in the world." He relished the title. Among his many other curious beliefs, Crowley was convinced that he was the reincarnation of Éliphas Lévi.

Crowley was born in England in 1875 to an extremely religious and strict family. As a child he rebelled against his parents' Christianity, eagerly accepting his distraught mother's accusation that he was the Great Beast, or 666, the Antichrist foretold in the book of Revelation. Aleister Crowley declared a personal war against Christianity, and he insisted that such had been his true mission throughout several reincarnations.

In his early twenties, he claimed to have experienced the presence of a terrifying mystical power, and thereafter he devoted himself to the study of the occult. He traveled throughout the world seducing both men and women, occasionally persuading his lovers to play the role of his favorite character—the biblical Scarlet Woman, the so-called Mother of Harlots.

In 1944, three years before his death, Crowley published a guide to his mystical theories of the Tarot in a small limited edition of a work called *The Book of Thoth.* In it, he emphasized the erotic imagery of the Major Arcana—not an entirely new interpretation, though no one before him had been quite so explicit. Other occultists had regarded the sword and scales held by the woman in the Justice card as male sex symbols, but Crowley, always alert to erotic possibilities, renamed the card "Woman Satisfied."

Those who reject the Tarot and the other forms of symbolic divination often point to such extravagances as Crowley's and rest their case. And indeed many of the devotees of numerology, the *I Ching,* and the like offer tempting targets for ridicule. Even some of the more serious-minded practitioners find themselves on the defensive in light of certain recent research.

For example, in a group experiment conducted jointly in North Carolina and England in 1983, volunteers participated in separate Tarot readings without being informed about the detailed character analyses derived through the cards. Later, the subjects were asked to pick their own analysis from among those of the entire group. Most volunteers were unable to determine which of the readings pertained to them.

Other tests have indicated that a reading or consultation is almost totally unimpressive unless there is direct, face-to-face contact between inquirer and diviner. This is usually taken as evidence that the subject is affected not by the efficacy of the symbols or the method being used but by the dramatic talents of the diviner.

Sympathizers dismiss such criticism. It misses the point, they say, that the subconscious link between inquirer and diviner is essential to enlightenment. In this view, the method—shuffling cards, sorting sticks, adding numbers, drawing hexagrams, and the like—should be regarded as an aid to meditation and communion, not as a simplistic key to ready answers. A related viewpoint holds that the Tarot, for example, is every bit as legitimate as the widely accepted Rorschach test, in which subjects are asked to comment on what they see in various inkblots. The Tarot, and perhaps the *I Ching* as well, can be said to substitute symbolic images for amorphous blots, freeing the subject's mind to make those associations and connections that are most meaningful.

But in the end, such debate seems to have little effect on these remarkably tenacious systems of divination. Neither social disapproval nor religious condemnation has been able to deter their adherents in the past and seems unlikely to do so in the future. To those who believe, these systems offer a glimpse of cosmic order, a point of contact with the deepest workings of the universe. Why should they give up such a gift?

The Magic of the Tarot

With the complex, controversial, and abstruse Tarot, certainties are elusive. Nevertheless, it is generally agreed among believers that the cards have a dual significance: They are at once mystical and divinatory.

Their supposed occult nature rests primarily with the twenty-two cards of the Major Arcana, or Trumps Major. These are regarded widely as allegories for the soul's journey from ignorance to enlightenment, or the human sojourn through life, or as mystical keys to the secrets of the universe and the place of humans therein. For thousands who believe in its power, the Tarot also evaluates the past, elucidates the present, and predicts the future. Both the Major Arcana and the fifty-six-card Minor Arcana—which is divided into suits of Wands, Cups, Swords, and Pentacles—are used in divinatory readings. Some say the cards tap the psychic awareness of the reader, the inquirer, or both. Others contend the cards carry their own meanings, intrinsic and absolute.

But what meanings? Hundreds of different Tarots are used today, and interpretations of cards may vary from deck to deck and from reader to reader. Each reader—and each inquirer, for that matter—brings his or her own imprint to the cards. Moreover, perceived meanings can be altered by the cards' positions relative to each other and by whether a card falls upright or inverted. On the following fifteen pages are the seventy-eight cards of the Major and Minor Arcana, drawn from representative decks, along with some of the cards' purported mystical and prophetic meanings.

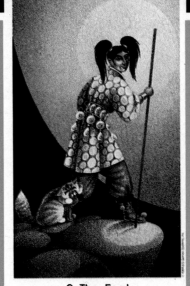

0 The Fool

THE FOOL

0   THE FOOL

The Fool

O·IL MATTO·THE FOOL·

THE FOOL.

THE FOOL

Depicted here in seven different decks, the Fool, number zero in the Major Arcana, is the sojourner setting out toward truth. Innocent, ignorant, and with no fixed number, he can wander among the other cards, exploring *their secrets. He is nothing, with the potential for all. As for his divinatory meanings, upright, the Fool denotes immaturity and hasty or ill-considered judgment. Inverted, he signifies wrong choices, hesitation, apathy, negligence.*

The Renaissance Tarot

Serious Tarot students see the Major Arcana as the soul's map in its quest for self-awareness and integration into the cosmic whole. The cards are tools, they say, and diligent meditation on them can unlock mystic truths.

Modern occultists of a psychological bent lend their own twist to the process. They divide the Major Arcana's twenty-one numbered cards into three groups, symbolizing the conscious, subconscious, and superconscious minds. The first seven cards—consciousness—describe life's out-ward aspects, its social and material reality, the physical matrix of life. The next seven are inner-directed toward contemplation and self-knowledge, and the last—superconsciousness—are keys to spiritual enlightenment.

Cards I through VII, as they are shown on these two pages, are from the so-called Renaissance deck, Pre-Raphaelite renderings by American artist and printmaker Brian Williams, who worked on the deck for nine years before completing it in 1987.

I. The Magician. He is called by many names—the Juggler, the Magus, the Mountebank—and his mercurial nature lies between instinct and intellect, the sublime and the mundane. He is a master manipulator, a con man and trickster, but perhaps also a miracle maker and sage. In divination he denotes skill, craft, cunning, eloquence, the mastery of arcane science. Inverted, he signifies fraud and chicanery, demagoguery, sophistry, lies, corrupt technology, cheap tricks.

II. The Priestess. She is the keeper of mysteries, the mistress of hidden knowledge. Her wisdom is feminine, creative, intuitive, spiritual, and nonrational. In divination she stands for female influences, passive power, the cyclical balance of nature, magic, and the arts of natural healing. She may predict change, a secret revealed, or a problem illuminated. Inverted, she is a warning against irrationality and implies obfuscation.

III. The Empress. The Empress is Mother Goddess and Mother Earth—fertile, bountiful, and nurturing. She embodies worldly sovereignty and pleasure, as well as female power, love, beauty, luxury, stability, well-being; she is also a civilizing influence and a symbol for domesticity, child rearing, growth, creativity, and prosperity. Inverted, she indicates cloying domesticity, family discord, dominating matriarchy, bourgeois small-mindedness, dissipation, jealousy, insecurity, problems with sexual matters or with career.

IV. The Emperor. A male symbol and patriarchal figure, he is consort of the Empress. The Emperor is temporal power, professional or political success, social status, rationality, strong will, energy, and decisiveness. At the negative extreme, he may also mean war and conquest. Usually propitious for a male inquirer, he bodes ambitions realized through force of personality. However, his presence in a woman's reading indicates a dominating male. Inverted, the Emperor means despotism, pomposity, and self-indulgence, or he may warn against weakness.

V. The Hierophant. Often called the Pope or High Priest, the Hierophant rules a spiritual kingdom. He is the male counterpart of the Priestess, and his realm is rational knowledge, creative intellect, inspiration, insight, established order, religious tradition, occult knowledge. He forecasts the acquisition of profound understanding and may stand for an important teacher or adviser. The card inverted means dogma, rigidity, and effete philosophizing, and it cautions against lies and bad advice.

VI. The Lovers. The obvious symbolism has to do with love, passion, the tension between flesh and spirit, and in addition, the responsibility for making choices. On a more mystical level, the Lovers denote inspiration, impulse, psychic gifts, and creativity. They illustrate duality unified, the male and female completing each other. In divination, the Lovers suggest courtship or a sound relationship or marriage. Inverted, they represent bad romantic choices, sexual difficulties, infidelity, ill-fated or unrequited love.

VII. The Chariot. The image of two horses drawing a chariot suggests a male-female metaphor, feminine pacifism subduing masculine bellicosity, or female seductiveness sapping male energy. The Chariot also signifies movement, travel, achieving a goal, reaching an important milestone in worldly attainment. It indicates triumph, good health, and success, although they may prove impermanent. Inverted, the card suggests ruthlessness, bullying, and defeat.

V·IL PAPA·THE HIEROPHANT·☊

VI·GLI AMANTI·THE LOVERS·♑

VIII·IL CARRO·THE CHARIOT·♋

Tarot of the Witches

As the Fool continues his metaphysical journey, he meets seven cards from the Tarot of the Witches, a contemporary deck designed by the Scottish surrealist Fergus Hall.

Tarot encyclopedist Stuart R. Kaplan suggests the Tarot has special significance for witches, who supposedly use it often for prophecy. Kaplan has written that the Tarot's Priestess symbolically presides over and completes the thirteen-member witches' coven, whose other members correspond to certain cards in Tarot suits. Situated inside witchcraft's occult magic circle, emblematic of the universe, the Priestess protects the coven and rules it with benevolence and wisdom. Kaplan also contends the four cardinal points of the circle correspond to the Tarot's suits: North is represented by Swords, south by Wands, east by Cups, and west by Pentacles. The circle's center, where lines from the cardinal points intersect, is said to be a sacred point of immense power and to symbolize the Major Arcana as a whole.

VIII — JUSTICE

VIIII — THE HERMIT

VIII. Justice. According to the Witches deck, this benevolent card follows the implication of its name, denoting equity, fairness, reasonableness, harmony, and balance. It carries additional meanings of honor, integrity, sincerity, virtue and virginity, good intentions, and well-meant acts. It may promise deserved rewards. In divination, the Tarot of the Witches makes no distinction as to whether a card appears upright or inverted in a reading.

VIIII. The Hermit. The reclusive cowled figure suggests withdrawal and solitude, an abandonment of the world and its pleasures. He denotes judiciousness, prudence, and circumspection, but he may also symbolize a person who is expressionless, insensitive, reluctant to face facts, wary of expending emotion, protective of privacy to the point of fear. The Hermit is a loner, misguided himself and with a tendency to misguide others. More esoteric Tarots are kinder to the Hermit, contending he is a seeker after divine wisdom

and truth. He has secluded himself not as a misanthrope but as pilgrim on an interior voyage toward enlightenment.

X. Wheel of Fortune. The Wheel may bode well or ill, depending on the cards that accompany it in a reading. Its possible meanings include good fortune, happiness, something opportune or heavensent, the answer to a question or the solution to a problem. It also carries neutral connotations of destiny, fate, inevitability, approaching change, a culmination, or an ending. If its neighboring cards are not propitious, the Wheel may mean an unhealthy intoxication with success or worldly honors and rewards.

XI. Strength. As its muscular avatar suggests, Strength signifies physical power, courage, fortitude, liberation, achievement gained at considerable risk. It may also imply determination, strength of will and resolution of mind, as well as strong convictions, confidence, energy, an orientation toward action, a capacity for attain-

ment and accomplishment. The card's more belligerent aspects are defiance, strife, contention, and conquest.

XII. Hanged Man. Martyrdom, sacrifice, suffering, and punishment are all suggested by this mysterious card. It may also signify surrender, abandonment, renunciation, stifled progress, or action or thought held suspended. On the other hand, regeneration is suggested, along with transition with the influx of new life. The Hanged Man is suspended not from a gallows but from a living tree, suggesting spring's rebirth. Students who use the Tarot as an esoteric spiritual guide rather than for fortune-telling attribute great mystical significance to the Hanged Man. For them, the card has far more to do with resurrection than with death, and it is a profound expression of the relationship between the divine world and the material one.

XIII. Death. This card need not be altogether as ominous as its name and number and its grisly image would imply. It

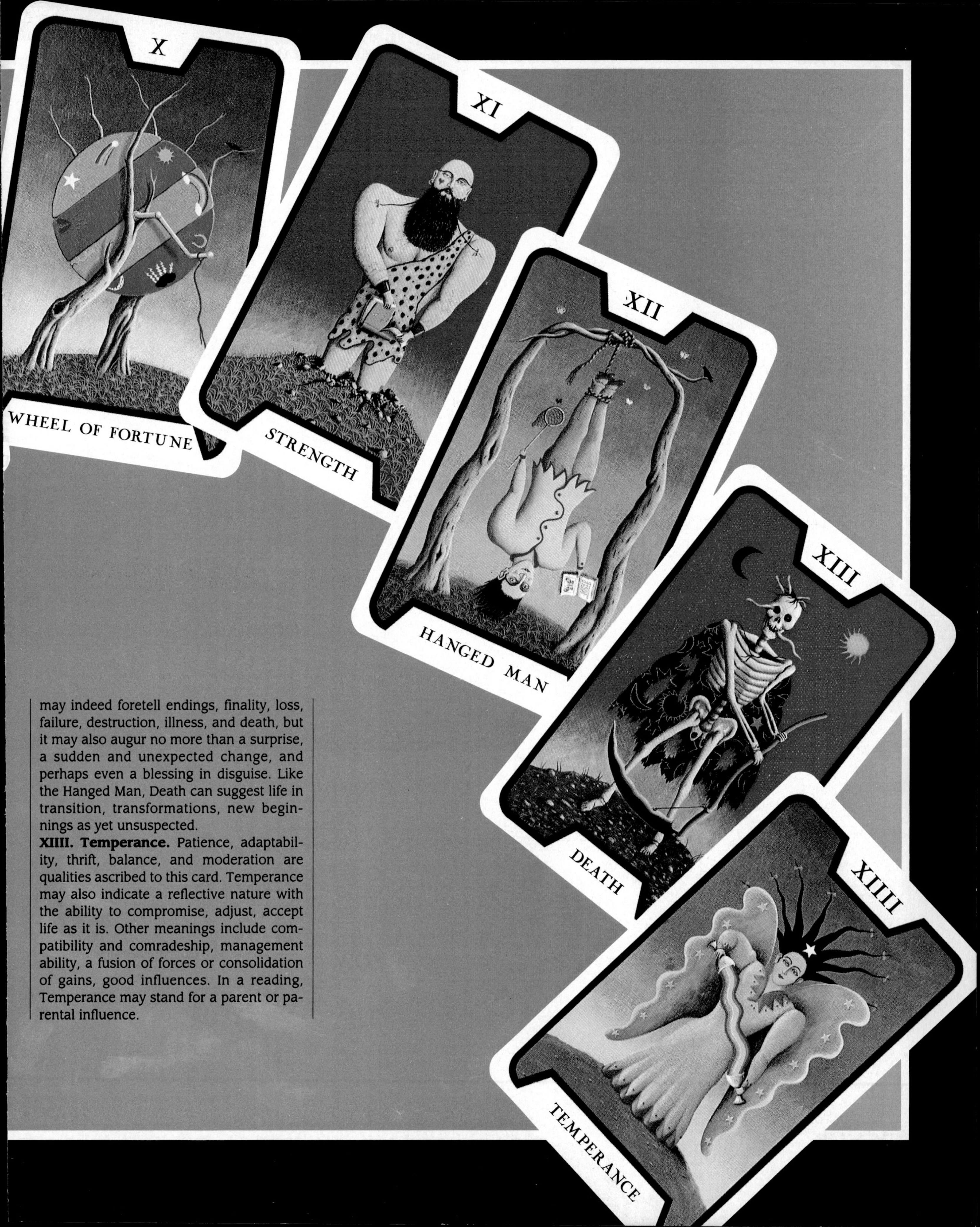

X

WHEEL OF FORTUNE

XI

STRENGTH

XII

HANGED MAN

XIII

DEATH

XIIII

TEMPERANCE

may indeed foretell endings, finality, loss, failure, destruction, illness, and death, but it may also augur no more than a surprise, a sudden and unexpected change, and perhaps even a blessing in disguise. Like the Hanged Man, Death can suggest life in transition, transformations, new beginnings as yet unsuspected.

XIIII. Temperance. Patience, adaptability, thrift, balance, and moderation are qualities ascribed to this card. Temperance may also indicate a reflective nature with the ability to compromise, adjust, accept life as it is. Other meanings include compatibility and comradeship, management ability, a fusion of forces or consolidation of gains, good influences. In a reading, Temperance may stand for a parent or parental influence.

XV. The Devil. Satan represents the chains of materiality, holding men and women in thrall after their fall from spiritual grace. Allegorically, the man and woman are Adam and Eve, and their chains are a commentary on the fatality of a purely material existence. In divination, the Devil signifies material power and the temptations of the flesh, obsession, violence, fate, prodigious effort, and weakness and pettiness. The Golden Dawn Tarot makes no provision for different meanings if cards fall reversed, but it does caution that the relationships between the cards can alter their meanings.

XVI. The Tower. The Tower struck by lightning depicts ruin in its several forms, stemming from the materialization of the spiritual world. It may also symbolize the destruction of the human mind, which pridefully seeks to penetrate sacred mysteries, as well as the futility of all knowledge apart from God. The Tower denotes strife, war, destruction, danger, adversity,

The Golden Dawn Tarot

Although it existed only fifteen years, the Hermetic Order of the Golden Dawn left an indelible stamp on Western occultism. Its initiates melded the Tarot and astrology with the mysteries of the Jewish Cabala to create an occult construct of staggering complexity.

The first Golden Dawn Tarot supposedly appeared by magic to the Order's leader, MacGregor Mathers. In fact, the cards were probably designed by Mathers himself and painted by his wife, Moina MacGregor Mathers. They were only for initiates, however, and a Golden Dawn deck for the public did not exist until 1978, when occult scholar Robert Wang, using old notebooks of the order's members, collaborated with colleague Israel Regardie to recreate the deck represented here.

"As Above, So Below" was a Golden Dawn motto. It meant that man was a microcosm of the universe, and in understanding himself he could understand all things. For Golden Dawn members, divination was only incidental to the Tarot's true purpose: instructing initiates in the most profound secrets of the cosmos.

misery, poverty, disgrace, deception, unforeseen disaster. It may also foretell despotism and imprisonment. In its only positive aspect, it indicates courage.

XVII. The Star. The Star is immortal beauty and truth unveiled, pouring blessings on the soul. The card also carries the mystic meaning of universal understanding devolving on those who are ready to receive it. It promises immortality and enlightenment. The Star augurs hope, faith, and rosy prospects. If ill-favored by other cards, however, it can also mean hope deceived, arrogance, and loss of power, and it may indicate a person who is excessively disposed to dreaminess.

XVIII. The Moon. The Moon symbolizes the life of the imagination venturing into the unknown. It also stands for reflected light from a dazzling prime source that remains as yet unrevealed—an analogy, perhaps, to the light of the intellect reflecting dimly a more absolute spiritual truth. The Moon illuminates humanity's animal na-

ture. It portends dissatisfaction, error, lies, deception, slander, terror, danger, darkness, hidden enemies, and occult forces at work, as well as silence, instability, and inconstancy.

XIX. The Sun. The Sun is emblematic of passage from the light of this world to the light of the next. Some of the card's symbolism also deals with enlightenment through self-knowledge, which leads to humanity's rescue from its animal nature and a union with transcendental consciousness. The Sun's divinatory meanings include wealth, gain, glory, material contentment, a good marriage. If a number of ill-favored cards surround the Sun in a reading, it takes on the negative aspects of vanity, ostentation, and arrogance.

XX. Judgment. The card is sometimes called the Last Judgment, and to a certain extent it does represent the usual Christian notion of that event. But it also has mystic significance involving the transformation of the soul in response to a summons from

its higher self. In addition, it implies resurrection and eternal life. In divination, Judgment denotes final decisions, judgments, and sentences, the ultimate settlement of a matter with no further appeal possible. It may foretell the loss of a lawsuit or some kind of change or renewal in the inquirer's life.

XXI. The Universe. Called the World in several other Tarot decks, this card is usually propitious when it occurs in a reading, ensuring success and just payment. It may also suggest travel, the material world, a kingdom. If it is badly positioned in a reading, however, it can mean stagnation and inertia. It often stands for the inquirer or for the subject of his or her question. In esoteric terms, the card signifies the rapture and perfection of the universe when, as A. E. Waite put it, "it understands itself in God." It is the end of the soul's metaphysical journey, where self-knowledge brings a new and higher consciousness that unites the one with the all.

Tarof of the Caf People

In general, divination with the Major Arcana is said to reveal one's spiritual condition and potential, while the Minor Arcana cards deal with more mundane realities: occupation, social position, domestic situation. Nevertheless, occultists associate each suit with mystical kinetic forces symbolized by the elements fire, water, air, and earth. The suit of Wands—also known as Rods, Staffs, Batons, or Scepters—is the so-called fire suit. In occult terms, it represents the archetypal world of pure spirit. Wands govern growth, self-development, creativity, ingenuity, energy, ideas, inspiration, passion. They are depicted not as sterile artifacts but as living branches, befitting the suit's generative aspect.

The Wands shown here are from the Tarot of the Cat People, an imaginative modern deck rendered by Karen Kuykendall, a painter, sculptor, and cat lover.

Ace of Wands

Two of Wands

Ace of Wands. A card of female fertility, the Ace denotes creation, genesis, a new undertaking, industry, luck, profit, inheritance, birth. Inverted, it stands for false starts, thwarted goals, dim prospects, frustrated plans, emptiness, and decadence.

Two of Wands. This represents a dominant individual, mature, bold, brave. The card also signifies reaching goals and fulfilling needs. Inverted, it implies trouble, loss of faith, sadness, impediments imposed by others.

Three of Wands

Four of Wands

Five of Wands

Six of Wands

Three of Wands. Practicality, business sense and industriousness, trade negotiations, and commerce are indicated by the Three. Inverted, its meaning changes to lessening troubles, assistance with ulterior plans, wariness of help that is offered.

Four of Wands. The Four represents sociability, harmony, peace, serenity, new wealth, harvest after labor, rest after strife, romance. Inverted, it predicts insecurity, diminished beauty, incomplete happiness and unfulfilled romance, lost tranquility.

Five of Wands. The ill-favored Five means unsatisfied desires, violent struggle, effort, conflict, barriers. Inverted, complexity, contradictions, and trickery are its messages. It gives warning against indecision.

Six of Wands. This card forecasts victory, gain, good tidings, advancement, the achievement of desires, the realization of goals. Inverted, the meaning changes to fear, disloyalty, superficial or meaningless profit.

Seven of Wands

Eight of Wands

Nine of Wands

Ten of Wands

Seven of Wands. The Seven suggests surmounting obstacles on the way to success, victory, and gain. Inverted, it means anxiety, indecision, doubt, confusion, embarrassment, and loss.

Eight of Wands. The Eight describes quickness, progress that may come too fast, and hasty decisions or, if it is inverted, family quarrels, discord, jealousy, stagnation, and aggravation.

Nine of Wands. This card augurs changes, the expectation of problems, awaiting trouble, a hiatus during a struggle, hidden enemies, anticipation, discipline, order. Inverted, it denotes ill health, obstacles, delays, adversity.

Ten of Wands. This is a card of excessive burdens, pressures, or problems, though they may soon be resolved; it also signifies effort to maintain position, the selfish use of power. Inverted, it portends trouble, duplicity, intrigue, deceit, loss.

Page of Wands

Knight of Wands

Queen of Wands

King of Wands

Page of Wands. He stands for a loyal person, trusted friend, or well-intentioned stranger, a consistent person, an envoy bearing important news. Inverted, the card means indecisiveness, reluctance, displeasure. It may warn of a gossip, an emissary with bad news, or a heartbreaker.

Knight of Wands. He augurs departure, possibly into the unknown, flight, change of address, a journey, absence. Inverted, the meaning is strife, interruption, quarrels, surprising change, the rupture of a relationship.

Queen of Wands. She is emblematic of a loving, outgoing person—chaste, poised, practical, charming, and gracious. The inverted meanings are jealousy and duplicity, possible unfaithfulness, fickleness, intransigence, obstacles, opposition.

King of Wands. A paternal, benevolent person, wise, well-educated, mature, honest, and conscientious. Inverted, the card divines a deliberate person prone to dogma, severity, and austerity.

The Mythic Tarot

These cards are adorned with Greek deities and legendary mortals, primal figures symbolizing nature and the human psyche. The device points up the archetypal quality often ascribed to the Tarot. Psychologist Carl Jung, among others, believed the Major Arcana were archetypes, images that are stored in the collective unconscious and that resonate in all subconscious minds.

Designed by Juliet Sharman-Burke and Liz Greene and illustrated by Tricia Newell, the Mythic Tarot was introduced in 1986. Its romanticism is well adapted to the suit of Cups, shown on these two pages. The suit, whose element is water, is emblematic of the creative world. Cups flow with love, dreams, fantasies, and with psychic and intuitive artistic gifts. The Mythic deck's Cups deal mostly with the story of the love god, Eros, and his mortal lover, Psyche. It is a tale of love found, lost to mistrust, and finally regained through courage.

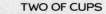

ACE OF CUPS

Ace of Cups. The card's divinatory meaning involves an outrush of raw emotion, a nascent relationship, the start of a journey of love. Unlike many decks, the Mythic Tarot suggests no alternate meanings for inverted cards.

TWO OF CUPS

Two of Cups. Like the Ace, the Two predicts the beginning of a relationship; in addition, it signifies reconciliation after a separation, friendships, contracts between business partners.

THREE OF CUPS

Three of Cups. The Three bodes emotional satisfaction and promise: a celebration of marriage, a new love affair, a child's birth, or a deeper exploration of love.

FOUR OF CUPS

Four of Cups. A disaffected relationship leading to depression, disappointment, boredom, and possible unexpressed resentment is indicated. The effect can be positive only if the negatives prompt one to put aside old fantasies and expectations in favor of a more realistic view of love.

FIVE OF CUPS

Five of Cups. The Five warns of a betrayal with subsequent sorrow and remorse; a possible separation, but without the likelihood of permanent endings; a challenge to commitment in the affairs of the heart.

SIX OF CUPS

Six of Cups. Nostalgia about old loves; the possible return of a former lover; the tempering of past romantic fantasies, leading to serenity and strength; and the possible revival and recapturing of former love are all predicted by the Six.

SEVEN OF CUPS

Seven of Cups. The card implies an emotional situation—possibly a love relationship—with great potential, which will be realized only if correct and realistic choices are made.

EIGHT OF CUPS

Eight of Cups. The Eight involves surrendering an emotional tie in a doomed relationship. It also means depression, mourning, emptiness, an unknown and intractable future.

NINE OF CUPS

Nine of Cups. The Nine promises pleasure, fulfillment, the realization of a treasured wish, the reward of effort, the consummation of commitment.

TEN OF CUPS

Ten of Cups. The contentment augured by the Nine of Cups continues into the Ten, which also connotes permanent love, a lasting relationship.

PAGE OF CUPS

Page of Cups. New emotions, a new relationship, new feelings about an old relationship, and renewal of the capacity to love, beginning with self-love forged in a time of disappointment and withdrawal, are implied by the Page. The regeneration encompasses the possibility of the birth of a child.

KNIGHT OF CUPS

Knight of Cups. This card promises emerging romanticism, the intoxication of romantic love, falling in love, a marriage proposal. Exalted artistic or poetic expression is also possible.

QUEEN OF CUPS

Queen of Cups. Profound, mysterious, and paradoxical emotions or fantasies that may have been lying hidden previously; the romantic, seductive female, possibly the inquirer, or the "other woman," and a deepening of inner awareness—these are the messages of the Queen.

KING OF CUPS

King of Cups. The King represents the wounded healer, one who, because of pain in past relationships—possibly with parents—must control the course of love in order to avoid new hurt. The card may symbolize either the inquirer or someone in his or her life.

The Rider-Waite Tarot

If there is such a thing as a standard Tarot, that distinction belongs to the one conceived by British editor, writer, and occultist Arthur Edward Waite. Waite had his ideas executed by a young American artist, Pamela Colman Smith, his colleague in the Hermetic Order of the Golden Dawn. The resulting deck was published in 1910 in London by William Rider & Son Limited, hence the name Rider-Waite. It remains the world's most widely used Tarot.

Waite claimed his deck purged much nonsense previously ascribed to the cards. A devoted mystic, he sneered at divination as a corrupt use, although he did offer divinatory meanings for those who wanted them.

The suit of Swords, symbolic of form and matter, is the air suit, generally representing the rational, logical mind. Swords also have to do with strife, struggle, the quest for truth, and the need for discriminating decisions and decisive actions. In the main, Swords are an ominous suit.

Ace of Swords. A very forceful card, it connotes triumph, conquest, great extremes, as well as very passionate love or hate. It has the same meanings when inverted, but catastrophic outcomes are implied.

Two of Swords. The Two suggests balance, courage, and comradeship, brotherhood in arms, plus fondness and intimacy. Inverted, the meanings change to duplicity, lies, disloyalty.

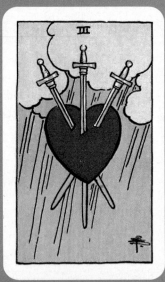

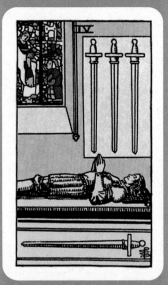

Three of Swords. The Three augurs separation, absence, disruption, dispersion, delay. Inverted, it entails mistakes, loss, confusion, distraction, and mental alienation.

Four of Swords. Withdrawal, solitude, the recluse's repose, vigilance, exile, the coffin, and the tomb are all foretold by the Four. Inverted, it signifies wise management, prudence, thrift, and precaution, but also greed.

Five of Swords. Hallmarks of the Five are degradation, infamy, destruction, and loss. The meanings persist when the card is inverted, but with the additional unpleasant connotations of death and burial.

Six of Swords. The Six charts a pathway or route, a sojourn by water, a messenger or envoy, an expedient. Inverted, it portends a confession, a declaration, or publicity.

Seven of Swords. This card implies plans, attempts, hopes, but at the same time it signifies discord, annoyance, an ill-fated plan. Inverted, the Seven denotes good advice or instruction, but also slander and babbling.

Eight of Swords. The Eight brings bad news, crisis, rebuke, terrible disappointment, conflict, sickness, calumny, power enchained. Inverted, it means unease, difficulty, treachery, opposition, the unforeseen, fatality.

Nine of Swords. A grim card, the Nine predicts desolation, failure, delay, deceit, miscarriage, despair. Inverted, it means imprisonment, justifiable fear, doubt, or shame.

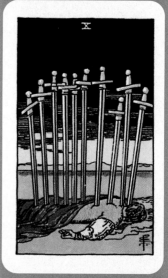

Ten of Swords. The Ten bodes pain, death, desolation, affliction, sorrow. Inverted, it presages success, profit, and favor—but all of them impermanent—and power and authority.

Page of Swords. The Page indicates authority, management, secret duties, spying, vigilance. Inverted, the card denotes the same qualities, but with an evil cast, as well as illness and things unprepared for and unforeseen.

Knight of Swords. The Knight signifies skill, capability, courage, hostility, anger, war, defense, resistance, destruction, ruin, possibly death. Inverted, it means inability, extravagance, bad judgment.

Queen of Swords. The unhappy Queen symbolizes female sorrow, embarrassment, need, sterility, separation, widowhood. Inverted, the meanings are spite, bigotry, guile, prudery, deceit.

King of Swords. He is King of judgment, power to decree life or death, combative intelligence, law. Inverted, he stands for cruelty, treachery, barbarity, perversity, malice.

The Thoth Tarot

Erotic and highly stylized, the Thoth deck was the brainchild of eccentric British diabolist Aleister Crowley, another Golden Dawn initiate. He designed it, and Lady Frieda Harris painted it, between the years 1938 and 1943.

The Thoth Tarot is replete with cabalistic and astrological symbolism, and Crowley exercised a free hand in renaming certain Trumps. With the Minor Arcana, he designated the court cards as Prince, Princess, Queen, and Knight rather than the traditional King, Queen, Knight, and Page. He also added names to the numbers of cards Two through Ten in each suit, and he used the term Disks for the suit shown here instead of the more common Pentacles or Coins. Crowley made no distinction as to whether cards fell upright or inverted; rather, he called them "well-dignified" or "ill-dignified," depending on neighboring cards.

Pentacles, the earth suit, represents activity and governs physical expression, money, work, and materiality.

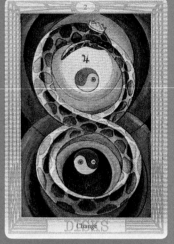

Ace of Disks. Crowley said the card represented "the root of the powers of earth" and the mystical unity of sun and earth, spirit and flesh. It stands for work, power, financial riches, satisfaction, materiality.

Two of Disks: Change. This card denotes harmonic change with alternating gain and loss, strength and weakness, joy and sadness. It ma signify changing occupation, traveling, visiting friends. It also represents someone who is at the same time diligent and unreliable.

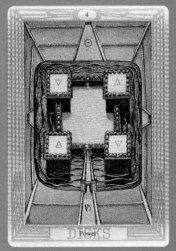

Three of Disks: Works. The Three governs employment, trade, construction, material increase, growth, beginnings. Ill-dignified, it represents someone selfish, avaricious, prejudiced, unrealistic in expectations.

Four of Disks: Power. The Four deals with law and order, increased wealth and influence, status, physical skill, power limited to the earthly sphere. Ill-dignified, its meanings are greed, suspicion, bias, unoriginality.

Five of Disks: Worry. The Five signifies labor, building, agriculture, intelligence applied to work. An ill-dignified position indicates stressful inaction, anxiety over money matters, lost wealth, penury.

Six of Disks: Success. The Six foretells nobility, power, and material success, although all of them may be ephemeral and somewhat illusory. Its ill-dignified aspects are conceit, wastefulness, and insolence.

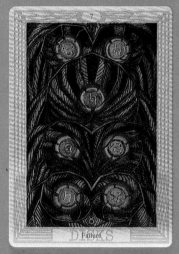

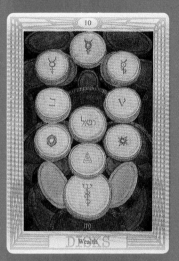

Seven of Disks: Failure. The Failure card means eventual growth, honorable work undertaken for its own sake and without hope of reward. Ill-dignified, it means laziness, abandoned work, profitless speculation, empty promise.

Eight of Disks: Prudence. The Eight reveals intelligence, skill, cunning, and industry applied to material things, including building and agriculture. An ill-dignified Eight indicates greed and miserliness, punctiliousness about small things at the expense of more important matters.

Nine of Disks: Gain. It promises material good fortune, inheritance, and greatly increased wealth, but when ill-dignified, covetousness, theft, and dishonorable behavior.

Ten of Disks: Wealth. The Ten brings riches; the completion of a fortune, but with no future prospects in the absence of creativity; and old age. Ill-dignified, its message is sloth, diminished mental acuity and material profit, heaviness.

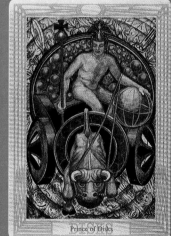

Knight of Disks. The Knight represents a farmer, somewhat plodding and overconcerned with material things but patient, hardworking, and clever with his hands. Ill-dignified, he is a petty, surly, jealous, grasping man.

Princess of Disks. She is a beautiful, strong young woman, generous, diligent, kind, nurturing, filled with life and attuned to its secret wonders. Ill-dignified, she is wasteful, at odds with her own dignity.

Queen of Disks. She is a kind, charming, affectionate woman—practical, quiet, and domestic, but ambitious in useful ways. Stupid, slavish, and whimsical when ill-dignified, she is also moody and somewhat prone to debauchery.

Prince of Disks. The Prince denotes an energetic and industrious young man, competent and practical, if dull. He tends to resent those more spiritually inclined and, though slow to anger, he is relentless once aroused.

Divination with the Tarot

With the Tarot, nothing is simple. Mastering all the possible meanings of all the cards as they appear in the various decks is an arduous job, but still it falls short of preparing a would-be Tarot reader to practice cartomancy. The next step is deciding which cards in the deck should be used and how they should be laid out. Some readers employ all seventy-eight cards, others only the Major Arcana. In either case, the cards may be arranged in any number of configurations. Some provide readings lasting only a few minutes, while the more complicated layouts can take hours to interpret. The cards may be used to answer an inquirer's specific question or to provide general information.

Three of the more common spreads are shown below and on the next three pages, using the standard Rider-Waite deck. The readings were done by Fredrick Davies, a psychic adviser with a large celebrity following in the United States and Great Britain. His interpretations do not necessarily follow the meanings given in the foregoing pages. Davies is an astrologer as well as a Tarot reader, so the stars figure in his analyses. Moreover, like many advisers, he brings his own purported psychic gifts to the interpretations.

His three-card reading was given for a woman artist, a Pisces; the seven-card, for a Cancer businessman; and the ten-card reading, for a female writer, a Gemini.

The Three-Card Spread. This is among the simplest spreads, ideal for short readings. At the outset, all of the cards should face in the same direction. The notion is that after shuffling they will then fall upright or reversed as fate decrees. As with most readings, this one began with the inquirer shuffling and cutting the cards and presenting them to the reader. He then fanned the deck and the inquirer selected three cards with her left hand. The reader laid them down.

Following the numbers on the small diagram next to the spread, card number one represents the inquirer's past, number two the present, and number three the future. Here, the cards are the Nine of Swords, the Seven of Cups, and the Seven of Swords. Davies interpreted them as follows:

The Nine indicates the inquirer is troubled by some person or event in her past. She wants to air her grievance, but to do so at detailed length would be fruitless. She should not be inhibited from speaking, but at the same time she should keep the complaint short, lest she regret later having said too much.

The Cups card bodes changes in her social schedule. Perhaps someone she loves will make a spur-of-the-moment suggestion regarding mutual plans. She ought to be open to possibilities and flexible in adapting to such situations.

The Seven of Swords suggests that the lover of her choice will not have the approval of well-meaning family members and friends. They will try to protect her by criticizing him, but she should not listen. Her best course is not to be intimidated by them but to follow her own instincts. The card might also be an analog of her professional life, meaning that she will be successful following her own course, regardless of criticism.

The Seven-Card Spread. This is also called the Horseshoe Spread because of its shape. After the inquirer shuffled and cut the cards, the reader laid them out from left to right. In sequence, the cards represent (1) the inquirer's past, (2) his present, (3) his future, (4) the particular matters on his mind, (5) others in his life, (6) obstacles, and (7) the outcome of a particular question, situation, or condition. The cards that fell in the businessman's reading were the Lovers, the Eight of Wands, the Three of Cups, the Five of Cups, the Three of Swords, the Four of Pentacles, and the Nine of Swords. Davies interpreted them in the following way:

In his past, the inquirer had to make a choice between two loves, perhaps one more romantic and serious and the other more passionate. Just next to the Lovers, the Eight of Wands counsels diplomacy and tact, especially in dealing with the current beloved. It recommends that the man temper honesty with discretion, especially if some third person is involved, but it also indicates a choice or decision is imminent. The Three of Cups indicates thoughts of marriage, or a happy marriage if the inquirer is married. (He is.) However, the card once again indicates the presence of a third person. It is not necessarily a lover and does not seem to represent a threat to the marriage. It could be a child, an ex-wife or ex-husband, perhaps a parent, or even an in-law.

The romantic theme carries over to the Five of Cups, which indicates that affairs of the heart are of current concern to the inquirer. The Three of Swords says that if he is embroiled in a romantic complication, a separation from one of the parties might be good. The inquirer is left to determine from which person he should separate, but the move is seen as bearing on his main-taining a happy marriage in the future.

Davies suggests that the Four of Pentacles might mean that the third party in the reading's suggested triangulation is not another woman but simply work. Perhaps the man is concentrating on his job to the detriment of his relationship with his wife. He should strive for balance, giving proper attention to his home life.

The Nine of Swords cautions again that tact is imperative if the situation is to have a propitious outcome. "It says, whatever you do, don't say anything to anybody about it in too much detail," Davies specifies. "If you say anything, you'll regret saying it. It will come back to haunt you. It's better just to plead total ignorance." If the inquirer feels that some kind of romantic choice is inevitable, he is cautioned against making it or revealing it precipitously. He should exercise restraint and wait for the appropriate moment.

The Ten-Card Spread. Also known as the Celtic cross, this spread has been used for many years and is quite popular among Tarot readers. After the inquirer shuffled and cut the cards, the reader laid them out in the sequence indicated by the diagram. In order, they represent (1) the inquirer herself, (2) what is on her mind, (3) future goals, (4) her past, (5) her more recent past, (6) the immediate future, (7) the inquirer again, (8) changes in her environment, (9) her emotional state, and (10) the outcome of her concerns and situation.

The cards in this reading were the World (inverted), the Two of Cups, the Ace of Wands, the Queen of Cups (inverted), the Eight of Wands, the Five of Cups, the Ace of Pentacles, the Seven of Cups, the Four of Pentacles, and the Magician (inverted). This was Davies' assessment:

Having the World trump represent the inquirer is extremely promising, despite the fact that the card is reversed. There is no such thing as an unlucky World in a reading, Davies says, no matter how it falls. Here it indicates spectacular prospects for the inquirer, including the possibility of work-related travel to far-flung ports, possibly in the Caribbean or South America. Everything is falling into place in both her professional and domestic lives.

However, the card's inversion may mean that she is feeling rather restless or uneasy despite the good fortune. "Everything should be wonderful for you at this time," Davies comments, "but you're still not totally convinced that it is."

Crossing the World, the Two of Cups indicates the inquirer's thoughts about her marriage. The card is among the happiest of marriage symbols, the reader relates, and in this case it indicates the inquirer is secure in her marriage and inclined to turn her thoughts to other matters, probably relating to her career. She is cautioned not to be so complacent that she neglects her marriage or fails to enjoy it.

The Ace of Wands suggests "something wonderful" is in the offing regarding the inquirer's future goals. The card predicts great opportunities, possibly with a publishing or television project. The past has been somewhat less satisfactory, according to the inverted Queen of Cups. Coupling the Queen with the writer's Gemini birth sign, Davies surmises that past obstacles and difficulties are clearing and that the future will be much brighter. The Queen's reversal indicates the inquirer might be able to look forward to a more amusing and eventful love life.

The Eight of Wands implies that the woman has recently entered a situation in which political skills and tact are essential.

The Five of Cups suggests that her near future will hold good romantic prospects. Perhaps her marriage will become more exciting. A love affair is possible, although it is just as likely that some new person entering her life will become a valued platonic friend or a collaborator in a professional venture.

The Ace of Pentacles reveals the writer has the ability to make a great deal of money. Prospects for gain are enhanced further, Davies says, because the ace is one of two in the reading. Unusual financial success is ensured. Changes in the writer's environment are indicated by the Seven of Cups. Perhaps she should make some alterations in her home to facilitate her working there. The next card, the Four of Pentacles, indicates that her career is, in fact, uppermost in the inquirer's thoughts and feelings. Her concern for it could be an obstacle to her domestic life unless she takes care to show her husband the attention he needs.

The final card, the Magician, is particularly auspicious for Geminis. The inquirer has magic with words; she is a master manipulator who can make anything happen with her writing and in her life. "The final outcome is wonderful," Davies says. "This is like a brand-new beginning for you."

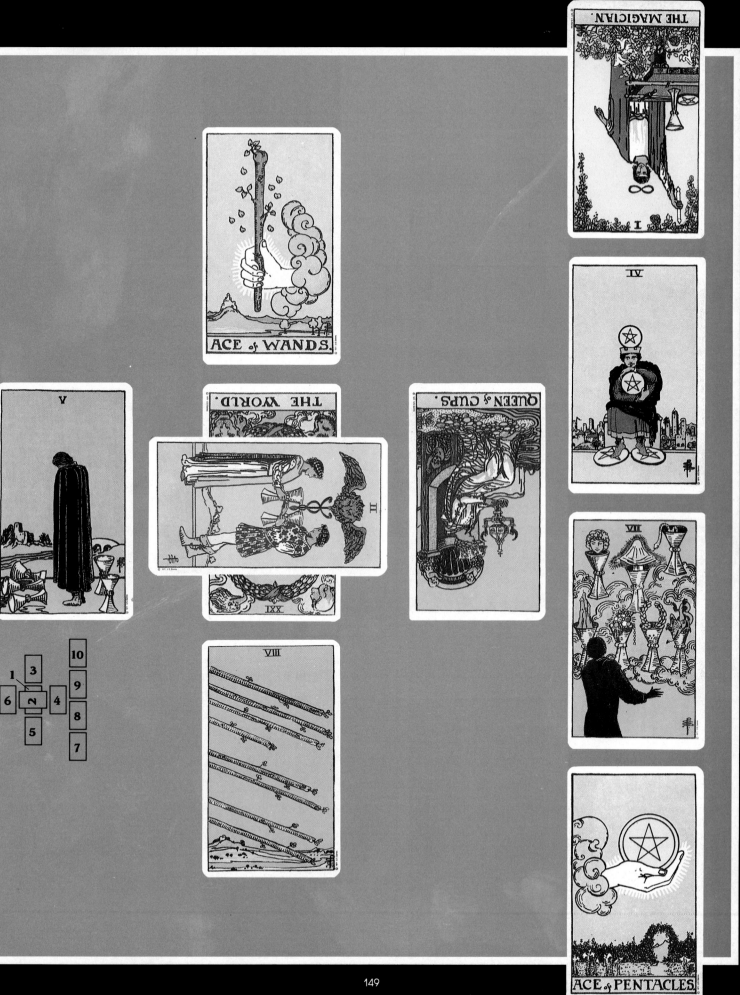

ACKNOWLEDGMENTS

The index for this book was prepared by Hazel Blumberg-McKee. The editors wish to express their appreciation to the following individuals and organizations:

Brigitte Baumbusch, Scala, Florence, Italy; Helen Bradford, Alexandria, Va.; Dr. Hans Bender, Institut für Grenzgebiete der Psychologie und Psychohygiene, Freiburg, West Germany; Philip Dunn, Labyrinth Publishing, Zug, Switzerland; Leif Geiges, Staufen, West Germany; Michael Goodrich, Cosmic Contact Psychic Services, New York, N.Y.; John Hogue, Bellevue, Wash.; Kathleen Jacklin, John M. Olin Library, Cornell University, Ithaca, N.Y.; Patricia McCarver, Labyrinth Publishing, Zug, Switzerland; Steve McCurry, New York, N.Y.; Patricia McLaine, Arlington, Va.; Professor Dr. Johannes Mischo, Institut für Psychologie und Grenzgebiete der Psychologie, Freiburg, West Germany; Singh Modi, New York, N.Y.; Rolla Nordic, New York, N.Y.; Marie-Christine Roquette, Musée de Salon et de la Crau, Salón-de-Provence, France; Marvin Schwab, Chevy Chase, Md.; Barbara A. Shattuck, *National Geographic* Magazine, Washington, D.C.; Rolf Streichardt, Institut für Grenzgebiete der Psychologie und Psychohygiene, Freiburg, West Germany; Jeanette Thomas, Edgar Cayce Foundation, Virginia Beach, Va.; Dr. Thomas A. Tufo, The A. N. Palmer Company, Hebron, Ill.; Dr. Jing Nuan Wu, Washington, D.C.; Matthew Zalichin, Takoma Park, Md.

BIBLIOGRAPHY

Altman, Nathaniel, *The Palmistry Workbook.* Wellingborough, Northamptonshire, England: Aquarian Press, 1984.

Avedon, John F., *In Exile from the Land of Snows.* New York: Alfred A. Knopf, 1984.

Avery, Kevin Quinn, *The Numbers of Life.* Garden City, New York: Doubleday, 1974.

Benham, William George, *The Laws of Scientific Hand Reading.* New York: Duell, Sloan and Pearce, Essential Books, 1946 (reprint of 1901 edition).

Besterman, Theodore, *Crystal-Gazing.* New York: University Books, 1965.

Bjornstad, James, *Twentieth Century Prophecy: Jeane Dixon, Edgar Cayce.* Minneapolis: Bethany Fellowship, 1969.

Blackmore, Susan J., "Divination with Tarot Cards: An Empirical Study." *Journal of the Society for Psychical Research,* June 1983.

Blofeld, John, transl., *I Ching: The Book of Change.* New York: E. P. Dutton, 1968.

Brasch, Rudolph:
Strange Customs: How Did They Begin? New York: David McKay, 1976.
The Supernatural and You! Victoria: Cassell Australia, 1976.

Bunker, Dusty, *Numerology and Your Future.* Gloucester, Massachusetts: Para Research, 1980.

Butler, Bill, *Dictionary of the Tarot.* New York: Schocken Books, 1975.

Butler, Christopher, *Number Symbolism.* New York: Barnes & Noble, 1970.

"Can the World Survive Economic Growth?" *Time,* August 14, 1972.

Capra, Fritjof, *The Tao of Physics.* Boston: Bantam New Age Books, 1975.

Carroll, David, *The Magic Makers.* New York: Arbor House, 1974.

Cavendish, Richard:
The Black Arts. New York: G. P. Putnam's Sons, 1967.
The Tarot. New York: Harper & Row, 1975.

Cavendish, Richard, ed.:
Encyclopedia of the Unexplained. New York: McGraw-Hill, 1974.
Man, Myth & Magic. 11 vols. New York: Marshall Cavendish, 1985.

Cayce, Edgar Evans, and Hugh Lynn Cayce, *The Outer Limits of Edgar Cayce's Power.* New York: Harper & Row, 1971.

Cazeau, Charles J., "Prophecy: The Search for Certainty." *The Skeptical Inquirer,* fall 1982.

Cheiro. *See* Hamon, Count Louis.

Chou, Hung-hsiang, "Chinese Oracle Bones." *Science America,* April 1979.

Christie-Murray, David, "Cayce: The Sleeper Speaks." *The Unexplained* (London), Vol. 10, Issue 115.

Clark, Clifford E., Jr., *Henry Ward Beecher.* Urbana: University of Illinois Press, 1978.

Coe, William R., "Resurrecting the Grandeur of Tikal." *National Geographic,* December 1975.

"Computer Sees 'Person' in Penmanship." *Science Digest,* October 1983.

Cooper, Helen, and Peter Cooper, *Heads: Or the Art of Phrenology.* London: London Phrenology Company, 1983.

Corliss, William R., comp., *The Unfathomed Mind: A Handbook of Unusual Mental Phenomena.* Glen Arm, Maryland: The Sourcebook Project, 1982.

Cowell, F. R., *Cicero and the Roman Republic.* New York: Pelican Books, 1967.

Crowley, Aleister, *The Confessions of Aleister Crowley.* Ed. by John Symonds and Kenneth Grant. New York: Hill and Wang, 1969.

Davies, John D., *Phrenology Fad and Science: A 19th Century American Crusade.* Hamden, Connecticut: The Shoe String Press, 1971.

Davis, Andrew Jackson:
The Penetralia: Being Harmonial Answers to Important Questions. Boston: Bela Marsh, 1856.
The Principles of Nature, Her Divine Revelations, and a Voice to Mankind. New York: S. S. Lyon, and Wm. Fishbough, 1847.

Dee, Nerys, *Fortune-Telling by Playing Cards.* Wellingborough, Northamptonshire, England: Aquarian Press, 1982.

Delfano, M. M., *The Living Prophets.* New York: Dell Publishing, 1972.

Delmonico, Damyan, *I Was Curious—a Crystal Ball Gazer.* Philadelphia: Dorrance, 1972.

The Diagram Group Visual Information:
How to Predict Your Future. London: Treasure Press, 1987.
Predicting Your Future. New York: Ballantine Books, 1983.

Dixon, Jeane, *My Life and Prophecies.* New York: William Morrow, 1969.

Dlhopolsky, Joseph G., "A Test of Numerology." *The Skeptical Inquirer,* spring 1983.

Dossey, Larry, *Space, Time & Medicine.* Boston: Shambhala Publishing, New Science Library, 1982.

Douglas, Alfred, *The Tarot.* London: Victor Gollancz, 1972.

Dummet, Michael, *The Game of Tarot.* Stamford, Connecticut: U.S. Games Systems, 1980.

Dunne, J. W., *An Experiment with Time.* New York:

Macmillan, 1927.

Easton, Thomas A., "Psychics, Computers, and Psychic Computers." *The Skeptical Inquirer,* summer 1987.

Ebon, Martin, *Prophecy in Our Time.* New York: New American Library, 1968.

Ebon, Martin, ed., *The Psychic Reader.* New York: World Publishing, 1969.

Edelson, Edward, *The Book of Prophecy.* New York: Doubleday, 1974.

The Editors of Time-Life Books, *Barbarian Tides* (Time Frame series). Alexandria, Virginia: Time-Life Books, 1987.

Edmonds, I. G., *Second Sight.* Nashville: Thomas Nelson, 1977.

Edwards, Paul, ed., *The Encyclopedia of Philosophy.* Vol. 1. New York: Macmillan, 1967.

Eggering, Susan, "Handwriting: What Experts See in Loops, Slants, Spaces." *The Anniston Star* (Alabama), October 5, 1986.

Ellis, Keith, *Prediction and Prophecy.* London: Wayland Publishers, 1973.

"Famous Last Words." *The Unexplained* (London), Vol. 7, Issue 74.

Farren, David, *Sex and Magic.* New York: Simon and Schuster, 1975.

Fisher, Joe, *Predictions.* New York: Van Nostrand Reinhold, 1980.

Flacelière, *Greek Oracles.* Transl. by Douglas Garman. New York: W. W. Norton, 1965.

Fontenrose, Joseph, *The Delphic Oracle.* Berkeley: University of California Press, 1978.

Forman, Henry James, *The Story of Prophecy.* New York: Tudor Publishing, 1940.

Fowler, Orson S., *The Octagon House.* New York: Dover Publications, 1973.

Franz, Marie-Louise von, *Time: Rhythm and Repose.* London: Thames and Hudson, 1978.

Frazier, Kendrick, and the Editors of Time-Life Books, *Solar System* (Planet Earth series). Alexandria, Virginia: Time-Life Books, 1985.

French, Peter J., *John Dee.* London: Routledge & Kegan Paul, 1972.

Gardini, Maria, *The Secrets of the Hand.* New York: Macmillan, 1984.

Gardner, Martin, *Knotted Doughnuts and Other Mathematical Entertainments.* New York: W. J. Freeman, 1986.

Garrett, Eileen, *Sense and Nonsense of Prophecy.* Toronto: Creative Age Press, 1950.

Garrison, Omar V., *The Encyclopedia of Prophecy.* Secaucus, New Jersey: Citadel Press, 1978.

Gattey, Charles Neilson, *They Saw Tomorrow.* London: Harrap, 1977.

Gettings, Fred:
The Book of Palmistry. London: Hamlyn, 1974.
The Book of Tarot. London: Hamlyn, 1973.

Gibson, Walter, and Litzka Gibson, *The Complete Illustrated Book of Divination and Prophecy.* New York: Doubleday, 1973.

Glass, Justine:
The Story of Fulfilled Prophecy. London: Cassell, 1969.
They Foresaw the Future. New York: G. P. Putnam's Sons, 1969.

Goran, Morris, *Fact, Fraud, and Fantasy.* South Brunswick, New Jersey: A. S. Barnes, 1979.

Goudsmit, Samuel A., Robert Claiborne, and the Editors of Time-Life Books, *Time* (Life Science Library series). Alexandria, Virginia: Time-Life Books, 1980.

Gould, Stephen Jay, *The Mismeasure of Man.* New York: W. W. Norton, 1981.

Grant, James, *The Mysteries of All Nations.* Detroit: Gale Research, 1971.

Greenhouse, Herbert B., *Premonitions: A Leap into the Future.* (no city available): Bernard Geis, 1971.

Gustafson, Frans, "Inside the Fortune Cookie." *San Francisco Sunday Examiner & Chronicle,* December 3, 1972.

Haber, Joyce, "Confucius Say: Future Is Bright for Fortune Cooky." *Los Angeles Times,* September 22, 1966.

Haining, Peter, *Superstitions.* London: Sidgwick & Jackson, 1979.

Halifax, Joan, *Shaman: The Wounded Healer.* New York: Thames and Hudson, 1982.

Hall, Alice J., "A Traveler's Tale of Ancient Tikal." *National Geographic,* December 1975.

Hall, Angus, *Signs of Things to Come.* Garden City, New York: Doubleday, 1975.

Hall, Edward T., *The Dance of Life: The Other Dimension of Time.* Garden City, New York: Anchor Press, 1984.

Hamon, Count Louis (born William Warner):
Cheiro's Complete Palmistry. Ed. by Robert M. Ockene. New York: University Books, 1968.
[Cheiro, pseud.], *Cheiro's Palmistry for All.* New York: Prentice Hall, 1987.

Harrison, William H., *Mother Shipton Investigated.* London: Norwood Editions, 1976 (reprint of 1881 edition).

Hawkins, Hildi:
"Numbered among the Great." *The Unexplained* (London), Vol. 6, Issue 69.

"The Sum of Human Knowledge." *The Unexplained* (London), Vol. 6, Issue 66.
"The Thought That Counts." *The Unexplained* (London), Vol. 6, Issue 67.

Hayward, Jeremy W., *Perceiving Ordinary Magic: Science and Intuitive Wisdom.* Boston: Shambhala, New Science Library, 1984.

Heichelhein, Fritz M., and Cedric A. Yeo, *A History of the Roman People.* Englewood Cliffs, New Jersey: Prentice-Hall, 1962.

Hill, Douglas, "The Meaning of Coincidence." *The Unexplained* (London), Vol. 3, Issue 33.

Ho, Peter Kwok Man, Martin Palmer, and Joanne O'Brien, *Lines of Destiny: How to Read Faces and Hands the Chinese Way.* Boston: Shambhala, 1986.

Hoebens, Piet Hein, "The Modern Revival of 'Nostradamitis'." *The Skeptical Inquirer,* fall 1982.

Hogue, John, *Nostradamus & the Millennium.* Garden City, New Jersey: Doubleday, 1987.

Holroyd, Stuart, *Magic, Words, and Numbers.* London: Aldus Books, 1975.

Howe, Ellic:
Astrology and Psychological Warfare during World War II. London: Rider and Company, 1972.
The Black Game: British Subversive Operations against the Germans during the Second World War. London: Michael Joseph, 1982.

Hyman, Ray, " 'Cold Reading': How to Convince Strangers that You Know All about Them." *The Zetetic,* spring /summer 1977.

Inglis, Brian, *Natural and Supernatural.* London: Hodder and Stoughton, 1977.

Innes, Brian:
"Coming Up Trumps." *The Unexplained* (London), Vol. 9, Issue 99.
"I Ching: Enquire Within." *The Unexplained* (London), Vol. 9, Issue 97.
"On the Other Hand . . ." *The Unexplained* (London), Vol. 9, Issue 100.
"The Pattern of the Future." *The Unexplained* (London), Vol. 8, Issue 96.
The Tarot: How to Use and Interpret the Cards. London: Orbis, 1979.

Jahoda, Gustav, *The Psychology of Superstition.* London: Penguin Press, 1969.

Jastrow, Joseph, *Wish and Wisdom: Episodes in the Vagaries of Belief.* New York: D. Appleton-Century, 1935.

Jastrow, Morris, Jr., *Aspects of Religious Belief and Practices in Babylonia and Assyria.* New York: Benjamin Blom, 1911.

Jung, C. G.:

Memories, Dreams, Reflections. Ed. by Aniela Jaffé, transl. by Richard Winston and Clara Winston. New York: Random House, Vintage Books, 1965.

The Portable Jung. Ed. by Joseph Campbell, transl. by R. F. C. Hull. New York: Viking Press, 1971.

Kahn, Herman, William Brown, and Leon Martel, *The Next 200 Years: A Scenario for America in the World.* New York: William Morrow, 1976.

Kaplan, Justin, *Walt Whitman: A Life.* New York: Simon and Schuster, 1980.

Kaplan, Stuart R., *The Encyclopedia of Tarot.* Vols. 1 and 2. New York: U.S. Games Systems, 1978.

King, Francis, "On the Side of the Angels." *The Unexplained* (London), Vol. 9, Issue 99.

Kline, Morris, *Mathematics in Western Culture.* New York: Oxford University Press, 1953.

Krauss, Franklin Brunell, *An Interpretation of the Omens, Portents, and Prodigies Recorded by Livy, Tacitus, and Suetonius.* Philadelphia: University of Pennsylvania Press, 1930.

Kunz, George Frederick, *The Curious Lore of Precious Stones.* New York: Dover Publications, 1913.

La Fay, Howard, "Children of Time." *National Geographic,* December 1975.

Leary, David M., compl., *Edgar Cayce's Photographic Legacy.* Garden City, New York: Doubleday, 1978.

Lee, Albert, *Weather Wisdom.* New York: Doubleday, 1976.

Leek, Sybil:
Phrenology. London: Macmillan, 1970.
The Sybil Leek Book of Fortune Telling. New York: Collier Books, 1969.

Lemesurier, Peter, *The Armageddon Script.* New York: St. Martin's Press, 1981.

Lester, David, *The Psychological Basis of Handwriting Analysis.* Chicago: Nelson-Hall, 1981.

Lévi, Éliphas, *Transcendental Magic: Its Doctrine and Ritual.* Transl. by Arthur Edward Waite. New York: Samuel Weiser, 1970 (reprint of 1896 edition).

Lewinsohn, Richard, *Science, Prophecy and Prediction.* New York: Bell Publishing, 1961.

Liggett, John, *The Human Face.* London: Constable, 1974.

Line, David, and Julia Line, *Fortune-Telling by Dice.* Wellingborough, Northamptonshire, England: Aquarian Press, 1984.

Logan, Jo, and Lindsay Hodson, *The Prediction Book of Divination.* Dorset, England: Blandford Press, 1984.

Loye, David, *The Knowable Future.* New York: John Wiley & Sons, 1978.

McCoy, Robert W., "Phrenology and Popular Gullibility." *The Skeptical Inquirer,* spring 1985.

McKinnie, Ian, *Fun in a Teacup.* Millbrae, California: Celestial Arts, 1974.

Mainwaring, Marion, " 'Phys/phren'—Why Not to Take Each Other at Face Value." *Smithsonian,* November 1980.

Mar, Timothy T., *Face Reading.* New York: Dodd, Mead, 1974.

Marin, Pamela, "Dear Mom, Can You Read What I Can't Say?" *Redbook,* October 1985.

Markham, Ursula, *Fortune-Telling by Crystals and Semiprecious Stones.* Wellingborough, Northamptonshire, England: Aquarian Press, 1987.

Martin, Michael, "Bumps & Brains: The Curious Science of Phrenology." *American History Illustrated,* September 1984.

Melville, John, *Crystal Gazing and Clairvoyance.* New York: Samuel Weiser, 1970 (reprint of 1896 edition).

Miller, Walter James, *The Annotated Jules Verne: From the Earth to the Moon.* New York: Thomas Y. Crowell, 1978.

Montague, Nell St. John, *Revelations of a Society Clairvoyante.* London: Thornton Butterworth, 1926.

Moolman, Valerie, and the Editors of Time-Life Books, *The Road to Kitty Hawk* (The Epic of Flight series). Alexandria, Virginia: Time-Life Books, 1980.

Mykian, W., *Numerology Made Easy.* North Hollywood, California: Wilshire Book Company, 1979.

Nielson, Greg, and Joseph Polansky, *Pendulum Power.* Wellingborough, Northamptonshire, England: Aquarian Press, 1986.

Obregón, Gonzalo, ed., *Los Tlacuilos de Fray Diego Durán.* Mexico: Cartón y Papel, 1975.

O'Neill, Robert V., *Tarot Symbolism.* Lima, Ohio: Fairway Press, 1986.

Park, Michael Alan, "Palmistry: Science or Hand-Jive?" *The Skeptical Inquirer,* winter 1982-83.

Parke, H. W., *A History of the Delphic Oracle.* Oxford: Basil Blackwell, 1939.

Pelton, Robert W., *Ancient Secrets of Fortune-Telling.* Cranbury, New Jersey: Barnes and Company, 1976.

Pern, Stephen, and the Editors of Time Life Books, *Masked Dancers of West Africa: The Dogon* (Peoples of the Wild series). Amsterdam: Time-Life Books, 1982.

Pernety, Antoine Joseph, *La Connaissance de l'homme moral par celle de l'homme physique.* Berlin: G. J. Decker, 1776-1777.

Pfister, Harold Francis, *Facing the Light.* Washington, D.C.: Smithsonian Institution Press, 1978.

Piggot, Stuart, *The Druids.* New York: Thames and Hudson, 1968.

Poe, Edgar Allan, "A Chapter on Autography." *American Heritage,* February 1975 (reprint of 1841 article).

Pollack, Rachel, *Seventy-Eight Degrees of Wisdom: A Book of Tarot.* Part 1. Wellingborough, Northamptonshire, England: Aquarian Press, 1980.

Priestley, John B., *Man and Time.* Garden City, New York: Doubleday, 1964.

Randi, James:
"Edgar Cayce: The Slipping Prophet." *The Skeptical Inquirer,* fall 1979.
"Nostradamus: The Prophet for All Seasons." *The Skeptical Inquirer,* fall 1982.
" 'Superpsychic' Vaughan: Claims vs. the Record." *The Skeptical Inquirer,* summer 1981.

Rawcliffe, D. H., *Occult and Supernatural Phenomena.* New York: Dover, 1952.

Rawlins, Dennis, "What *They* Aren't Telling You: Suppressed Secrets of the Psychic World, Astrological Universe, and Jeane Dixon." *The Zetetic,* fall/winter 1977.

Reader's Digest, *Strange Stories, Amazing Facts.* Pleasantville, New York: The Reader's Digest Association, 1976.

Roberts, Henry C., ed. and transl., *The Complete Prophecies of Nostradamus.* Oyster Bay, New York: Nostradamus Co., 1982.

Rohmann, Laura, "Write You Are." *Forbes,* March 9, 1983.

Rothman, Tony, "The Seven Arrows of Time." *Discover,* February 1987.

Roy, Archie, "The Waiting Future." *The Unexplained* (London), Vol. 7, Issue 84.

Russell, Jeffrey Burton, *Witchcraft in the Middle Ages.* Ithaca, New York: Cornell University Press, 1972.

Sargent, Carl, "Jung: No Shame in Psi." *The Unexplained* (London), Vol. 13, Issue 149.

Saxon, Kurt, *Keeping Score on Our Modern Prophets.* Eureka, California: Atlan Formularies, 1974.

Schafer, Edward H., and the Editors of Time-Life Books, *Ancient China* (Great Ages of Man series). New York: Time-Life Books, 1967.

Seligman, Kurt, *Character Reading from Handwriting.* New York: Pantheon Books, 1971.

Shadowitz, Albert, and Peter Walsh, *The Dark Side*

of Knowledge: Exploring the Occult. Reading, Massachusetts: Addison-Wesley Publishing, 1976.

Shafer, Elizabeth, "Phrenology's Golden Years." *American History Illustrated*, February 1974.

Shakabpa, Tsepon W. D., *Tibet: A Political History*. New Haven, Connecticut: Yale University Press, 1967.

Shepard, Leslie, ed., *Encyclopedia of Occultism & Parapsychology*. Detroit: Gale Research, 1984.

Sheraton, Mimi, "Demise of Fortune Cookies Is Near?" *Chinatown News* (Vancouver, British Columbia, Canada), July 3, 1983.

Sherrill, W. A., and W. K. Chu, *An Anthology of I Ching*. London: Routledge & Kegan Paul, 1977.

"666 and All That." *Discover*, February 1985.

Smith, Christine, *The Book of Divination*. London: Rider, 1978.

Smith, Richard Furnald, *Prelude to Science*. New York: Charles Scribner's Sons, 1975.

Smyth, Frank, "Prophet by Appointment." *The Unexplained* (London), Vol. 7, Issue 73.

Stern, Madeleine B., *Heads & Headlines: The Phrenological Fowlers*. Norman, Oklahoma: University of Oklahoma Press, 1971.

Stern, Madeleine B., compl., *A Phrenological Dictionary of Nineteenth-Century Americans*. Westport, Connecticut: Greenwood Press, 1982.

Stuart, George E., "Riddle of the Glyphs." *National Geographic*, December 1975.

Sugrue, Thomas, *There Is a River: The Story of Edgar Cayce*. New York: Holt, Rinehart and Winston, 1942.

Tan, Sheri, "Judge Settles S.F. - L.A. Clash—S.F. Wins." *Asian Week* (San Francisco), November 4, 1983.

Taylor, Thomas, *The History of Animals of Aristotle, and His Treatise on Physiognomy*, translated from the Greek. London: Robert Wilks, 1809.

Trungpa, Chögyam, *Born in Tibet*, as told to Esmé Cramer Roberts. Boulder, Colorado: Shambhala Publications, 1977.

Vallentin, Antonina, *Leonardo da Vinci: The Tragic Pursuit of Perfection*. Transl. by E. W. Dickes. New York: Viking Press, 1938.

Vandenburg, Philipp, *The Mystery of the Oracles*. New York: Macmillan, 1979.

Vaughan, Alan, *Patterns of Prophecy*. New York: Hawthorn Books, 1973.

Verne, Jules, *From the Earth to the Moon and All around the Moon*. Transl. by Edward Roth. New York: Dover Publications, 1962.

Wagar, W. Warren, "Toward a World Set Free: The Vision of H. G. Wells." *The Futurist*, August 1983.

Wagner, Carl E., Jr., *Characterology: The Art & Science of Character Analysis*. York Beach, Maine: Samuel Weiser, 1986.

Wallace, Robert, and the Editors of Time-Life Books, *The World of Leonardo* (Time-Life Library of Art series). New York: Time Inc., 1966.

Wang, Robert, *An Introduction to The Golden Dawn Tarot*. York Beach, Maine: Samuel Weiser, 1978.

"Watch Their P's and Q's." *Personal Report for the Executive*, August 15, 1987.

Wells, Charlotte Fowler, *Sketches of Phrenological Biography: Some Account of the Life and Labors of Dr. Francois Joseph Gall*. Vol. 1. New York: Fowler & Wells, 1896.

West, Peter:
Graphology: Understanding What Handwriting Reveals. Wellingborough, Northamptonshire, England: Aquarian Press, 1981.
Life Lines: An Introduction to Palmistry. Wellingborough, Northamptonshire, England: Aquarian Press, 1980.

Westcott, W. Wynn, *Numbers: Their Occult Power and Mystic Virtues*. London: Theosophical Publishing House, 1974.

"Whence Came the Fortune Cookie?" *Asian Week* (San Francisco), October 21, 1983.

Whincup, Greg, *Rediscovering the I Ching*. Garden City, New York: Doubleday, 1986.

Whitrow, G. J., *The Nature of Time*. New York: Holt, Rinehart and Winston, 1972.

Wiener, Philip P., ed., *Dictionary of the History of Ideas*. Vol. 4. New York: Charles Scribner's Sons, 1973.

Wilhelm, Richard, transl. (Cary F. Baynes, English translation). *The I Ching or Book of Changes*. Princeton, New Jersey: Princeton University Press, 1950.

"The Worst Is Yet to Be?" *Time*, January 24, 1972.

Wu, Jing Nuan, "The I Ching." Washington, D.C.: Unpublished Manuscript.

Yates, Francis A., *Theatre of the World*. Chicago: University of Chicago Press, 1969.

Zohar, Danah, *Through the Time Barrier: A Study of Precognition and Modern Physics*. Ed. by Brian Inglis. London: Heinemann, 1982.

PICTURE CREDITS

The sources for the illustrations in this book are shown below. Credits from left to right are separated by semicolons; credits from top to bottom are separated by dashes.

Cover: Art by Stephen R. Wagner. 7: Art by Rebecca Butcher. 8: Mary Evans Picture Library, London. 9: © 1948 Karsh, Ottawa/Woodfin Camp & Associates. 11: Royal Air Force Museum, London. 12, 13: Museo de America, Madrid, photograph by Otis Imboden and Victor Boswell, © 1975 National Geographic Society. 15: Jean-Loup Charmet, Paris. 16, 17: Courtesy the Trustees of the British Library, London. 19: from *Nostradamus and the Millennium*, produced by Labyrinth Publishing S.A.; Archiv für Kunst und Geschichte, Berlin (West). 20: Imperial War Museum, London. 21: BBC Hulton Picture Library, London. 24: Photograph courtesy Edgar Cayce Foundation Archives. 25: AP/Wide World Photos. 26, 27: Larry Sherer. 28: Bulloz, Paris, courtesy Institut de France, Paris. 29: From *From the Earth to the Moon: All Around the Moon*, space novels by Jules Verne, Dover Publications, Inc., New York, 1962. 31: Art by Rebecca Butcher. 32: Scala, Florence, courtesy Museo Civico, Piacenza. 33: © Eric Valli. 34: From *Fire and Ice: A History of Comets in Art*, by Roberta M. Olson, Walker & Company, New York, 1985. 36, 37: Bryan and Cherry Alexander, Dorset(2); Bryan and Cherry Alexander, © 1982 Time-Life Books B.V., from *Peoples of the Wild: Masked Dancers of West Africa: The Dogon*(2). 38, 39: Harald Sund © 1979 Time-Life Books B.V., from *The Great Cities: Mexico City*. 40: Roger-Viollet, Paris. 42, 43: Tom Tracy, courtesy U.S. Geological Survey, © 1982 Time-Life Books Inc., from *Planet Earth: Earthquakes*. 44: Stone Routes, London. 45: AP/Wide World Photos. 47: Ann Ronan Picture Library, Taunton, Somerset. 48: Werner Forman Archive/British Museum, London. 49: Ashmolean Museum, Oxford. 51: Larry Sherer, courtesy Olde Towne Gemstones. 53: Art by Kathleen Bober, detail from page 57. 54-59: Art by Kathleen Bober. 61: Courtesy Nathaniel Altman. 65: Art by Rebecca Butcher. 67: From the book *Cheiro's Complete Palmistry*, by Count Louis Hamon, © 1968 published by arrangement with University Press, Inc. and Lyle Stuart, Inc. 68: Archiv für Kunst und Geschichte, Berlin (West). 70, 71: Paul Lau. 72: Roger-Viollet, Paris. 73: © Explorer Archives, Paris. 74: Drawings by Constance Joan Naar for *Fortune* Magazine. 75: Yale Medical Historical Library, New Haven. 76: From *Heads & Headlines: The Phrenological Fowlers*, by Madeleine B. Stern, University of Oklahoma Press, Norman, 1971. 77: Museum of American History, Division of Medical Sciences, Smithsonian Institution, photographed by Kim Nielsen; from *Heads or the Art of Phrenology* by Helen and Peter Cooper, London Phrenology Company Ltd., © 1983. 78: Department of Manuscripts and University Archives, Cornell University Libraries, Ithaca, New York. 79: From *The Octagon House: A Home for All*, by Orson S. Fowler, republished by Dover Publications, Inc., New York. 80: Beecher Family Papers, Yale University Library, New Haven; courtesy American Antiquarian Society—Oscar Lion Collection of Walt Whitman, Rare Books & Manuscripts Division, The New York Public Library, Astor Lenox & Tilden Foundations. 83: BBC Hulton Picture Library, London. 84: Brown Brothers—Images Colour Library Ltd., London/Leeds: The Charles Walker Collection. 85: Roger-Viollet, Paris. 87: Brown Brothers. 88, 89: Roger-Viollet, Paris—© Evelyn Hofer/Archive Pictures Inc.; Brown Brothers. 90, 91: Frank Scherschel for *Life*; Dmitri Kessel for *Life*. 93: Ceil O'Neil, detail from page 94—alphabet provided by Macmillan Publishing Company/Palmer Method Handwriting. 94, 95: Ceil O'Neil—alphabet provided by Macmillan Publishing Company/Palmer Method Handwriting. 96, 97: Alphabet provided by Macmillan Publishing Company/Palmer Method Handwriting. 99-103: Art by Kimmerle Milnazik. 105: Art by Rebecca Butcher. 106: Detail of a painting by Botticelli, photograph by Scala, Florence, courtesy Galleria deglia Uffizi, Florence. 107: Austrian National Library, Vienna. 108, 109: Fresco by Andrea del Castagno, photograph by Scala, Florence, courtesy Cenacolo di S. Apollonia, Florence. 110, 111: Dice by John F. Schmidt, ovals by John Drummond. 112, 113: Art by John F. Schmidt. 114, 115: Larry Sherer, courtesy Jason Newman. 116: Horace Bristol/Photo Researchers, Inc. 117: From *Fortune Telling*, © Marshall Cavendish Ltd., 1974, photo by Malcolm Scoular. 118: Painting by Ma Lin, courtesy National Palace Museum, Taipei (Takeyoshi Tanuma). 119: Institute of History and Philology, Academia Sinica, Taipei. 120: Michael Holford, Loughton, Essex, courtesy Science Museum/Wellcome Collection. 122,123: © 1958 Karsh, Ottawa/Woodfin Camp & Associates. 124: Bibliothèque Nationale, Paris. 125: Scala, Florence, courtesy Accademia Carrara, Bergano. 126: Mary Evans Picture Library, London/Harry Price Collection, University of London. 128: Painting by Alexei Venetsianov/Edimedia, Paris. 131: U.S. Games Systems, Inc., except top left, from *The Mythic Tarot*, by Juliet Sharman-Burke and Liz Greene, published in U.K. by Century Hutchinson and in U.S. by Simon & Schuster. Card © Tricia Newell 1986. 132-137: U.S. Games Systems, Inc. 138, 139: Border art by Alicia Austin—U.S. Games Systems, Inc. 140, 141: Border art by Alicia Austin—from *The Mythic Tarot*, by Juliet Sharman-Burke and Liz Greene, published in U.K. by Century Hutchinson, in U.S. by Simon & Schuster. Cards © Tricia Newell, 1986. 142-145: Border art by Alicia Austin—U.S. Games Systems, Inc. 146-149: U.S. Games Systems, Inc.

Index

Time-Life Books Inc.
is a wholly owned subsidiary of
TIME INCORPORATED

FOUNDER: Henry R. Luce 1898-1967

Editor-in-Chief: Jason McManus
Chairman and Chief Executive Officer: J. Richard Munro
President and Chief Operating Officer: N. J. Nicholas, Jr.
Editorial Director: Ray Cave
Executive Vice President, Books: Kelso F. Sutton
Vice President, Books: George Artandi

TIME-LIFE BOOKS INC.

EDITOR: George Constable
Executive Editor: Ellen Phillips
Director of Design: Louis Klein
Director of Editorial Resources: Phyllis K. Wise
Editorial Board: Russell B. Adams, Jr., Dale M. Brown,
Roberta Conlan, Thomas H. Flaherty, Lee Hassig, Donia
Ann Steele, Rosalind Stubenberg, Henry Woodhead
Director of Photography and Research:
John Conrad Weiser
Assistant Director of Editorial Resources: Elise Ritter Gibson

PRESIDENT: Christopher T. Linen
Chief Operating Officer: John M. Fahey, Jr.
Senior Vice Presidents: Robert M. DeSena, James L. Mercer,
Paul R. Stewart
Vice Presidents: Stephen L. Bair, Ralph J. Cuomo, Neal
Goff, Stephen L. Goldstein, Juanita T. James, Hallett
Johnson III, Carol Kaplan, Susan J. Maruyama, Robert H.
Smith, Joseph J. Ward
Director of Production Services: Robert J. Passantino

Editorial Operations
Copy Chief: Diane Ullius
Production: Celia Beattie
Library: Louise D. Forstall

MYSTERIES OF THE UNKNOWN

SERIES DIRECTOR: Russell B. Adams, Jr.
Series Administrator: Myrna Traylor-Herndon
Designer: Susan K. White

Editorial Staff for *Visions and Prophecies*
Associate Editors: Sara Schneidman (pictures),
Pat Daniels (text)
Writers: Janet P. Cave, Laura Foreman
Assistant Designer: Lorraine D. Rivard
Copy Coordinators: Darcie Conner Johnston, Mary Beth
Oelkers-Keegan
Picture Coordinator: Betty H. Weatherley
Researchers: Christian D. Kinney, Susan Stuck, Elizabeth
Ward
Editorial Assistant: Donna Fountain

Special Contributors: Christine Hinze (London, picture
research); Patricia A. Paterno (picture research); Dusty
Bunker, Marfé Ferguson, Thomas A. Lewis, Daniel
Stashower, Donia Ann Steele, John R. Sullivan, William
Triplett, Michael Webb, Robert H. White (text); John
Drummond (design); Vilasini Balakrishnan, Melva
Holloman, Sharon Obermiller (research)

Correspondents: Elisabeth Kraemer-Singh (Bonn), Vanessa
Kramer (London), Maria Vincenza Aloisi (Paris), Ann
Natanson (Rome).
Valuable assistance was also provided by Angelika
Lemmer (Bonn); Bing Wong (Hong Kong); Judy Aspinall
(London); Trini Bandrés (Madrid); Elizabeth Brown,
Christina Lieberman (New York); Dag Christensen (Oslo);
Ann Wise (Rome); Janet Huseby (San Francisco); Dick
Berry (Tokyo); Traudl Lessing (Vienna).

The Consultants:
Nathaniel Altman became involved in hand analysis in
1968 and since then has read more than 10,000 palms. He
has lectured on palmistry in the United States and abroad
and has written a number of books on the practice.
Among his works are *The Palmistry Workbook,* and *Career,
Success and Self-Fulfillment: How Scientific Palmistry Can
Change Your Life,* which he coauthored with Andrew
Fitzherbert.

Dusty Bunker conducts lectures and workshops throughout the country on the subject of numerology. She has
frequently appeared on radio and television broadcasts
and is the author of *Numerology and Your Future* and
Numerology, Astrology and Dreams, among other works.

Frederick Davies, a British astrologer living in New York
City, performed the Tarot readings that begin on page
146. He has published columns in magazines and news-
papers in the U.S. and abroad and is the author of two
books on astrology, *Signs of the Stars* and *Money Signs.*

Stuart R. Kaplan is president of U.S. Games Systems, Inc.,
which publishes Tarot decks and related books and
games. He is considered an authority on Tarot card
symbolism and has written several books on the subject,
including *The Encyclopedia of Tarot.*

Marcello Truzzi, professor of sociology at Eastern
Michigan University, is also director of the Center for
Scientific Anomalies Research (CSAR) and editor of its
journal, the *Zetetic Scholar.* Dr. Truzzi, who considers
himself a "constructive skeptic" with regard to claims of
the paranormal, works through CSAR to produce
dialogues between critics and proponents of unusual
scientific claims.

Gloria Weiss, a member of the American Handwriting
Analysis Foundation, is a professional handwriting analyst
and identification expert. She specializes in personality
evaluation, assessing clients in such areas as intellect,
vocational aptitude, and emotional responsiveness.

Other Publications:

THE TIME-LIFE GARDENER'S GUIDE
TIME FRAME
FIX IT YOURSELF
FITNESS, HEALTH & NUTRITION
SUCCESSFUL PARENTING
HEALTHY HOME COOKING
UNDERSTANDING COMPUTERS
LIBRARY OF NATIONS
THE ENCHANTED WORLD
THE KODAK LIBRARY OF CREATIVE PHOTOGRAPHY
GREAT MEALS IN MINUTES
THE CIVIL WAR
PLANET EARTH
COLLECTOR'S LIBRARY OF THE CIVIL WAR
THE EPIC OF FLIGHT
THE GOOD COOK
WORLD WAR II
HOME REPAIR AND IMPROVEMENT
THE OLD WEST

*For information on and a full description of any of the
Time-Life Books series listed above, please call 1-800-621-
7026 or write:*
  Reader Information
  Time-Life Customer Service
  P.O. Box C-32068
  Richmond, Virginia 23261-2068

This volume is one of a series that examines the history
and nature of seemingly paranormal phenomena. Other
books in the series include:
*Mystic Places
Psychic Powers
The UFO Phenomenon
Psychic Voyages
Phantom Encounters*

Library of Congress Cataloging in Publication Data
Visions and prophecies.
  (Mysteries of the unknown).
  Bibliography: p.
  Includes index.
  1. Prophecies (Occultism).
I. Time-Life Books.   II. Series.
BF1791.V57 1988   133.3   87-33638
ISBN 0-8094-6320-2
ISBN 0-8094-6321-0 (lib. bdg.)

Time-Life Books Inc. offers a wide range of fine record-
ings, including a *Rock 'n' Roll Era* series. For subscription
information, call 1-800-621-7026 or write Time-Life Music, P.O. Box C-32068, Richmond, Virginia 23261-2068.